Into

Silence

and

Servitude

. . . .

McGILL-QUEEN'S STUDIES IN THE HISTORY OF RELIGION
Volumes in this series have been supported by the Jackman Foundation of Toronto.

Series One: G.A. Rawlyk, Editor

Into
Silence
and
Servitude

. . . .

How
American
Girls
Became
Nuns,
1945–1965

. . . .

BRIAN TITLEY

McGill-Queen's University Press
Montreal & Kingston · London · Chicago

© McGill-Queen's University Press 2017

ISBN 978-0-7735-5141-1 (cloth)
ISBN 978-0-7735-5172-5 (ePDF)
ISBN 978-0-7735-5173-2 (ePUB)

Legal deposit third quarter 2017
Bibliothèque nationale du Québec

Printed in Canada on acid-free paper that is 100%
ancient forest free (100% post-consumer recycled),
processed chlorine free

McGill-Queen's University Press acknowledges the support of the
Canada Council for the Arts for our publishing program. We also
acknowledge the financial support of the Government of Canada
through the Canada Book Fund for our publishing activities.

Library and Archives Canada Cataloguing in Publication

Titley, E. Brian, author
Into silence and servitude : how American girls became nuns,
1945–1965 / Brian Titley.

(McGill-Queen's studies in the history of religion. Series two ; 79)
Includes bibliographical references and index.
Issued in print and electronic formats.
ISBN 978-0-7735-5141-1 (cloth). – ISBN 978-0-7735-5172-5 (ePDF). –
ISBN 978-0-7735-5173-2 (ePUB)

1. Convents – United States – History – 20th century.   2. Girls –
Religious life – United States – History – 20th century.
3. United States – Church history – 20th century.   I. Title.
II. Series: McGill-Queen's studies in the history of religion.
Series two ;79

BX4220.U6T58 2017   271'.90097309045   C2017-901903-1
                                              C2017-901904-X

Set in 10/13.5 Baskerille 10 Pro
Book design & typesetting by Garet Markvoort, zijn digital

Contents

· ·

Tables and Figure

. . . .

TABLES

FIGURE

Acknowledgments

. . . .

Writing is a solitary enterprise. You spend a lot of time alone at a desk – preferably without distractions or interruptions and for hours at a time. But history books can only be written after many months – even years – of research and reading. You cannot simply make it up or fill in the gaps with conjecture. Everything must be documented as the disparate pieces of the puzzle are assembled, evaluated, and arranged in a coherent manner. The time spent in archives and libraries is as important as that spent at the writing desk. During the initial stages of this book I was fortunate to meet archivists and librarians who readily welcomed me to their workplaces and provided the kind of assistance and guidance that made research both enjoyable and productive. I would like to acknowledge the following people:

Kevin Cawley and Charles Lamb, the University of Notre Dame Archives, Big Bend, Indiana;
Emily Dominic and Peter Schmid, Providence Archives, Seattle, Washington;
Marianne Mader, Sisters of Providence Archives, St Mary-of-the-Woods, Indiana;
Ellen Pierce, Maryknoll Archives, Ossining, New York;
Lenore Rouse, Rare Books and Special Collections, Mullen Library, Catholic University of America, Washington, DC.

I owe a word of special gratitude to the reviewers who assessed the manuscript for McGill-Queen's University Press. Their thoughtful and constructive comments drew attention to shortcomings in my work that needed attention. I am aware of the enormous commitment of time and effort required for these assessments, and I do appreciate it.

Kyla Madden at McGill-Queen's University Press played a key role in moving matters forward ever since we discussed what I was working on in June 2015. Meticulous in her attention to detail, and committed to the highest standards of excellence, no one could ask for a better editor.

I have always been aware of the special privilege of working in an academic milieu of congenial and stimulating colleagues, and the Faculty of Education at the University of Lethbridge has been such a place par excellence for many years. When I needed a break from the solitary confinement of scribbling, there were always friends nearby who were ready to listen, discuss, and even disagree. To list everyone would be tedious, but I will mention a few who have been particularly supportive and eager to engage in serious and not-so-serious dialogue.

Kas Mazurek and I go back a long way – to our doctoral studies at the University of Alberta, to be precise. We share a similar sense of humour and our views on most issues – including religion – tend to coincide. I recall a lively discussion we had some years ago about Saint Faustina Kowalska upon his return from a trip to Poland, where he had visited her convent. Where are you going to find a colleague who has even heard of Saint Faustina?

Lance Grigg is a philosopher who enjoys disagreeing with me. Our vigorous debates over the years on the origins of Christianity and on Catholicism before and after Vatican II have been entertaining to say the least. Lance is also an excellent chess player and always presents a challenge when we sit down across from one another at our favourite game. A game of chess, a few beers, an argument about religion – does academic life get any better?

At first glance, Richard Butt and I should not even be friends. To begin with, he is English and I am Irish. He has a weak spot for phenomenology, while I am contemptuous of it. And he actually prefers rugby to soccer. And yet we recognized early on that we were both restless proletarians who refused to accept the low station in life into which God had been pleased to place us. A patient listener and stimulating conversationalist, Richard has always supported me when I needed it and challenged me when I deserved it.

I owe a special debt to Craig Loewen, dean of education, who facilitated completion of this book by allowing me to retain my office and access to other university facilities after my retirement in 2013. The Faculty of Education is well served under Craig's leadership.

Moving outside the faculty, I wish to acknowledge the advice and insight of Heidi MacDonald in our History Department. Heidi's own work on the history of women religious in Canada has already achieved national recognition, and there is a lot more to come. Although incredibly busy with a bewildering array of commitments, she still finds time to discuss our mutual research interests.

On the other side of the globe, Tom O'Donoghue at the University of Western Australia has never been short of words of encouragement since we first met at a conference in 1997. His book, *Catholic Teaching Brothers* (2012) was extremely helpful to me as I pieced together a structure for my own work. Tom was generous enough to read a few of the early chapters as my writing progressed and provided his habitual astute commentary.

I wish to extend the most heartfelt gratitude of all to my wife, Jane O'Dea, who has been steadfast in her support for everything I have done or tried to do for over four decades. A university colleague in her own right, Jane readily put time aside to read the manuscript in its entirety, giving me the benefit of a feminist philosopher's perspective that enabled me to avoid – I hope – the more obvious hazards arising when men write about women. As someone who had experienced both the best and the worst of the Irish convent system during her youth, her insight was invaluable. And there is more. In 2000 Jane became dean of the Faculty of Education at what was probably the lowest point in its history. During the decade of her leadership she initiated a radical transformation of institutional culture, saved us from postmodernism and schoolmarmery, and created a community of scholars and teachers in which it has been a pleasure to work. A book like this would never have been written without the transformation that Jane brought about.

I would like to dedicate this book to Jane O'Dea, the most remarkable woman that I have ever been privileged to know. *Exceptionnelle*, as the French would say. And I would like to provide a second dedication to my late sister, Irene O'Connell, whose education was terminated by the Sisters of Mercy when she was only fifteen. As Irene used to say to me over the years: "How different my life might have been had I been raised in a country with a public school system." Wise words from another remarkable woman.

(OPPOSITE, ABOVE) *Aspirants in chapel, Ancilla Domini High School, Donaldson, Indiana, 1950s (GHJC-24-15-03. Reproduced with permission, the University of Notre Dame Archives, South Bend, Indiana)*

(OPPOSITE, BELOW) *Aspirants dancing, Ancilla Domini High School, Donaldson, Indiana, 1950s (GHJC-24-15-01. Reproduced with permission, the University of Notre Dame Archives, South Bend, Indiana)*

(ABOVE) *Postulant receiving her veil, the Poor Handmaids of Jesus Christ, Donaldson, Indiana, 1950s (GHJC-25-17-01. Reproduced with permission, the University of Notre Dame Archives, South Bend, Indiana)*

(OPPOSITE, ABOVE) *Postulants at the doorway of the Sisters of Charity of Providence novitiate, Seattle, Washington, 1950 (140.C1.18. Reproduced with permission, Providence Archives, Seattle, Washington)*

(OPPOSITE, BELOW) *Religion class with Fr A. Throckmorton, Sisters of Charity of Providence novitiate, Seattle, Washington, 1950s (140.C5.3. Reproduced with permission, Providence Archives, Seattle, Washington)*

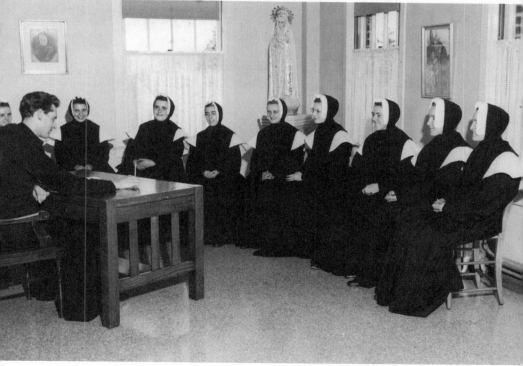

First profession ceremony, Sisters of Charity of Providence novitiate, Issaquah, Washington, 1963 (1963.002. Reproduced with permission, Providence Archives, Seattle, Washington)

Into

Silence

and

Servitude

· ·

Introduction

. . . .

THIS IS A BOOK THAT I STUMBLED INTO, one that slowly took on a recognizable form as I explored a number of questions that had perplexed me since my early years. Some would say that anything to do with nuns or women religious is an odd choice of subject for a male secular historian. It begins to make more sense, however, when I explain that nuns and convents were part of the inescapable landscape of my youth. Every girl that I knew growing up in Ireland was educated by nuns. In fact, I spent my first two years of school at "South Pres," the convent on Douglas Street, Cork, where Nano Nagle established the Sisters of the Presentation in 1776. On my way back and forth from school, I passed by the Convent of the Reparation on Windmill Road, the home of a congregation of contemplative nuns. At times my family attended Mass in the church attached to that convent, during which we listened to the nuns singing part of their Office. My father used to describe their singing as "glorious" or "brilliant" – words of praise indeed, since Cork people are rarely heard saying anything positive, except in reference to their hurling team. Nuns seemed to control all the hospitals and girls' schools in the city, and their convents were everywhere. On the north side stood the largest convent of them all – that of the Sisters of the Good Shepherd in Sunday's Well. During the 1950s and 1960s few people were *au courant* with its dark secrets. It was just another convent.

At times we would catch glimpses of postulants being ushered through the city streets. Nobody took much notice of these "apprentice nuns" – to use the local parlance; nobody wondered who they were, what they were doing, or why. Much the same could be said about the small groups of nuns that turned up in some of my

university classes. Content to stick together, they avoided the lively
social activities of the general student body. Their lives remained a
mystery, and they appeared to want it that way. The world of nuns
and convents was simply an impenetrable *terra incognita*. But questions were unavoidable, especially when some of my peers had sisters and girlfriends who left suddenly to enter religious life. Why
would girls and young women become nuns in the first place? And
what was it like to become one? These seemed like obvious questions, but answers remained strangely elusive.

Some years later, while studying the relationship between the
Canadian state and that country's native population, I came across
the system of residential schools that had been established in the
nineteenth century as a joint state/church venture for the purposes of cultural assimilation and religious conversion. At the time,
nothing had been written about these schools, but they have since
acquired a reputation as the darkest chapter in Canadian history.
About half of them were conducted by agencies of the Catholic
Church and nuns did most of the classroom teaching. I could discover little about these nuns except that many of them were French
or French-Canadian, that they were often poorly educated, and
that their command of the English language was sometimes inadequate for the competent performance of their work. And yet they
laboured on, often for many decades of their lives, in remote and
inhospitable places.

I had many questions, but the existing histories of women religious were not particularly helpful. Far too often the literature took
the form of congregational chronologies penned by insiders under
titles such as *Joyous Service*, *Legacy of Mercy*, and *Odyssey of Love*.
Stories of heroic personal sacrifices filled these pages, but there was
little of a critical nature that would have addressed my concerns.

Then, by a strange coincidence, three books were published in
1987 that showed a different way: Caitríona Clear, *Nuns in Nineteenth
Century Ireland*; Marta Danylewycz, *Taking the Veil: An Alternative to
Marriage, Motherhood, and Spinsterhood in Quebec, 1840–1920*; and
Geneviève Reynes, *Couvents de femmes: La vie des religieuses cloîtrées
dans la France des XVIIe et XVIIIe siècles*. These were works by secular
historians who probed the inner workings of convents and gave
some attention to the questions of recruitment and training that

had long been a source of curiosity for me. They also introduced me, if briefly, to the existence of lay/coadjutrix sisters – a subcategory of servant nuns whose lives challenged the prevailing heroic interpretation of history.

The literature on the history of women religious in the United States began to follow a similar path too, as more archives were opened to academic researchers. Leaving behind the old hagiography, the new scholarship set a high standard of research and writing. Books such as Anne Butler, *Across God's Frontier: Catholic Sisters in the American West, 1850–1920* (2012), Carol Coburn and Martha Smith, *Spirited Lives: How American Nuns Shaped Catholic Culture and American Life, 1836–1920* (1999), and Kathleen Sprows Cummings, *New Women of the Old Faith: Gender and American Catholicism in the Progressive Era* (2009) made extensive use of primary sources and provided the sort of detailed accounts of their subjects that earned deserved praise. Later, as my research progressed, Margaret McGuinness, *Called to Serve: A History of Nuns in America* (2013) appeared. It was a most welcome general synthesis. I learned much from these historians and their books, but their tendency to emphasize institution-building and the achievements of prominent nuns – while important – left many of my questions still unanswered.

As I delved into the subject, I encountered, *par hasard*, an oblique reference to aspirancies – institutions that seemed to play a significant role in the recruitment of American girls to religious life and about which nothing had been written. Aspirancies were convent boarding schools providing secondary education to adolescents interested in becoming nuns. Heavily subsidized by the congregations that operated them, their purpose was to protect and cultivate the religious vocations their students were presumed to have. In looking further into this topic, I realized that aspirancies were both instruments of recruitment and an initial stage of religious formation and could only be properly understood in reference to both. This took my research in two directions: to the postulancy and novitiate programs where many aspirants were going, and to the context in which recruitment in its many dimensions was taking place.

As my research horizon broadened to take on the form of a book, it occurred to me that the period from 1945 to 1965 had a compelling logic as a chronological focus. This was the era of the baby-boom children, when the number of students in American Catholic schools and the total number of nuns in the country reached a mutual pinnacle. That these parallel trends were intimately connected soon became clear. Very few nuns were recruited from among the many Catholic girls who attended public schools; they came almost exclusively from the ranks of those in Catholic schools. Was there something unique about the experience of a Catholic education that would bring this about? The fact that the vast majority of nuns were employed as teachers in parochial and diocesan schools raised further questions. Was there an economic imperative at play? Was their wageless labour a means of curbing costs and making education in a private school system more affordable?

The questions around recruitment – how and why it operated as it did – are complex and interrelated, and these are the focus of the first half of the book. In order to break down the complexity, I felt that a general excursion into the history of female monasticism was warranted that I might explain how it originated and evolved over the centuries. Phenomena such as cloister, the vows, distinctive clothing, and routines of work and prayer would not be readily understood without such a background. The same could be said for the distinction between contemplative and active congregations. The key role played by active congregations in building up America's Catholic school system became part of this background.

It was generally understood that girls and young women became nuns in response to a special call from God, from the realization that they were in receipt of the religious vocation. But there was much more to it than a sudden awareness of divine favour, and especially in circumstances where the Church was in desperate need of nuns to staff its expanding school system. My inquiry led me to a rather obscure body of literature on the sociology of vocations, to the idea that social science methods could be employed to discover the optimum circumstances under which the divine call might be heard. The idea was by no means free of controversy in view of the traditional conception of a vocation as a purely supernatural phenomenon and the Church's suspicion of sociology as a product of secular and modernist thought.

Nor was it readily accepted that agents of the Church should engage in active recruitment – that they should give God a helping hand in revealing the divine call to suitable girls and young women. And yet, this became accepted practice. Many congregations even employed the services of recruitment professionals to boost the numbers entering their religious-formation programs. The strategies of these professionals are examined in detail.

In investigating active recruitment, I came to question an assumption made by some historians of women religious: that Catholic families felt honoured when daughters entered the convent. The truth proved a bit more elusive and complicated and required an entire chapter unto itself.

As we move into the second half of the book, we follow girls entering religious life as they negotiated the sequence of formation stages known as aspirancy, postulancy, and novitiate – each stage bringing its unique challenges respecting decorum, autonomy, personal relations, work, and study. Of the many who were called, not all were chosen, or, more precisely, reached the stage where they took their vows of poverty, chastity, and obedience. Dismissals punctuated each of the stages. Religious congregations were bent on expansion, but only with new members able to adapt to the age-old rituals and routines of convent life. Voluntary withdrawals were also of note, as candidates came to realize what was expected of them in religious life and demurred. By the early 1960s, convent novitiates were crowded and the number of nuns in the country continued to grow. By 1965, when the system reached its high point, there were almost 180,000 nuns in total.

It would not do to bring matters to a conclusion in 1965, and in a postscript I examine the unexpected decline that set in immediately afterwards. The decline was marked by significant desertions by those already in religious life and a collapse in recruitment. The connection between the rise of the convent system and its dramatic fall is also explored.

It would not have been possible to write a book like this without employing a complex diversity of sources. Archival material provided me with valuable insight into programs of formation – what was studied, how was it studied, and so forth. There were also useful statistics on admission and perseverance, as well as the sorts of judgments made about candidates as they progressed through the programs. A body of rather obscure literature, mainly from the pens of priests, led me to a better understanding of recruitment and of the operations of certain aspects of convent life.

But these sources left much that was untold. What was it like to be there, to decide to enter a convent, and to experience the various stages of formation? To make sense of this, I turned to oral history and to the memoirs of nuns and former nuns who entered in the decades following the Second World War. Employing these memoirs allowed me to populate the pages of the book with real people rather than vague collectivities. Individuals who first appear as objects of recruitment or in conflict with their parents over their religious vocations often turn up later as aspirants, postulants, and novices. In this way continuity between the chapters is forged. Besides, the processes of recruitment and formation were one continuum, where selection and rejection were constantly at play both on the part of congregations and of the young people attracted to religious life.

Some may be surprised at the scant attention I give to theory in this book. But I decided that theorizing was much less important than recording the experiences of ordinary girls and young women who spent part of their youth training to become nuns and several subsequent years working in convent institutions. Rescuing their lives and voices from obscurity while positioning them in the historical context of postwar America was one of my purposes. French philosopher Paul Ricoeur once said: "To be forgotten is to die twice." If these ordinary nuns are not forgotten, then I will have accomplished something.

. . . .

CHAPTER 1

Brides of Christ ...

and Why So Many

Were Needed

If we wish to go forward as the inspired zeal
of the Bishops would have us go forward,
how many vocations do we need in this
country? Most conservative estimates tell us
that in addition to 45,000 priests we should
have 60,000 more; in addition to 7,000
Brothers we should have 75,000 more;
in addition to 125,000 Sisters we should
have 400,000 more.[1]
The Boston Pilot, *11 October 1952*

A religious community is an economical
and efficient source of women workers
in the Church. By binding women
into a community life, the Church
has low-cost personnel for its schools,
hospitals, and charitable institutions. Its
extensive American operations would
collapse without them.[2]
*Edward Wakin and Fr Joseph
F. Scheuer, 1965*

NUNS WERE ALWAYS A BIT OF A MYSTERY, even to Catholics who
had spent time, willingly or not, in one or more of their institutions.
The popular image of women shrouded in billowy black garments
with faces encased in starched white linens was by no means universal. Since nuns belonged to hundreds of different congregations,
with diverse mandates and national origins, their habits varied in
ways that were sometimes striking, sometimes subtle. For example,
the pointy white cornets of the Sisters of Charity of St Vincent
de Paul set them apart from the ordinary, and they were known
affectionately as "God's geese."[3] At the more subdued end of the
scale, the totally black attire of the Passionist Sisters was indistinguishable from a Middle Eastern chador. Nor was black necessarily
always the dominant colour. The Sisters of Our Lady of Charity of
the Refuge wore white habits with black veils, the white symboliz-
ing their purity, the black their death to the world.[4] The robes of the
Discalced Carmelites were of a coarse brown material and, as their
name implied, they eschewed the standard black shoes for sandals;
the colour brown symbolized poverty and humility.[5] The Sisters of
Charity of Montreal wore habits of grey topped with black hoods,
and were popularly known as the Grey Nuns. Whatever the differences and distinctions, a nun's habit covered her entire body except
for face and hands and ensured that all traces of feminine curves
were obscured by layers of cloth.

While many of the habits were variations on a similar theme, the
same could be said of the names of the different congregations.
As we have already seen, there were at least three different kinds
of Sister of Charity; in fact, there were many more, the Sisters of
Charity of the Blessed Virgin Mary and the Sisters of Charity of
the Incarnate Word, for example. Sometimes congregations took
their names from events and phenomena associated with the lives of
Jesus and Mary – the Assumption, the Holy Cross, the Immaculate
Conception, Nazareth, and even such combinations as the Poor
Sisters of Jesus Crucified and the Sorrowful Mother. Some of the
names sound remarkably similar and can lead to confusion: the Sisters of the Precious Blood, the Sisters of the Most Precious Blood,
and the Sisters Adorers of the Most Precious Blood. And there were
congregations whose names implied acceptance of a subservient
role: the Poor Handmaids of Jesus Christ and the Servants of the
Pierced Hearts of Jesus and Mary, for example.

What the names may indicate is the origin of the constitution or set of rules under which the congregation operates. If St Benedict, St Dominic, or St Francis is mentioned directly or in adjective form in the name, the congregation in question probably follows governing principles devised by that saint.[6] Holy rules are essential to any understanding of religious life, and they make little sense unless we probe their origins during the early centuries of Christianity.

Chastity has always been the most defining characteristic of nuns. It is believed to place them on a higher moral plain than ordinary women, whether single or married. The Christian idea that chastity is a necessary condition of the truly virtuous life can be traced to the cult of the Blessed Virgin, and in particular to the belief that Mary was a virgin both before and after the birth of Jesus.[7] As this idea found acceptance in the early Church, it became possible to argue, as St Augustine did, that all sexual activity – even in marriage for the purposes of procreation – was somehow tainted with sin.[8] The moral superiority of chastity was reinforced in biographical accounts of early Christian female martyrs. These stories followed a predictable pattern: a beautiful Christian woman takes a vow of chastity, rebuffs the advances of a pagan male authority figure, and is tortured and killed, while preserving her virginity intact. Many of these stories are now acknowledged to be historically suspect, but they do indicate a tradition of consecrated virginity in the Church long before monasticism emerged as an institutional form.[9]

Monasticism had its origins in dilemmas arising from the successful expansion of Christianity. The early followers of Jesus readily renounced worldly pleasures in anticipation of his imminent return, but with the passing of time the community of believers acquired members with little taste for self-denial and austerity. With the conversion of the Emperor Constantine in 313 CE, the Church was on the road to total domination in Rome and the enjoyment of wealth and power. In the new order of things, the sacred objects associated with Christian rituals came to be crafted in precious metals, while bishops and popes adorned themselves in costumes woven from the richest of fabrics. The Church and the World had found accommodation. Monasticism represented a rejection of the encroaching worldliness.[10] It was rooted in the idea of *contemptus mundi* – contempt for the world. And it implied a critique of the Church's embrace of temporal goods and concerns. Moreover, the Church triumphant eliminated the possibility of martyrdom, at least in the Roman Empire, and monasticism stepped into the breach, creating new roads to sainthood. Renouncing the world behind convent and monastery walls became the new form of martyrdom.

The Egyptian desert became a favourite place of refuge for a class of Christian hermits who sought to flee the corrupting influences of civilization – St Anthony being the best known among them.[11] As the number of hermits proliferated in the early 300s, the idea of organizing them into communities became compelling. Pachomius, a contemporary of Anthony, was the first to experiment with this idea when he gathered a group of ascetically minded men together in an abandoned village on the Nile around 320 CE. His sister established a parallel community of women on the other side of the river. Pachomius devised a simple set of rules to guide both communities in their daily routines of prayer, work, and study. Female monasticism, then, made its appearance at the same time as its male equivalent.[12]

Pachomius's rules were adapted and refined by later saintly figures – Basil of Caesaria, Augustine of Hippo, Benedict of Nursia – as they designed governance structures for monasteries and convents. While there were differences in the details of the various rules, some concepts remained constant: absolute obedience to the abbot or abbess; strict schedules of work and prayer; property held in common; chastity and its accoutrements: modesty in dress and restricted contact with the outside world and with the opposite sex in particular.[13]

The schedule of prayers, known as the Divine Office or the Liturgy of the Hours, was one of the defining characteristics of monasticism. It had its origins in the Jewish practice of praying at regular hours. Early Christians adopted this practice, and it was later incorporated into monastic constitutions. St Benedict's Rule required monks and nuns to pray eight times a day at three-hour intervals. Beginning at midnight, the prayers, which consisted of combinations of psalms, hymns, and Scripture passages, went by the following names: Matins, Lauds, Prime, Terce, Sext, None, Vespers, and Compline. Chanting the prayers in antiphons – call and response, with two choirs interacting – appears to have been the practice from the beginning. During the Dark Ages, reliance on sundials, hour glasses, and marked candles to measure the passing of time meant that the three-hour intervals had to be interpreted loosely and rules were written accordingly. For example, Prime was to take place at "cock-crow," while Vespers was at "the lighting of the lamps." Days in convents and monasteries were punctuated by bells ringing to indicate prayer time.[14]

Limiting contact with the world was known as enclosure, clois-ter, or *clausura*. It meant staying inside the monastic compound and keeping visitors out. Enclosure was much stricter in female monasticism than in its male counterpart, chastity being the major concern. It was assumed that women were frivolous and weak by nature and more easily beguiled by Satan – an idea linked to the story of Eve and to the Church's fear of female sexuality, or what historian Jacques Solé called "le mythe clérical de la lascivité fem-inine."[15] The preservation of chastity was fundamental to the logic of the convent. From the earliest days, women religious or nuns were considered spouses of Christ whose bodies were off limits to ordinary mortals. Caesarius of Arles, who founded a convent in the sixth century, described nuns as "consecrated virgins, souls vowed to God, who await the coming of the Lord with lighted lamps and a tranquil conscience."[16]

The rule on modest dress was a further safeguard for chastity. By the sixth century, religious women wore distinctive, if plain, cloth-ing that covered the body almost completely and that included a veil on the head. Showing hair had sexual connotations, and it had to be kept from view. Being dressed in the habit for the first time – taking the veil – became a ritualized beginning of a nun's new life in Christ, and the uniformity of habits symbolized a loss of indi-viduality and a commitment to the community and its goals.[17] The ritual of veiling was accompanied by the taking of the three vows of poverty, chastity, and obedience – in effect, making a solemn com-mitment to following the rules or constitutions in their essentials.

What persuaded women to take the veil in the first place? While mystical experiences did play a role, there were some practical advantages to religious life. Nuns were able to avoid the hazards of childbirth and the risk of an unhappy marriage. Moreover, the convent as a place of refuge took on a new importance as bar-barian tribes dismantled the western part of the Roman Empire.

Although it was not always true, nuns believed that they were better positioned in their walled sanctuaries to avoid the bed of Vandal, Visigoth, or Hun. Monastic literature popularized this view by portraying convents as oases of prayerful tranquility in a world ruled by fear and uncertainty.[18]

The reasons for entering convents became more complex and diverse as the centuries passed. Patronage by the medieval elite allowed the system to expand in the belief that those on earth and the souls in Purgatory benefited from nuns' prayers. Moreover, wealthy benefactors began to see convents as convenient places of retirement for widows of their own class. By the tenth century some estimates put the proportion of nuns who were widows as high as 25 per cent.[19]

Whether single or widowed, the influx of upper-class ladies fundamentally changed the original egalitarianism of religious life. Some willingly embraced menial labour as ascetic discipline, but this was not always so. Others entered on the understanding that they could bring their slaves and/or servants with them to do the physical work, allowing them, the ladies, to concentrate on prayer. And so the class system established itself inside the convent, with a clear distinction being made between choir sisters – the elite – and lay or coadjutrix sisters – the servants. While choir sisters chanted the Divine Office in chapel, lay sisters were preparing the meal they would serve them later. Lay sisters acquired distinctive habits that signalled their inferior status and were excluded from participation in the governance of the community. It has been estimated that lay sisters may have comprised up to 30 per cent of Italian and Spanish communities in the Early Modern period.[20]

Not everyone entered willingly. In Renaissance Italy, convent dowries – required for choir sisters – were only a fraction of those required to secure a decent husband. Families who could not afford the latter, or who simply wanted to preserve their wealth, sometimes placed daughters in convents as a measure of economy.[21] Or if a daughter were considered unmarriageable because of some physical defect, she might be similarly disposed of, as in the case of the Venetian Arcangela Tarabotti (1604–1654), who bitterly resented her fate.[22] Powerful abbesses also were known to persuade their relatives to hand over very young daughters to be raised in their convents – a sure method of recruitment.[23]

Placing women in convents against their will was sometimes related to moral judgments on their behaviour. Louis the Pious (778–840), son and successor of Charlemagne, began his reign by sending his unmarried sisters, who were living with their lovers in the royal palace, to the convent.[24] In the later Middle Ages, French, German, and Italian convents were established for the special purpose of housing "fallen women" and former prostitutes who were persuaded to reform their lives and seek salvation in prayer and penance.[25]

Because of the complexity of circumstances under which women entered convents, not all were happy to be there. Some nuns had taken their vows reluctantly or under duress, and proved difficult to deal with. From the later Middle Ages into the Early Modern period, loose enforcement of the rules was common enough, resulting in pregnancy scandals and even outbreaks of mass sexual hysteria that were attributed to the Devil.[26]

By the 1200s there were Benedictines, Carmelites, Cistercians, Dominicans, and Franciscans – to name the major orders – in male and female versions. Monks were officially known as the First Order and nuns the Second Order. There were also Third Orders, male and female. The tertiaries, as they were called, were lay auxiliaries, who might live in the world or in community, who retained control of their property, and who took simple vows that could easily be renounced. Beguines and canonesses were some of the names by which female tertiaries were known.[27] Although their status was only quasi-religious, their mortifications and mystical experiences could match those of fully cloistered nuns. Agnes Blannbekin (died 1315), a Viennese beguine, had a vision in which she saw naked nuns and monks dancing with Jesus in Heaven.[28] Experiments with Third Orders provided models for the active congregations that appeared in Early Modern Europe – congregations that found it possible to modify enclosure to allow for some engagement with the world outside the walls.

The Reformation was a disaster for monasticism, and for the convent system in particular. Martin Luther proclaimed his rejection of monasticism in leaving the Augustinian Order and in marrying Catherine von Bora, an ex-nun. As Protestantism spread through central and northern Europe in the 1500s, convents and monasteries were suppressed and their properties confiscated by ambitious princes and monarchs. Monks sometimes had the possibility of seeking office in newly established Protestant churches, but no such course was open to nuns, many of whom faced great hardship when evicted from their convents.[29]

But monasticism consolidated its position and took on new forms in the parts of Europe remaining loyal to Rome. The Council of Trent (Trentino), was called by the Pope to redefine Catholic doctrine and practice in light of Protestantism's challenge. Meeting between 1545 and 1563, the council decreed a tightening of monastic rules and better enforcement of them. The threat of investigation by the Inquisition encouraged compliance.[30]

The spirit of the Counter Reformation, as the movement emanating from Trent is called, can be seen in St Teresa's austere reform of the Carmelites in Avila, Spain.[31] Although successful in many respects, the Discalced Carmelites did not represent real innovation in female monasticism. A new type of congregation emerged in Italy around the same time that better meets that description and ultimately transformed convents in their mode of operation. In the 1530s Angela Merici established the Company of St Ursula in Brescia. The Ursulines, as they were known, were originally a "company of virgins" who took simple, private vows, lived together in houses rather than in convents, and wore no distinctive habit. Relying on the example of the tertiaries, they avoided directives on enclosure and went about their charitable and educational work with considerable freedom. Their schools for girls were immediately popular with the wealthy classes. And the company attracted many young women to its ranks for whom the austerities and mortifications of the older contemplative congregations had little appeal.

In time the Ursulines encountered opposition within the Church and were pressured to adopt more conventional forms of religious life, a transformation in place by the mid-1600s. In becoming a congregation, however, they forged for themselves modifications to cloister. Their convents were designed with an enclosed living space for the sisters and an attached but separate school annex that was open to students but to nobody else.[32] The prayer schedule of the Divine Office also needed to adapt under the circumstances, since teaching nuns needed a decent night's sleep if they were to be effective in the classroom. After some experimentation, a different schedule of prayers, known as the Little Office of Our Lady, was approved by Pope Paul V in 1585.[33] The Ursulines were the prototype of the new active congregations arising from the Counter Reformation – enclosed, but not completely, spending less time in prayer, and providing a useful service to society.[34]

The Ursulines spread into France, where they experienced great success. They became part of the "devotional revival" that gripped that country during the first half of the 1600s. This revival was a movement of sustained religious fervour that saw a remarkable proliferation of convents and congregations. Most of the new foundations were of the active kind and their useful work found support at all levels of society.[35] Several of them later found their way to North America as the convent system put down roots on that continent. The following are worth noting in that respect: the Visitation Sisters, founded by Jeanne de Chantal and François de Sales in Annecy, Haute-Savoie, 1610; the Daughters of Charity, founded by Vincent de Paul and Louise Maraillac in Paris, 1633; the Sisters of St Joseph, founded by Jean-Pierre Médaille in Le Puy-en-Velay, 1650; and the Sisters of Our Lady of Charity of the Refuge, founded by Jean Eudes in Caen, Normandy, 1641.

The first three of these congregations directed a diversity of institutions concerned with education, health care, and charity. The Sisters of Our Lady of Charity of the Refuge established penitential asylums for the moral rehabilitation and salvation of fallen women and former prostitutes.[36]

Although the Reformation destroyed the Catholic Church's power in much of northern and central Europe, opportunities to establish new domains opened up with exploration and colonization in the Americas. The Thirteen English Colonies that eventually formed the United States were Protestant for the most part, but they were flanked north and south by French and Spanish settlements where the Church was asserting itself as a significant player in the subjugation of Aboriginal peoples and in shaping the lives of the colonists.

Spanish rule in Florida was never on a firm foundation, challenged as it was by Aboriginal resistance and incursions by the English and the French. When the territory was incorporated into the United States in 1821, the Church had little to show for its missionary exploits.[37] In Mexico, it was a different story. Here the Church was a key partner in the system of colonial administration from the beginning. Female monasticism made an early appearance with the establishment of the convent of La Concepción in Mexico City in 1550. Colonial Spanish convents were structured along the caste lines of society. Choir sisters usually had to be of European blood, while Indians and Mestizas were relegated to servant work as co-adjutrices.[38] Early in the twentieth century, Mexican congregations would come to play a role in the American convent system and some US-based congregations would look to Mexico for new recruits.[39]

North of the Thirteen Colonies the Church quickly put down roots in the French settlements along the St Lawrence River, and convents were part of the ecclesiastical infrastructure almost from the beginning. Marie Guyart, a young widow from Tours, played a significant role here. During the 1620s, Guyart had a mystical experience, during which she was swept through the city streets in a flood of precious blood. Further experiences followed and in 1631 she entered the Ursuline community, abandoning her twelve-year-old son, Claude, in doing so. In 1639, accompanied by two other Ursulines, Marie de l'Incarnation, as she was now known in religion, set sail for New France, arriving at the little settlement that would become Quebec City on 1 August. Here she established a convent that survives today. After futile efforts to Europeanize Aboriginal children, she and her community focused on educating the colonists' daughters.[40]

Almost a century later, in 1727, twelve Ursulines from France stepped ashore in New Orleans, intending to establish hospitals and schools. Educating girls in what was then a French colony soon became their major concern.[41] These two Ursuline initiatives set in motion a practice that evolved into an unquestioned convention: that schools for Catholic girls should ideally be conducted by nuns.

With the Louisiana Purchase of 1803, New Orleans became part of the United States, and it could be argued that the Ursuline convent in that city was America's first. The settlement along the St Lawrence had an enduring influence too, if in a different way. Incorporated into British North America after the Peace of Paris, 1763, it evolved into the preponderantly French-speaking and Catholic Canadian province of Quebec. During the nineteenth and twentieth centuries, French-Canadian congregations established a major presence in the American convent system.[42]

At the time of independence, there were an estimated twenty-five thousand Catholics in the United States, concentrated mainly in Maryland. There were only two dozen priests, no nuns, and no bishop. John Carroll, of a prominent and patriotic Maryland family, was chosen Bishop of Baltimore in 1789, becoming the leader of the Church throughout the nation. The survival of the Catholic community in a preponderantly Protestant state became Carroll's immediate concern, and to this end he set about creating a network of churches, schools, and related institutions.

In 1790 four Carmelite nuns, three of whom were American-born, arrived from Belgium and opened a convent in Port Tobacco, Maryland. Another contemplative congregation, the French Poor Clares, settled in Georgetown in Washington, DC, and were prevailed upon to open a school. Contemplatives tended to come to the United States seeking refuge from turmoil in their homelands – the French Revolution, for example – but they were not exactly what Bishop Carroll wanted. Carroll sought active nuns who would establish and run institutions important to the Catholic community, and trying to shoehorn contemplatives into that role just didn't work.[43] Matters improved in 1799 when three Irish immigrants, known as "the pious ladies," took over the school in Georgetown that the Poor Clares had abandoned. The "ladies" were successful as teachers, and in 1816 they were persuaded to take vows as Visitation Sisters.[44]

Elizabeth Seton, a widow and convert to Catholicism, was responsible for a similar initiative around the same time. It was fairly common for educated but impoverished widows to turn to school teaching for a living, and Seton did just that after her husband's death. Her results were uneven until, in 1808, she was invited to open a Catholic school in Baltimore with the assistance of the Sulpician Fathers, who were refugees from the French Revolution. The school was a success, and in 1809 Seton and her teaching companions were encouraged by the Sulpicians to form themselves into a religious community. Adopting the rule of St Vincent de Paul, they became the Sisters of Charity of St Joseph. The Sisters took as their habit Seton's black bonnet and "widow's weeds" rather than conventional religious attire.[45]

The Visitation Sisters and the Sisters of Charity forged new paths as religious congregations that were adaptable to American circumstances yet strongly linked to European monastic traditions. And they reinforced the idea, already established elsewhere, that the education of Catholic girls should ideally be the domain of nuns. The other side of this equation was that, when lay Catholic women, whether single or widowed, sought to make a living in teaching, they came under pressure to embrace some form of religious vows.

Between 1820 and 1870, more than five million Irish and German Catholic immigrants settled in the United States, transforming its ethnic and religious composition. The Church, with its fledgling network of parishes and schools, became a common meeting ground for the new arrivals.[46] Religious orders and congregations accompanied the immigrants, strengthening and expanding ecclesiastical institutions. Ireland's Sisters of Mercy, for example, established themselves in Pittsburgh in 1843, and after a few years had convents in New York City and Chicago, all places of heavy Irish settlement. German congregations followed the same pattern. In 1847 the School Sisters of Notre Dame came from Bavaria to teach the children of German immigrants in rural Pennsylvania.[47]

Nuns and settlers were not always a perfect ethnic match. France, experiencing another religious revival in the aftermath of the Revolution, became a major source of nuns for the American Church, in spite of a lack of French immigration. US bishops embarked on active recruitment, and French congregations responded. For example, the Sisters of St Joseph became a significant presence in frontier Missouri beginning in the 1830s.[48] The Sisters of Providence played a similar role in Indiana when they arrived in the 1840s.[49] And the Sisters of the Good Shepherd, an offshoot of the Sisters of Our Lady of Charity of the Refuge, set up in Louisville, Kentucky, in 1842 and subsequently expanded their operations to become the major custodians of "fallen women" across the land.[50] A number of French-Canadian congregations also deserve mention in this respect. The Sisters of Charity of Providence and the Sisters of the Holy Names were building Catholic institutions in the territories of Washington and Oregon as early as the 1850s – territories with few French-Canadian settlers.[51]

Purely American foundations were added to this mix, some reflecting the racist divisions in society. The Church had a limited presence among African-Americans, and even where it did have

adherents, there was no question of admitting them to existing
all-white religious congregations. In 1828 a small group of Carib-
bean immigrant and African-American women opened a "School
for Colored Girls" in Baltimore. Within a year these teachers were
persuaded to take religious vows and became the Oblate Sisters of
Providence. A second segregated congregation appeared in New
Orleans in the 1850s: the Sisters of the Holy Family. A third one was
founded in 1916: the Franciscan Handmaids of Mary. Hostility to
the Handmaids' school in Savanna, Georgia, prompted their reloca-
tion to Harlem, where their educational work met with success.[52]

Jim Crow rules for religious congregations should come as no
great surprise considering the dimensions of institutional racism
in the country. In the antebellum period some congregations even
owned slaves: the Ursulines in New Orleans and the Sisters of Charity of Nazareth in Kentucky and Tennessee, for example.[53] Some
bishops and priests were also slave-owners and openly opposed
abolition. Bishop Carroll himself owned a slave named Charles. The
Church's policy on America's "peculiar institution" was silence.[54]

In 1835 there were fewer than one thousand nuns across the land;
by 1861 that number had reached almost five thousand. One estimate had them divided into at least sixty different congregations,
many with distinctive ethnic identities.[55] The expanding network of
convents aroused Protestant suspicions that old-world popery was
threatening American values. These fears, and sometimes hysteria,
were spurred on by the publication of bizarre exposés allegedly
written by escaped nuns, the best known of them being Maria
Monk's *Awful Disclosures of the Hôtel Dieu Nunnery* (1836). There
were anti-Catholic riots in places and demands that convents be
inspected. When such inspections took place, however, evidence
of nuns being held captive – a popular Protestant fantasy – was
never found.[56]

Prejudice against nuns was mitigated by their involvement in
health care – an involvement that began early in the nineteenth century. Suffering and death loomed large in Catholic ideology. There
were prayers for the sick, dying, and dead. A last confession was seen
as the best preparation for the pending divine judgment, and much
was made of deathbed conversions. While nuns played no role in
the last sacramental rites, their work as nurses in the hospitals they

established served to fortify the faith of their patients. They did not become doctors, but hired seculars to do that work. Their hospitals charged patients who could afford to pay and offered subsidized and even free health care to those of lesser means.

Over six hundred nuns volunteered as nurses in the Civil War of the 1860s, and did so with both armies. Their hard work and dedication won them a grudging respect and often open admiration. As a consequence, nursing came to be seen as a respectable female profession.[57] Congregations opened nursing schools in connection with their hospitals, where both lay and religious nurses were trained. Catholic hospitals always had a strong lay presence among their employees, at least in part because nuns were forbidden to engage in surgical or obstetrical nursing – a ban not lifted by the Vatican until 1936.[58]

Collaboration with the laity was much less evident in the field of Catholic education, where the vast majority of nuns were deployed. Throughout the nineteenth century the bishops encouraged their flocks to establish and support Catholic schools. Their vision was that of a network of elementary schools organized in each parish, in which the teachers were either nuns or religious brothers. The system of parochial institutions came to be controlled exclusively by bishops, priests, brothers, and nuns. The laity was excluded from leadership roles and was relegated to paying, praying, and obeying, as historian Jay Dolan put it.[59]

The immigrant surge of the 1840s and 1850s coincided with and contributed to urbanization and industrialization in the northeastern states. The modernizing economy brought about a commitment to a universal, state-funded system of elementary schools that aimed to resocialize youth in new behaviours, self-discipline, and citizenship. The bishops, however, viewed public schools as tainted with Protestantism, or worse again, godlessness. They urged the faithful to avoid such schools, and in some cases even issued proscriptions.[60]

Agitation by the bishops to secure a share of state education funds for their schools got nowhere. Catholic parochial schools, then, were private institutions, reliant on fees, donations, and teachers willing to work for low pay. Catholic parents did not always send their children to the parochial system, perhaps because of poverty or the ready availability of public schools, which was often the case, for example, in Massachusetts. In New York there was a much more pronounced determination to cooperate with the bishops' educational agenda.[61]

The lack of universal compliance prompted the bishops to take a stronger stand when they convened for the Third Plenary Council of Baltimore in 1884. They decreed that every church should have a parochial school nearby and that Catholic parents should enroll their children in them. In effect, it was a commitment to build a national alternative to the system of public elementary schools. An ambitious plan to be sure, but it had no realistic hope of success without a massive expansion of the ranks of the religious sisterhoods and brotherhoods that were expected to staff classrooms at minimum cost.[62]

Getting more young men into the brotherhoods appealed to Catholic educators, since their low numbers suggested there was room for growth. Besides, it was believed that boys, when they reached "a certain age," were best taught by men. Brothers remained in short supply, however, perhaps because young men considering lives in religion found the priesthood more attractive. In the Archdiocese of Philadelphia, vocations to sisterhoods continued to surge ahead of those to brotherhoods so that by 1919 there were thirty-six sisters in the classroom for every one brother.

The bishops and leading Catholic educators had to accept that nuns were the answer. And, although vocations to the sisterhoods were plentiful, there were never enough of them to meet the demands of the expanding parochial school system. The vocations were there, it was assumed, but young people were clearly in need of nudging or prompting to become aware of the possibility of a special calling. Teaching sisters were encouraged to engage in "conscious propaganda" in favour of the religious life in their classrooms, marking the beginning of a school-centred recruitment drive that would acquire a professional sophistication between the 1940s and 1960s as the demand for more vocations became particularly acute.[63]

Anita Caspary attended Catholic Girls' High School in Los Angeles during the late 1920s and early 1930s, and her experience shows this approach in practice during the decades before the war.

The school was unique in that the principal was a priest and seven or eight different congregations of nuns in distinctive habits did the teaching. An intense rivalry prevailed among the congregations to secure recruits to their respective ranks from the student body. One nun made a special effort to recruit Caspary, but she was not ready at the time for such a decision. Later, in September 1937, she entered the Sisters of the Immaculate Heart of Mary and became Sister Mary Humiliata.[64]

Recruitment at home was supplemented by recruitment abroad. As soon as Irish congregations established themselves in the United States, they adopted the practice of sending emissaries home on recruitment drives. And congregations that were not even Irish in origin got in on the act upon realizing that Ireland was a fertile source of new blood. The poverty and poor marriage prospects of many Irish women following the devastation of the Great Famine of the 1840s made them vulnerable to alluring promises of education and respectable careers in the missionary field. The recruitment drives intensified after the Baltimore Council. Year after year, Irish convent schools were "deluged" with American recruiting nuns competing with one another to sign up "aspirants." The usual pattern was to persuade teenage girls – the aspirants – to cross the Atlantic and enter the sponsoring congregation's novitiate. According to one estimate, between 1812 and 1914 something in the region of four thousand to seven thousand Irish women immigrated to the United States, either as professed nuns or as aspirants intending to enter a novitiate.[65] The Sisters of St Joseph was one of several non-Irish congregations to participate in these recruitment campaigns. In 1898, thirty-seven of their fifty-five postulants in St Louis had been recruited in Ireland.[66] In 1890, Margaret Mary Murphy, a wealthy widow of Irish birth who was resident in Texas, founded the Congregation of the Sister Servants of the Holy Ghost and Mary Immaculate to create schools and orphanages for "the Dark Races." When postulants were slow in signing up, she made several recruitment drives to Ireland. Some of Murphy's recruits – and this was true for other congregations as well – manipulated the situation to their own advantage by a pretense of sincerity until they had secured a free passage to America, upon which they simply walked away.[67]

The promise of a career in religion at times disappointed Irish recruits, especially in the case of poorly educated women who found themselves with the inferior status of lay or coadjutrix sisters.[68] Kitchen duty could also be the destiny of those with an education. Johanna O'Connor, born in County Kerry in 1856, entered the Sisters of Providence, St Mary-of-the-Woods, Indiana, in July 1881 and took the religious name Sister Mary Assisi. Although she was educated, an interesting conversationalist, and "blessed with a bright mind," there was something about Mary that rendered her unsuitable for teaching in the eyes of the congregation: her "rich Irish brogue that she never lost." Her strong faith and "spirit of prayer," however, enabled her to accept the life of humble labour to which she was assigned. She died in 1940.[69] Many of the lay Sisters of Providence resented their second-class status, the long hours of work required of them, and their exclusion from certain devotional practices. Only in 1954, after many decades of agitation, was the distinction between lay and choir sisters abolished in that congregation.[70]

In accordance with the bishops' grand design, nuns became the workhorses of the parochial school system. They were principals, teachers, fundraisers, and willing volunteers for any task requiring attention. Some took on the additional duty of teaching religion classes on Saturdays or after regular school hours to Catholic children who attended public schools in a program known as the Confraternity of Christian Doctrine. Teaching younger children was perceived as a "natural" profession for women – being in harmony with maternal instinct. As public elementary-school systems expanded in the nineteenth century, the teaching force became largely feminized. This was due at least in part to women's willingness to work for lower wages than men. The exploitation of female labour in public schools was a mere shadow of that in parochial schools. Around 1900 the "salaries" of sister teachers were about one-third of those earned by female teachers in the public system.[71] The salaries were really stipends paid by the parish or diocese to the religious congregation staffing its school, and were supposed to cover the cost of living. Nuns, who rarely handled money, and who in any case were bound by vows of poverty, never got a cent of it for themselves.

Half a century later, not much had changed. In some ways, the exploitation was even worse. A study by the National Catholic Education Association (NCEA) in the early 1950s concluded that the average annual stipend earned by a teaching sister for her congregation was $511.25, while her living costs amounted to $489.50. The stipends were the equivalent of about one-quarter of what public-school teachers earned at the time. And religious brothers working in the parochial system were "taking home" twice as much as the nuns.[72]

When congregations agreed to staff parochial schools, they earned barely enough to make ends meet. Teaching girls of an older age, however, turned out to be a much more lucrative proposition. The private academy for "young ladies" was often the first institution to be established when a group of nuns arrived on American soil. Fee-paying academies enrolling the daughters of the elite, either as boarders or day students or both, were "cash cows" for teaching congregations. And if the congregation were French in origin this worked to its advantage, since wealthy parents believed that a "French education" was just what their daughters needed. Congregations deployed their most highly educated members as teachers in these institutions, while sending the lesser qualified to parochial schools.[73] Academies served another, and equally important, function. New American-born recruits to religious life came preponderantly from the ranks of academy girls. In Brewer's analysis of seven of these institutions between 1871 and 1925, an average of 13 per cent of students were recruited into their sponsoring congregations.[74]

Europe continued to be a major source of new blood for the sisterhoods, although arrivals in the second half of the nineteenth century were more diverse in their countries of origin. Until the 1880s, the vast majority of Catholic immigrants came from countries such as Ireland and Germany and the religious congregations that accompanied them reflected a corresponding ethnic identity. By the 1900s, the pattern of immigration had changed. Italians and Poles now dominated, and there were also large numbers of Croats, Lithuanians, and Slovaks added to the mix. Congregations that spoke their languages accompanied them. The Missionary Sisters of the Sacred Heart of Jesus came to New York from Italy in 1889. They were led by their founder, Mother St Francis Xavier Cabrini, who had been instructed by the Pope to make the journey in order to work with Italian immigrants. Another papal directive sent the Religious Sisters Filippini to Trenton, New Jersey, from Italy in 1910, and for the same reason.[75]

The Felician Sisters were the first Eastern European congregation to arrive on American shores. They came to Wisconsin from Krakow in the 1870s to work among Polish immigrants. The Sisters of St Joseph of the Third Order of St Francis were also Polish, but with an unusual origin. The congregation was founded in America in 1901 when forty-seven Polish sisters defected from the School Sisters of St Francis because of unpleasant relations with their German colleagues.[76]

Other ethnic congregations were also established on American soil. The Sisters of St Casimir, for example, were founded by Lithuanian-born Mother Maria Kaupas in Scranton, Pennsylvania, in 1907 to establish schools in Lithuanian parishes. And the Sisters of Saints Cyril and Methodius were also founded in Scranton in 1909 as a Slovak-American congregation.[77]

Between 1860 and 1900 almost half a million French Canadians migrated to the United States, attracted by the employment available in New England mill towns. They settled in French-speaking ghettoes known as *les petits Canadas* on the fringes of those towns. Accompanied by hundreds of priests and nuns, they established Catholic schools and other social institutions modelled on those of Quebec. The Grey Nuns of Montreal and the Sisters of the Assumption of the Blessed Virgin Mary were among the most notable congregations engaged in this work.[78]

Missionary zeal, Catholic immigration, and recruitment drives brought most, but not all, congregations to America. In political upheavals in Portugal and Mexico beginning in 1910, the Church, in its alliance with old elites, found itself on the wrong side of history. Stripped of their privileges under new regimes, some nuns sought refuge in the United States. The Institute of the Sisters of St Dorothy is an example of a refugee Portuguese congregation; the Sisters, Servants of Mary of Vera Cruz is a Mexican example.[79]

One consequence of these developments was the emergence of the ethnic parish school, in which instruction was in a language other than English. In contexts such as this, Catholic education took on a strong cultural-preservation purpose. Anti-foreign hysteria during the First World War brought the system under critical scrutiny. It was considered unpatriotic to teach in a foreign language – and in particular in languages associated with Germany and the Austro-Hungarian Empire. Teaching in another language also tended to reinforce the idea that there was something foreign about Catholicism. The Church hierarchy, mainly Irish in origin, had never been enthusiastic about ethnic schools and championed assimilation as an antidote to anti-Catholicism. It used its influence to eliminate the foreign languages in the 1920s. Besides, the end of mass immigration from Eastern and Southern Europe in 1924 meant fewer newcomers and nuns to sustain the ethnic parish. By the 1930s the parish school operating in Croatian, French, German, Polish, or Slovak was gone.[80]

Language loss and the recruitment of American-born women were part of the process of assimilation that all congregations experienced over time. Yet in some cases an ethnic identity was preserved in some measure through particular traditions, through reverence for a founder, or through contact with a foreign-based mother house. The Poor Handmaids of Jesus Christ were keeping some records in German until 1937,[81] and the Sisters of Charity of Providence (Seattle) were still corresponding in French with the mother house in Montreal in the 1950s. By then these nuns were preponderantly English-speaking and American-born, although their co-adjutrix sisters continued to be poorly-educated, French-speaking Québécoises, who were sent west from Montreal.[82]

Ethnic parishes in various stages of assimilation became known as the "Catholic ghettoes." In these tightly knit communities, the Church's network of schools, colleges, hospitals, and charitable organizations were generously supported by the faithful. The Church and its institutions served as a fortress protecting Catholics from a perceived hostile society given to moral relativism, materialism, and individualism. Insisting on its own institutions, and that they be subsidized or even supported by the state, was part of the Church's anti-modernist agenda that had its roots in the papacy of Pius IX (1846–78); it was an attempt to halt the state's intrusion into aspects of life in which faith and morals were at issue. The right to socialize the faithful in traditional morality was at the heart of it. Imparting a strict moral code in a disciplined environment became one of the hallmarks of Catholic education, and even made it appealing at times to some non-Catholics.[83]

The gulf between Catholic and public schooling widened later in the nineteenth century as the latter system embraced the ideas and practices of "progressive education." Although it had earlier antecedents, progressivism was rooted in the pragmatic philosophy of William James and John Dewey, which rejected dogma and absolute certainty. Pragmatists claimed that knowledge and values arose from human action and experience and were subject to change over time. In the classroom, it meant learning through inquiry, problem-solving, group activities, and initiatives from students arising from their interests. Dewey's aim was to produce democratic citizens, and he saw religious dogma as an obstacle barring his way. In fact, he was hostile to the very idea of a Catholic school system.[84]

Catholic philosophers returned the hostility, attacking pragmatism as a narcissistic delusion that sought emancipation from all authority. The scholasticism of St Thomas Aquinas, with its objective moral order, was their alternative.[85] And the most blistering critique of progressive education came from Pope Pius XI in his encyclical *Divini Illius Magistri* (1929). The Pope took "pedagogic naturalism" to task for undermining the authority of the teacher, for appealing to "the pretended self-government and unrestrained freedom on the part of the child," and for its denial of original sin and of the need to correct "disorderly inclinations."[86] Debates between Catholics and progressives over education served to reinforce the Church's determination to maintain and develop its own school system. The two solitudes were by no means exclusive, however. Liberal Catholics, such as the maverick New York priest Father George B. Ford, readily embraced the practices of the new education, while secular historian Arthur E. Bestor denounced them in his *Educational Wastelands* (1953).[87]

The emergence of the public high school in the second half of the nineteenth century presented a new challenge to Catholic education. Parental agitation for a modern and more practical secondary program of studies that led directly to employment was behind this development. By the 1870s many state systems had free high schools in place.[88] When Catholics began to enrol in these schools, the bishops were obliged to sponsor their own parallel system. Catholic high schools, as distinct from private academies owned and operated by religious orders and congregations, were due to episcopal initiative and aimed to attract students graduating from the parochial schools of the diocese. Teaching in these schools was contracted out to religious that specialized in the work. For example, when Chicago's Immaculata High School opened in 1921, it was placed under the direction of the Sisters of Charity of the Blessed Virgin Mary. Immaculata was a girls-only institution, and this was considered the ideal, but many Catholic high schools were coeducational simply because of low enrolment. Free public high schools attracted far more Catholic students than their fee-paying diocesan equivalents.[89]

The emergence of the Catholic high school put new pressures on the convent system. School accreditation systems required teachers with more academic qualifications. Yet, sending their members to college put enormous strains on the slim financial resources of many communities. Some turned to secular universities because of their geographical proximity and lower fees, in spite of what Sister Bertrande Meyers called "the evil inherent in such a policy." Sister Meyers's survey of Mother Provincials in the late 1930s found the vast majority of them opposed to attendance at secular institutions. Some nuns who had done so had returned "tainted with anti-Catholic ideas" that could be observed in their classroom teaching.[90]

The decline of ethnic schools as the twentieth century progressed was a symptom of a larger trend in American Catholicism. The faithful began to drift away from the old immigrant ghettoes with each generation. During and after the Second World War, the dissolving of the old neighbourhoods accelerated, bringing new challenges to traditions that flourished only in isolation.[91] And yet the Church was determined to resist integration of its flock into the mainstream in important ways. Sustaining and expanding its school system, even in challenging circumstances, was part of this determination.

In 1945 the Catholic population of the United States stood at 23,963,671. Ten years later it had increased by 35.9 per cent to 32,575,702. During the same decade, the number of nuns grew by 15 per cent, from 138,079 to 158,069. Nuns were not keeping up with the growth in the laity.[92]

The staggering growth was mainly a consequence of the postwar baby boom. As the baby boomers emerged from infancy, the Catholic schools system attempted to accommodate them in an unprecedented expansion. In 1949 Catholic elementary and secondary enrolment stood at just over 2 million; by the end of the 1950s it had more than doubled to 4.2 million and was continuing to grow. The growth was orchestrated by a generation of "builder bishops," who raised enormous sums of money to construct new schools. The most determined among them was Archbishop John O'Hara of Philadelphia, who wanted a Catholic education for every Catholic child, in classrooms staffed by men and women of the cloth. Despite his best efforts, however, he could never find enough priests, brothers, and nuns to do the job and was forced to rely increasingly on lay teachers.[93]

The employment of lay teachers was considered unsatisfactory, since they were thought to lack the dedication of those in religious vows. More importantly, they required salaries that drove up costs and fees and made Catholic schools less affordable. In an address to the First National Congress of Religious in the United States in 1952, Monsignor Carroll F. Deady, superintendent of schools for the Diocese of Detroit, called the employment of lay teachers in parochial schools "harmful" to their essentially religious character. But not all speakers at the Congress agreed. Some argued that, in order to be realistic, schools would have to content themselves with a certain proportion of lay teachers, although estimates on the ideal proportion varied from 20 to 50 per cent. It was acknowledged too that lay Catholic women graduates were often reluctant to teach in the system, because of low salaries, lack of security and social life, and the attitude of sisters to them.[94]

The only real solution to the long-term viability of the system was a major expansion in the number of nuns. Furthermore, many Catholic parents believed that it was the teaching nun that made parochial schools special.[95] Nuns were not only cheap, there were far more of them than priests and brothers, since women entered religious life in much greater numbers than men. In 1952 there were 16,000 priests and 8,000 brothers in the country. Nuns, however, numbered 157,000, of whom 86,000 were working in Catholic schools.[96]

The challenge of finding more nuns was complicated by new demands respecting teaching credentials. It was common practice in the decades following the Second World War to take sisters fresh from their novitiates and place them in charge of classrooms in

Catholic schools. Lack of professional training was not considered a problem, since it was assumed that the sisters would learn to teach by trial and error and with divine guidance. Mother Marie Helene, Superior General of the Sisters of Providence (St Mary-of-the-Woods) explained it this way: "The art of teaching, like all other arts, can be learned by practice, but the fundamental talent God seems to give in generous measure to our religious sisters. The ease with which a frail little sister can interest and gain the hearts of a group of children shows that God gives the tools to those who are willing to do His work."[97]

The lack of credentials threatened to harm the reputation of Catholic schools relative to their public counterparts, which were increasingly well funded and staffed by qualified professionals. In fact, thirty-three states by 1952 either required a college degree for teacher certification or were on course to do so.[98] A survey conducted in the same year showed that only 13 of 255 congregations providing data had programs in place enabling their members to pursue undergraduate degrees.[99]

Sister Madeleva Wolff, president of St Mary's College, South Bend, Indiana, addressed the issue in a presentation to the National Catholic Education Association conference in 1949. Noting that state agencies had hitherto been courteous in tolerating convent practices, Sister Madeleva argued that sisters should have appropriate academic qualifications before taking up teaching. She recognized the existing pressure from the Church's educational leaders to staff classrooms, but claimed that a college education would strengthen a sister's professional work and her vocational commitment.[100] There was some resistance to this proposal, but it was tempered by Pope Pius XII in 1952 when he spoke to delegates assembled in Rome for the First World Congress of Mothers General. The Pope was concerned that "excessively strict" rules and ministries undertaken without proper training had contributed to the alarming decline in religious vocations in many parts of postwar Europe. He urged that nuns be enabled to enter their schools with the same mastery of "profane knowledge" as seculars.[101]

American nuns immediately embraced the Pope's challenge. Discussions at the annual meetings of the National Catholic Education Association in the early 1950s led to the creation of the Sister Formation Conference, a body dedicated to the aim of a degree for all teaching sisters.[102] Nuns did get degrees before this initiative, but it usually took endless special summer schools to get there – the twenty-five-year plan, as many called it.[103] Sister Formation wanted at least two years of liberal arts studies – or better still, college graduation – for the next generation of nuns before they took up teaching, and release time for those already in the classroom in order to study full time. The need to maintain credential competitiveness with public schools was readily acknowledged by the nuns who led the movement. It was also recognized that, if congregations were to staff the expanding network of diocesan high schools, sisters would need the appropriate academic background for success in subject specialist teaching.[104]

Canon law required those wishing to enter religious life to pass through two distinct stages of training before taking their vows: the postulancy and novitiate. As a consequence of Sister Formation, a third period of training was added for newly professed nuns, although it was not mandatory or universally implemented. The new stage comprised two or more years of academic and professional study and became known as the juniorate. The choice of term led to confusion since aspirancies or preparatory schools had sometimes been called "juniorates" (Chapter 5).

The Sister Formation leadership favoured juniorates located in "sister colleges," or institutions run by religious congregations. In such an arrangement, problems associated with cost and violations of cloister could be controlled. There were forty-four sister colleges across the country in 1950, and by the end of the decade that number had more than doubled. Even so, the colleges were unequal to the task. Limited in capacity and with poorly qualified instructors, they often faced problems with accreditation bodies. The use of Catholic universities and even secular ones was unavoidable, even if it drove up costs and meant placing young nuns in mixed classrooms with exposure to "the distractions of the world."[105] By 1960 there were about 150 juniorate programs in operation.[106]

Juniorates presented parochial and diocesan schools with another challenge. Enrolment in the 1950s was far outstripping recruitment to sisterhoods and, if nuns went on to college, it would exacerbate the existing staff shortage. Bishops, parish priests, and superintendents of Catholic education were often dubious about Sister Formation, preferring to get nuns into classrooms as quickly

and as efficiently as possible, without regard to qualification. Although unenthusiastic at the idea of hiring lay teachers to fill the
void, they had little choice in the matter. Lay teachers constituted
9.8 per cent of Catholic school staff in 1950. A decade later the
percentage had risen to 26.2. Even so, their employment was seen
as a temporary expediency until more nuns could be recruited and
trained. There was no conception of a diminished role for nuns in
Catholic education.[107]

Sister Formation was clearly a necessity, but it placed new pressures on the convent system. Congregations were now obliged not
only to expand their personnel and operations, but to finance the
college education of new and existing members. And it greatly increased the demands being placed on individual nuns, whose daily
schedules left little time for additional tasks. A study conducted by
Sister M. William Kelley in 1956 found that nuns were being hos-
pitalized for mental illness at a much higher rate than laywomen.
When her data were compared to those gathered in a similar survey
done in 1936, it was clear that the problem was growing worse.
Sister Kelley hypothesized that the stress of overwork in crowded
classrooms and hospital wards, combined with the need to upgrade
qualifications, were at the root of the problem.[108]

The mental-health issue did not fade away. In an address to the
1959 Sisters' Institute of Spirituality, Sister Mary Annette acknowledged that impossible work assignments were driving teaching
nuns, many of whom were "living in a continual state of crisis,"
to the use of sedatives and other drugs.[109] Two years later, at the
Second National Congress of Religious in the United States, Father
Richard P. Vaughan spoke at length of the many stresses that
women religious experienced: "the demands of the vows, particularly obedience and chastity; the confining and close relationships
demanded by convent life; the near absence of the usual tensions
outlets; strict routine; and overwork." The novitiate was, in his opinion, a protected milieu, and the sister was only really tested when
"given the full responsibility for fifty wiggling children." He suggested psychological screening of candidates for the religious life
to ensure that they were ready for the challenges they would face.[110]

The concerns of Sister Kelley, Sister Mary Annette, and Father
Vaughan point to serious problems in the convent system and in

the Catholic schools linked to it. The image of order and tranquility presented to the laity was something quite different.

CONCLUSION

The history of monasticism tends to be untidy. It does not fit comfortably into the evolution of the Church's hierarchical structure of priests, bishops, and pope. Female monasticism is even more awkward to place. The friars and monks of male orders were normally ordained priests and could take on leadership positions in the Church. But this was not so for nuns, who were anomalous, in that they were neither clergy nor laity. And yet they were religious in the sense that their vows bound them to a special way of life, and their prayers were believed to be particularly effective in invoking divine favour. Nuns were holy in a sense that married women could never be.

Convents as places of prayerful refuge from a troublesome world have been around for centuries, as we have seen, and some continue to serve that function today. But by the Early Modern period the older contemplative congregations bound by enclosure began to give way to active congregations that provided useful services to society. In America, active congregations have always been important arms of the Church. Indeed, in the matter of establishing and maintaining a Catholic school system as a viable alternative to public education, no Church body has played a more vital role than the nuns. Without the tireless and cheap labour of tens of thousands of nuns, the very idea of a school in every parish would have been inconceivable.

Moreover, nuns in their distinctive habits were often the public face of the Church. In their roles as teachers, in particular, they were in more frequent contact with lay Catholics than priests and bishops. If congregations were to expand, and to do all that was expected of them, more girls and young women would need to feel drawn to convent life, to become aware that they were in receipt of the special grace of a religious vocation. The nature of this vocation, both human and supernatural, requires our attention.

CHAPTER 2

· · · · · · · · · · · · · · · · · · · ·

Seeking "Convent

Material"

"Vocation": this is the significant word
which springs to our lips when we think of
those girls and women who voluntarily renounce matrimony to consecrate themselves
to a higher life of contemplation, sacrifice,
and charity ... This vocation, this loving call,
makes itself heard in many different ways,
as many as the infinite variety of accents in
which the divine voice may speak: irresistible invitations, affectionate and repeated
promptings, gentle impulses.[1]
Pope Pius XII

Even human failings do not prevent a
teacher from influencing some one boy or
girl in a class. I could actually name people
who had one or the other of these human
failings and yet had a following of several
girls over whom they exerted tremendous
influence for good – in some instances
brought to the convent door, and the
vocations they attracted were
solid and sound.[2]
Sister Jean Claire (1961)

ENTERING A LIFE IN RELIGION was not simply a matter of choosing a career. A young woman did not decide to become a nun in the same manner as she might decide to become a lawyer or an electrician: depending on inclination or aptitude. In order to join a congregation, you had to have a "religious vocation" – defined by the Church as a special calling from God. In other words, God was doing the choosing and called those whom he considered suitable and worthy. A vocation then, was always a special gift or grace; it was never a right or just a decision about making a living.[3] The biblical quotation most often cited in support of the idea of divine initiative was John 15:6: "You did not choose me, but I chose you and appointed you so that you might go and bear fruit." And some nuns, when questioned about the call, paraphrased this very passage: "It is less a question of choosing than of being chosen."[4]

What were they being chosen for? The Church considered the religious life a "state of perfection" and infinitely superior to a life pursuing worldly ambitions. The Gospel story usually alluded to as authority for this idea is found in Matthew 19:20–2. A rich young man told Jesus that he had always kept the commandments and then asked if there was more that he could do. The reply was: "If thou wilt be perfect, go and sell what thou hast and give to the poor, and thou shalt have treasure in Heaven; and come follow Me."

The origin of the vows of poverty and obedience are usually traced to this story. But the "state of perfection" also required chastity, which was viewed as more pleasing to God than marriage. There was no shortage of endorsements of the superiority of virginity to sexual activity in the works of Church fathers and doctors over the centuries. The clearest modern pronouncement on the matter came from Pius XII in his 1954 encyclical, *Sacra Virginitas*. The Pope described virginity as "the angelic virtue," citing St Cyprian, who had claimed that the preservation of chastity made you equal to "the angels of God."[5] St Methodius and St Gregory were also quoted approvingly in declaring virginity the equivalent of martyrdom. The reasoning was that virginity was a difficult virtue, requiring "a constant vigilance and struggle to contain and dominate rebellious movements of body and soul, a flight from the importunings of this world, a struggle to conquer the wiles of Satan."[6]

Remaining a virgin was not, however, necessarily virtuous in itself. Motivation for doing so was important. It was no good if virginity were chosen in order to "shun the burdens of marriage" or because you wanted to "proudly flaunt your physical integrity."[7] Virginity became virtuous, it was said, only when accompanied by the deliberate act of consecrating it to God in a religious vow. And the consecration had to be until death; it wouldn't do if it were simply a temporary commitment, which had been the case with ancient Rome's vestal virgins, for example.[8]

A religious vocation, then, involved a special call from God to live a life of perfection – a perfection that was evident in the fact that the vast majority of saints had come from the ranks of those in religious vows, as one writer on the subject argued.[9]

How did you know if God was calling you? This question was of great importance to girls and young women who were being told that they might have a vocation and ought to be on the lookout for signs of it. The very notion of a "call" implied to many that they might expect to hear a voice or some other clear indicator of divine favour. The literature on the religious life – or "spiritual science" as Father John Hagan called it[10] – was at pains to dispel this misconception, lest it hamper recruitment to the cloister.

It was readily admitted, however, that God sometimes did his calling with dramatic gestures, such as knocking St Paul off his horse on the road to Damascus.[11] The lives of saints are replete with examples of similar epiphanies. Even in twentieth-century America, miraculous interventions were occasionally reported. This was the case with two of the nuns who responded to Father Thomas Bowdern's survey. The first of these respondents, a bookkeeper in her late twenties at the time, wrote that she had been lying in bed one cold morning when a "sweet voice" from a crucifix on the wall addressed her, saying: "Come, and I will take you to Me." She arose, went to Mass in deep snow, and later entered a convent. The second respondent had returned home from a party one night when, upon looking in the mirror, saw Jesus carrying his cross behind her. He said: "Follow me," and she did.[12]

Some vocations were revealed in a less striking manner – through "providential signs," for example. Such a sign might take the form of a "pious coincidence" or auspice which suggested that God had had a hand in it.[13] For the most part, however, "the call" took the form of an inclination towards the religious life; it was the "interior voice of conscience" guiding you to the convent door in response to a reading, sermon, retreat, or even a personal tragedy. Upon feeling such an inclination, all you really needed was the strength of will to go forward with it. Willpower was what it was all about – the moral courage to do what you felt God was asking of you.[14] The words of Boston's Archbishop Richard Cushing on the ordinary nature of the call are worth noting: "The ordinariness of the calling in the majority of instances is seldom appreciated. To say to such young Catholics that religious vocation is nothing more than average ability, decent character, and good will responding to God's grace which has come to one in ordinary ways, seems to them almost a be-littlement of God's dignity. How much these wonderful youngsters need to learn of God's ways of dealing with the human soul!"[15]

Whether you believed you had been chosen as a consequence of a sudden revelation, a providential sign, or an inclination of the will, your vocation still needed ecclesiastical validation. By admitting the young person to a training program and ultimately to religious vows, the Church gave its seal of approval to the vocation and con-firmed its supernatural origin.[16]

Admission was not automatic, for as canon law made clear, there were impediments: "Any Catholic who is not prevented by a legit-imate impediment, and who is moved by the right intention, and who is suitable for the burdens imposed by religious life can be admitted to a religious institute." A fairly obvious impediment was not being a Catholic, and you were usually required to produce a baptismal certificate to prove you were of the right faith. And you had to be a certain age: fourteen to become a postulant; fifteen to become a novice. It goes without saying that you could not be mar-ried – although widows were welcome. Other impediments of note included being liable for punishment for "a grave misdemeanour" or being burdened by debts that could not be paid. In other words, the convent could not serve as a refuge from the law or debtors.

Furthermore, Canon 544:7 had this to say: "Women, finally, should not be received unless there has been an accurate investi-gation of their character and morals, with due regard for the pre-scription."[17] What this meant was that those who had led lives of dissolute carnality were inadmissible. Even so, it was possible for such "fallen women" to enter a Good Shepherd convent as a

penitent and ultimately achieve the status of a "magdalen."[18] The
Sisters of Mercy in St John's, Newfoundland, added a special degree
of scrutiny to the moral assessment of candidates for admission:
before Helen Colgan could enter the community as a postulant in
1953, she had to be inspected by a gynecologist to ensure she was
a virgin.[19]

In addition to these and other impediments prescribed in canon
law, congregations could impose their own. It was common practice, for instance, to refuse admission to anyone over the age of
thirty. The reasoning here was that women of that age or older were
likely set in their ways and less readily adaptable to community
living.[20] Many congregations required their applicants to be of
legitimate birth and demanded a parental marriage certificate as
evidence.[21] Others would not admit those with "bodily defects" or
"deformities."[22] And some refused those of certain racial or ethnic
ancestries, such as "the children of gipsies and others without a
fixed place of residence."[23] There were cases, too, of congregations
attempting to cling to an identity linked to their country of origin
through exclusionary practices: for example, the Sisters of Mercy
in Brooklyn, founded in Ireland early in the nineteenth century, for
many decades would not accept candidates of Italian origin.[24]

The most common prejudice of this sort in the United States was
directed at African-Americans. When Mary Alice Chineworth, an
African-American, wished to become a sister in the mid-1930s, she
was turned down on racial grounds first by the Sisters of Charity of
the Blessed Virgin Mary, who were her teachers, and second by the
Sisters of the Blessed Sacrament for Indians and Colored People.
The latter congregation, as its name implied, conducted schools for
two of America's racial minorities, but the white nuns would not
admit young women of those same minorities to their own ranks – a
practice retained until the 1960s. Chineworth eventually joined the
Oblate Sisters of Providence, one of three segregated congregations
for African-Americans.[25]

The list of impediments may appear lengthy, but in practice very
few applied to the teenagers attending Catholic schools from whose
ranks the sisterhoods drew most of their new blood. A more important consideration was that candidates be "moved by the right

intention," as canon law put it. There was no ambiguity on what that meant: the first motivation ought to be securing your own salvation. You should also desire to "promote the glory of God by a good life" and contribute to the salvation of others.[26]

Canon law also prescribed that candidates be "suitable for the burdens imposed by religious life." This simply meant that congregations wanted workers; they wanted girls and young women of unsullied reputation, good mental and physical health, and average intelligence, who could be trained as teachers, nurses, and the like. In the case of lay or coadjutrix sisters, the intelligence/educational requirements were much more flexible.[27]

Suppose, then, that you felt called to the religious life, had no impediments, and met the moral, physical, and intellectual requirements. Were you obliged to join? Could you reject a vocation, sensing, perhaps, that the life was just too hard? The question was a difficult one and had serious implications for recruitment. Strictly speaking, since the "call" to the religious state was a counsel, advice, or invitation, and not a command, those receiving it were under no obligation to respond in the affirmative. Nor did they sin in saying "no."[28] Yet it is difficult to imagine a priest or nun saying to a teenage prospect: "You clearly have a vocation and you can take it or leave it."

Once theologians addressed the question, however, their lines of argumentation quickly disposed of the idea of genuine personal choice in the matter. According to A. Motte, if you rejected your vocation without giving it the thoughtful consideration it deserved, you were guilty of a "culpable imprudence" that originated in vices and passions. What this meant was that if you were aware that your disposition was such that you could only save your soul in the safety of the cloister and that living in the world would lead you to sin, then your "imprudence" constituted a mortal sin.[29] In making this argument, Motte was following the reasoning of St Alphonso di Ligouri, who had warned against living in the world while conscious of your "natural weakness in the midst of temptation."[30]

Another writer on the subject noted that a servant doing good work did not please her master if the work was not what the master had requested. By analogy, being a good wife and mother would not please God if he had called you to the convent. St Vincent had made this point when he said: "It is very difficult, not to say impossible, to save one's self in a state of life in which God does not wish one to be."[31]

To reject a vocation, then, was probably sinful and most certainly exposed you to a life of temptations that endangered your eternal salvation. Moreover, you were saying no to God, which entailed an obvious risk. This was a more compelling argument than "take-it-or-leave-it" when discussing religious vocations with impressionable teenagers who were often confused and apprehensive when the question was broached. Sister Mary Barrett's survey of Catholic girls in senior high school (1960) found 90 per cent of them admitting that they would have felt honoured to have a vocation. Yet their individual remarks showed great ambivalence, with many admitting a fear of following a vocation. The fear was sometimes expressed this way: "I just might have a vocation, and frankly, I'd rather not have one."[32] Similarly, a survey of girls attending three Sisters of Charity of Providence high schools around the same time discovered that 36 per cent of respondents were frightened at the prospect of having a vocation.[33]

Many of the girls in these surveys were uncertain of their ability to recognize the "call" and how they ought to answer it. Was there an active role here for the Church? Could young people be assisted in identifying their vocations and encouraged to pursue them? The answer was "yes" on both counts. If vocations were insufficient, which they were, the explanation was that people were failing to respond to God's invitation, which was being drowned out "in the shuffle of our materialistic, competitive civilization."[34] And since God worked through natural means, the Church was even obliged to provide assistance to his grace. In an address to the National Catholic Education Association in 1944, the Reverend William J. Ferrer put it this way:

> There is too much "Providentialism" in our appreciation of the grace of vocation. There are some Religious who will not discuss the matter with their boys and girls because they do not want to "interfere in the operations of grace" ... Let us once and for all face the fact that a vocation to the higher

life – great and supernatural a grace as it is – comes *normally* through precisely this "interference" which some of us profess to fear. Let us by all means "interfere" then, and interfere frankly – but intelligently, of course, so as really to "sell" the higher life and not make enemies for it.[35]

Active recruitment was not only acceptable; it was desirable and necessary. St Thomas Aquinas was often quoted in justifying this approach: "Those who induce others to enter religion, not only do not sin, but merit a great reward."[36] In *Sacra Virginitas*, Pius XII placed responsibility for recruitment squarely on "educators of youth," who were urged to "do what they can to provide every help for youth entrusted to their care who feel themselves called by divine grace to aspire to the priesthood or to embrace the religious life, in order that they may be able to reach so noble a goal."[37]

One question on the minds of those who grappled with the issue was the possibility of employing the research techniques of social science. The Catholic Church had always had a difficult relationship with sociology, viewing its intellectual lineage with suspicion and its confident, secular spirit with distain. Sociology's aim of social progress without reference to God or the supernatural was incompatible with the Church's world view. Even so, fearing that the faithful would seek it out in secular universities, the Catholic University of America appointed a professor of sociology in 1897. But Catholic sociology never constructed an alternative theoretical model based on Church teachings. Instead, it simply borrowed the discipline's research methods for application to questions of relevance to the Church.[38]

The religious life was certainly one of these questions, but there was a hesitancy in subjecting it to sociological analysis lest it compromise the understanding of vocation as a "supernatural reality." And all the more so since Pius XI, in *Divini Illius Magistri* (1929), denounced as "not only vain and false, irreverent and dangerous" the idea of research that was "purely natural and profane" on "those matters of education which belong to the supernatural order: as for example questions of priestly or religious vocation, and in general the secret workings of grace which indeed elevate the natural powers, but are infinitely superior to them, and may nowise be subjected to physical laws, 'for the Spirit breatheth where He will.'"[39]

Father Basil Frison, cognizant of the Pope's admonition, issued his own warning in his authoritative book on selecting individuals for the religious life: "The teachings of the Church on the essentially supernatural character of vocation render practically impossible the use of any scientific method in a definitive analysis."[40]

But these concerns were quickly put aside in recognition of the utility of statistics and other survey data in understanding historical trends and in discovering the "human conditions" in which people were more likely to respond to God's call. It was realized that some important questions simply could not be answered without resorting to social science. For example, were vocations increasing or decreasing, and, if the latter, how could it be explained? Father François Houtart, in championing a sociology of vocations, said it was not good enough to explain an insufficiency of candidates by claiming that the young of today lacked generosity and loved pleasure. It would be necessary, he argued, to examine socio-economic trends that might adversely affect the attractions of the convent, such as increasing educational and career opportunities for girls.[41]

This was a sensible suggestion and promised to have theoretical significance and practical relevance. But the sociology of vocations was never more than a plodding enterprise, relying on the dominant quantitative survey method that was strongly influenced by federal funding agencies in postwar America. Most university sociology departments endorsed this approach; the goal was to establish probable outcomes when humans were examined in relation to their behaviours, institutions, and social circumstances.[42]

The sociology of vocations was largely the work of nuns enrolled in graduate degrees at the Catholic University of America under the direction of the Reverend Thomas J. Harte.[43] The typical method was to survey nuns in their own congregations or those in a particular region to discover what had drawn them to the religious life. The idea was to gather "pertinent information" that would assist recruiters in "the prudent selection of prospective candidates to the sisterhoods."[44]

The Irish-born Harte was quite aware of the shortcomings in his students' work.[45] Since the surveys were confined to those already in the convent, nothing was learned about those who had no vocations, rejected their vocations, or were rejected by their chosen community, either upon application or during formation.[46] Constructing an image of the "vocation family" was usually part of the inquiry, but little consideration was given to ethnicity and social class, factors that often influenced which congregation a candidate might join. Nor was information gathered about families whose children all stayed in the world.[47]

The sociologists sought to establish three profiles:

- The candidate who was "convent material";
- The "vocation family" that raised her;
- The ideal school setting in which her vocation was cultivated.

Let's begin with the candidates for religious life. How had nuns spent their youth? Had they been typical adolescents who just suddenly felt the call and entered a convent, or had there been something in their habits or comportment that might have signalled their future in religious life? Was it possible to identify "convent material" among the young? Father Godfrey Poage, a priest heavily involved with recruitment during the 1950s, asked a gathering of nuns to name the one characteristic in a girl that provided the surest indicator of a vocation. The unanimous response was "piety." A pious girl, the nuns said, was one who attended the sacraments regularly, was an enthusiastic participant in school devotions, was modest in dress and deportment, read Catholic literature, and was in general polite and reverential towards religious. The converse, of course, was also true. A girl was considered a poor prospect if she adopted "unbecoming postures," wasted "hour after hour on silly romances," and attended movies once a week or more frequently, thereby "filling her mind with distractions and picking up ideas that [would] make her renunciation of the world all the harder."[48] The silver screen, it should be noted, was frequently attacked by the Church for its low moral character and baneful influence, and it seems that future nuns were heeding these warnings.[49]

The respondents to Sister Marie William Cahill's survey of 1955 consistently reported frequent attendance at Mass and Communion during their youth, and she concluded that it had to be one of the surest signs of a vocation. If priests and nuns observed such behaviour in a young person, she said, they should immediately attempt to recruit her.[50] And some of them clearly did so. A high-school student interviewed by Father Joseph Fichter a year or two later recalled her parochial school experience with this remark: "if you go to Holy Communion more often than usual, the Sisters think you've got a vocation. They pestered me so much about being a nun that I finally said I would, so that they let me alone."[51]

What sort of family did she come from? Information gathered about vocation families showed them to be typically urban, reasonably secure economically, and with fathers working in skilled trades or lower-middle-class occupations.[52] These were the families with the resources to send their children to Catholic schools, which, as we shall see, was an important factor in generating vocations. Both parents were practising Catholics, had attended Catholic schools themselves, were reverential to priests and nuns, and were regular in their receipt of the sacraments. Moreover, they maintained a religious atmosphere in the home, meaning that there were family prayers, subscriptions to Catholic periodicals, and holy pictures and statuary as domestic decor. They were the sort of families that were happy to spend quiet evenings together at home.[53]

Family size was a consideration. Sister M. Christina, while teaching sociology at Marygrove College, Detroit, in the 1940s, surveyed 1,700 sisters and discovered the following about their backgrounds:

- 3 per cent came from families with three or fewer children
- 40 per cent came from families with four to seven children
- 57 per cent came from families with more than seven children.[54]

Other sociologists found a similar pattern.[55] While we do not have comparative data for non-vocation families, the size factor is still a valid one in vocation families. In one sense, the figures should not surprise. Just on mathematical probability alone, the bigger the family, the more likely it was to produce vocations. Unfortunately, the researchers were unwilling or unable to present an analysis or interpretation to account for the significance of size, beyond raw probability. Was it possible, for example, that parents with many children were more supportive of vocations, secure in the knowledge that some of their offspring at least would remain in the world to carry on the family name and to care for them in old age? Was the converse also true? Were smaller families more opposed to their daughters entering religion? Linking family size to family attitude would have been interesting, but it was not done. Writing at the beginning of the 1960s, Joseph Fichter claimed that the idea that vocations tended to come from large families was a "persistent myth among Catholics." He argued that it was not a useful assumption, since too many other variables were missing.[56] Even so, the idea was widely accepted among those recruiting others to the religious life during the postwar decades.

It will be recalled that Pius XII had placed responsibility for recruitment on the "educators of youth." He had nuns in mind when it came to girls' education, since they were reputedly the best at the task. He was right. The sociologists were able to demonstrate something that had long been assumed: vocations were most plentiful among girls attending single-sex Catholic secondary schools in which the vast majority of teachers were nuns. Second place, according to this measure of success, went to coeducational Catholic schools. Public schools, which were also coeducational, brought up the rear.[57] Father John Hagan warned that public schools should not be neglected completely as sources of vocations, since a little over 10 per cent of the sisters in his study had completed four years of secondary education in such places.[58]

Sister M. Celestine Hoedl added another dimension to the sociology of vocations in 1961 with her discovery that, with schools, size was also a factor, but opposite to the way in which it applied to families. Smaller secondary schools were more effective in convent recruitment than larger ones, she said. She surmised that smaller numbers improved teacher-student relations, enabling sister-teachers to exert more influence on the young "in the direction of religious idealism."[59] In effect, then, a single-sex Catholic high school in which most of the teachers were nuns, and which had an enrolment of less than two hundred, was the ideal milieu for the incubation of vocations.

A bit more detail is needed to understand how the vocation dynamic actually worked in these schools. All surveys that asked nuns to identify "the most potent influence" on their vocation decision received identical responses: the inspiring example of the nuns who had taught them.[60] Here's how one of Sister Mary Barrett's respondents put it: "The sisters who taught me were full of love and the things of God. They were happy and kind towards one another. Their spirit of joy was the biggest inspiration."[61]

The fostering of vocations, however, required a bit more than just being a shining example of joy and happiness. Father Edward Garesché's summary of his own survey results in the 1940s probably best sums up what was really going on. He claimed that the teaching sister was most effective in encouraging vocations when she "gives individual study and attention in an enthusiastic, zealous way to the girls whom she considers evidently to have a vocation, giving them words of encouragement and books to read explaining the religious life."[62]

This was a frank admission that girls who were "convent material" were being singled out for special attention. Classroom dynamics of this sort were far more probable in the smaller single-sex schools described above than in other settings. And obviously, Catholic girls attending public schools would never have experienced the zealous solicitations of a friendly nun.

Even in the ideal milieu of the single-sex school, we cannot assume that the type of teacher-student interaction that fostered vocations necessarily prevailed. In truth, not all nuns were inspiring and full of joy. Some were grumpy and disagreeable; others were old-fashioned and disapproving. In three surveys conducted between 1954 and 1960, unpleasant nuns were identified as a major obstacle to recruitment.[63] One respondent said she would have more easily recognized her vocation had her teachers had a "sense of humor and ability to laugh so as to show us they are human."[64] During the late 1950s, Sister Mary George, mistress of postulants at the Sisters of Mercy novitiate in North Plainfield, New Jersey, sought the opinion of her postulants and novices in diagnosing their failure "to gather more laborers for the increased harvest." The response was unambiguous in identifying the types of nuns who were doing "outright harm to the cause." They were disgruntled, grouchy, indiscreet, jealous, pushy, and at times downright silly.[65]

Nasty and disagreeable nuns may have discouraged vocations, but they didn't necessarily kill them. In one survey, nuns were asked why they had joined a community other than the one that had educated them; more than half blamed the lack of friendliness and kindness of their teachers.[66] They still joined up, but at another convent.[67]

Or it could be a question of finding the right congregation. Sister Rosemary Dillmann attended an elementary school in Seattle run by the Dominicans and found the nuns harsh and unappealing. But everything changed for her when she moved to a high school under the Sisters of Charity of Providence. Inspired by the example of her new teachers, she joined the congregation in the early 1950s.[68]

Barrett discerned that older nuns had an image problem among cool teens and felt it might be better to have younger ones teaching at the high-school level where most vocation decisions were made: "Some of the older ones (50 and over) sure do have some old-fashioned ideas. If they'd keep them to themselves it wouldn't be so bad, but they try giving them to the young girls. What a mistake!"[69] Hagan made a similar suggestion, noting that congregations would do well to allocate nuns with attractive personalities where they were most likely to enjoy recruitment success: "it is manifestly to the advantage of the community to place in such positions those who seem gifted to exercise an appeal to young people."[70] Sister Marian Elizabeth's experience teaching at St Lawrence Academy in New York in the late 1940s led her to the same conclusion, with the proviso that the "cool" nuns be situated at the lower high-school grades:

Those communities are wise that place their spiritually attractive young sisters in the freshman classes. By "spiritually attractive young sisters" I mean those who understand youth in such a way as to win their confidence without sacrificing religious ideals. It is in our freshman classes that the seeds of vocations are best sown. Here the soil of pliable minds is most fertile, the climate of a zealous young religious teacher most invigorating, for youth calls to youth. Under her direction the fogs of doubt and indecision are lifted.[71]

A significant number of Catholic high schools organized at the diocese level were coeducational, not by design but because limited enrolment made segregation impractical. Students in such settings had priests, nuns, and laity as their teachers.[72] How did these schools compare with single-sex institutions in vocation productivity?

Hoedl compared the figures for 151 all-girl schools and 177 co-educational schools for the period 1954 to 1959. The percentage of vocations from the former was 1.16, and from the latter, 0.71. These figures might be better represented this way: for every 116 vocations from single-sex settings, there were only 71 from mixed settings. This was a significant difference. Unsurprisingly, when Hoedl questioned 595 sisters on the relative advantages of both kinds of school respecting "the favorable growth of religious vocations," 82 per cent preferred single-sex institutions.[73]

What was it about the coeducational high school that impaired recruitment to the convent? The sisters surveyed by Barrett said that mixed Catholic high schools were beginning to imitate their public counterparts in providing a rich panoply of extracurricular activities in which boys and girls socialized freely together – dances, clubs, shows, sporting events, and so forth. In such settings, a life in religion appeared too much of a sacrifice. One of the respondents put it like this: "If they are not careful, girls lose their sense of values and think, why give up having such a good time and bury yourself in a convent?" Another said: "dating, dances, and clothes give Christ more competition than we give them credit for." Students at these schools, in explaining the reasons for their decision to stay in the world, confirmed their teachers' observations: "I made up my own mind, but I think that a coeducational high school failed my vocation." And: "I guess in all honesty, it would be my boyfriend."[74] Father Fichter agreed. The culture of dating and going steady was more pronounced in coeducational schools, he observed, and it had to have a negative effect on vocations.[75]

The emphasis so far has been on secondary schools and on the adolescents that attended them – and with good reason, since young people entered religion at that age. A number of writers on the subject felt that the parochial elementary school should not be neglected as ground in which the seeds of a future vocation could be sown. Father Basil Frison advised his readers that teaching sisters in Italy claimed that they could detect the signs of a vocation in second- or third-grade students, and that early vocations had a higher perseverance rate than older ones.[76] Hagan concurred and cited a survey that asked nuns about the age in which they had been "conscious of the desire to enter the consecrated state." The numbers showed a significant clustering between the ages of ten and fourteen, with 70 per cent of respondents reporting the desire by the latter age.[77] Barrett found a similar result, leading her to conclude that the period between twelve and fourteen years of age was particularly "fruitful" for "serious thoughts on religious vocations."[78]

Serious thoughts were not the same as a decision to enter. By the latter half of the 1950s, the decision to answer a vocation was being made primarily in Grades 11 and 12, and it was being made after a number of years thinking about it.[79] The conventional wisdom was that once a decision was made, it should be acted on immediately. Hagan argued that it was folly to test the vocation by "living in the world" for some time.[80] One Mother Superior, cited by Garesché, remembered at least fifty girls with strongly marked vocations at high-school graduation who went on to further studies and ultimately rejected the call.[81] A priest, writing on the subject, urged seclusion from the world between the times of decision and entry, lest a "trifling circumstance" derail the vocation: "A day of amusement, a discouraging word, even from a friend, an unmortified passion, or a conversation, especially with a person of the opposite sex, often suffices to bring to naught the best resolution of giving one's self entirely to God."[82]

In accumulating this corpus of knowledge about candidates, their families, and schools, the sociologists discerned a number of worrisome trends, which, if projected forward, boded ill for the future of religious life.

The Catholic teenager, with whom much hope rested, was changing. A survey of senior high-school girls in the early 1950s noted that fewer of them were satisfied with staying home in the evenings.[83] The youth-oriented popular culture of that decade was beginning to make an impact. The prevalence of social activity was also observed a decade later, when it was even more pronounced. Moreover, by the 1960s, academic achievement and career preparation seemed to be outflanking moral growth as a personal goal for many. Girls were being attracted more than ever by the wage-earning possibilities of the teaching, nursing, and social work professions, and without the constraints of convent life.[84] As one nun remarked in resignation, or perhaps despair: "During senior year there is so much talk of going to college. The world seems to be more inviting than ever when pictures of campuses, double rooms, and collegiate clothing are circulating."[85]

What about the Catholic home? It was observed that parents were increasingly ambitious for their daughters in a materialist sense, a worrisome trend probably reflected in the youngsters' career aspirations.[86] As families participated in postwar prosperity, they began to drift away from ethnic parishes or the "Catholic ghetto" to settle in the suburbs, where social networks rooted in Church-sponsored institutions were more difficult to construct and sustain.[87] And an emerging Catholic elite that sought integration into the mainstream began to question the need for confessional schools and other faith-based entities.[88]

Another development of concern was a steady increase in mixed marriages. A non-Catholic parent could not be expected to support a vocation, let alone encourage it.[89] But even in families where both parents were of the faith, objections to the religious life were on the rise.[90] It was also found that family prayer was in decline; radio and television were providing irresistible competition for the Rosary and other devotions.[91]

And then there was the Catholic high school. A study of one congregation's schools in the Midwest in the first half of the 1950s showed a pattern of consolidating smaller single-sex institutions into larger coeducational ones, doubling the negative impact on vocations.[92] Several studies reported an increasing emphasis on academic achievement, whether in single-sex or coeducational schools – a challenge to preserving their religious ethos. A crowded curriculum, combined with expanding class sizes, little preparation time, and a lack of professional-development opportunities, put enormous pressure on teaching nuns. Pushed to the limits by overwork, the nuns found it difficult to convey the joy of their vocations and inspire imitation among their students.[93]

CONCLUSION

Most of the challenges facing Catholic schools in the 1950s were related to an enrolment surge as baby boomers arrived at their doors. More nuns than ever were required to staff classrooms, but young women were not entering religion in sufficient numbers to meet the demand. It was both a source of annoyance and hope to the social scientists to discover that significant numbers of high-school girls reported seriously considering the religious life at some stage during their adolescence,[94] yet most of these girls were not making the commitment. Why were so many getting away? Could the Church do better at recruitment? Was a more systematic approach possible?

The sociology of vocations, although often limited in its methods and assumptions, showed the way. It amassed a body of knowledge that indicated a focused strategy in which resources could be deployed in such a way as to secure better results. Its appearance was a necessary prelude to professionalized recruitment.

. . . .

CHAPTER 3

Called or

Chosen?

For the friends I gave up, He has supplied
me with a host of new ones. Each nun is as
dear to me as a real sister. Living with such
sweet friends of Christ, I can but strive to
imitate their fine qualities. In the gardens
of our convent, no turmoil, rush, or worry
disturbs the serenity. There is no bother
about the proper dress to wear, or anxiety
about curls to fix – just peace, and calm
of heart and mind.[1]
Sister M. Claudette (1947)

To train the minds of the young, to mold
them into solid characters, to build a
superstructure of faith upon a natural
foundation of Christian virtue – what more
noble vocation for any young woman who
is willing to sacrifice the passing delights of
the world for the hundred-fold
reward of eternity?[2]
Archbishop Richard J. Cushing (1965)

CHURCH LEADERS WERE REALISTIC ENOUGH to acknowledge that God's call was insufficient in itself to sustain and increase the desired flow to the cloister. Was the "vocations crisis," persisting as it did from decade to decade, inevitable? Could human activity assist God in meeting the demand? Was it possible for priests and nuns to be "His instruments in ferreting out good material and extending His invitation to a life of perfection in His name?"[3] As we have seen, the theologians approved initiative in the matter, but how did it work in practice?[4]

Godfrey Poage, CP (1920–2001), was a significantly influential figure in promoting a more interventionist approach to recruitment. A member of the aggressive preaching order the Passionist Fathers, he was national director of American Vocational Clubs and director of the Pontifical Office for Religious Vocations (1957–67), and devoted himself full-time to vocations recruitment.[5] Moreover, he wrote extensively on the subject and was convinced that human activity was indeed required: "The conviction we must make our own is that while many boys and girls are given the grace of a priestly or religious vocation, they often fail to recognize or carelessly reject the divine call. So if we want more vocations to our seminaries or convents we must get busy and help such favored individuals."[6]

Jude Senieur, OFM, Cap., was another champion of active recruitment. A native of Charleston, West Virginia, he served as vocational director for the Capuchins and taught at their St Fidelis Seminary in Herman, Pennsylvania.[7] In his prolific writings he readily acknowledged that, while only God could grant the grace of a vocation ("a mysterious process"), recruiters could be instruments in his hands, just as Andrew led Peter to Jesus, and Phillip brought Nathanael.[8] We shall encounter Poage and Senieur frequently in these pages.

Religious congregations were well aware that their own schools were the best sources of new recruits. The sociology of vocations had removed any doubts on that question. Wherever convent schools were established, the number of vocations increased noticeably. And teaching congregations expanded more rapidly than non-teaching ones as a consequence.[9]

Although it was recognized that firm commitments to the religious life were unusual before the mid-teenage years, many involved in recruitment felt that it was never too early to encourage young minds in that direction, even in the elementary grades. Father Barnabas Mary, CP, assured his audience at the National Catholic Educational Association (NCEA) Convention in 1951 that, according to St John Bosco, God gave the seed of a vocation to one-third of all Catholic school children. The seed, however, needed nurturing, he said, and that work was "the solemn duty and sublime privilege of every elementary school sister."[10]

Most sisters needed little encouragement to exercise their "sublime privilege." The motto of Sister Mary Isabel, community supervisor with the Sisters of St Joseph in Pittsburgh in the early 1950s, was: "Let every teacher in every grade be a vocation recruiter." In order to make this happen, she devised a plan for her congregation's elementary schools that integrated the topic of vocation across the curriculum throughout the year. The plan was organized into themes that reflected the liturgical calendar and featured lots of practical tips for classroom application. Before Advent, for example, teachers in the primary grades, in explaining the Creation, might address their students as follows: "God made me for a special reason. God wants some boys and girls to be His special helpers. God wants us to be holy, to grow better every day so that we will be ready to do His Will."

The Virgin Mary's preparation for her vocation was the theme between Advent and Lent. Here the teacher might guide her class with these words: "Mary was ready when God's message was brought to her. From the time she was a little girl Mary did everything to please God ... When God chooses helpers He looks for boys and girls who try to be like Mary – obedient, pure, humble, kind, unselfish, and generous in acts of sacrifice." Between Lent and Easter, the spirit of sacrifice was the theme. Students were to be told that sacrifice and denial made them spiritually strong and was excellent preparation for those who would "give up all things to follow Christ." In effect, sister teachers were leading children aged six, seven, and eight to believe that God might call them to be his special helpers one day, and that they should be ready to do his bidding. In the upper grades the themes were different. Here teachers were to "glorify missionaries as the vanguard of civilization" and assign research projects on different congregations and orders.[11]

Father Poage urged teachers to use the catechism class to "put in a plug for vocations." In explaining the importance of prayer and the sacraments, he suggested that they emphasize "the deplorable condition of those outside the Church" and the need for more religious to preach the Gospel to them. He also recommended that teachers create a "vocational atmosphere" in their classrooms. This might be done, he said, by having students cut out photographs of priests, brothers, and nuns "in action" from Catholic magazines and put them on display.[12]

Claire Perkins, who attended Our Lady of Mount Carmel Elementary School in Bayonne, New Jersey, in the late 1940s and early 1950s, recalled the large bulletin board adorning the back of her Grade 6 classroom, featuring pictures of nuns in various stages of formation, interspersed with statements encouraging the students to give their lives to Christ. Her teachers, the Felician Sisters, never lost an opportunity to promote the religious life, saying it was a special honour and not for everyone.[13]

At the high-school level, it was sometimes possible to incorporate the recruitment theme into aspects of the curriculum. Sister M. Carrol of St Augustine's Convent, Kalamazoo, Michigan, made vocational literature required reading in her English classes and had her students report on it.[14] Sister Martina, while teaching at the Holy Angels Academy in Seattle, used Francis Thompson's poem, "The Hound of Heaven," to convey the idea that God was calling her students, that they were failing to respond, and might have to answer to his wrath one day:

I fled Him, down the nights and down the days;
I fled Him, down the arches of the years;
I fled Him, down the labyrinthine ways
Of my own mind; and in the midst of tears.[15]

In some high schools, girls were assigned research projects on the religious life that required them to prepare presentations on the work of different congregations and dress up dolls in the habits of their chosen nuns.[16] Spiritual reading was strongly encouraged, and the lives of saints were given special attention. In the school attended by Mary Jane Masterson in 1940s Cleveland, the religious teacher offered a reward to the student who read the greatest number of saintly biographies. Mary Jane read forty-two in all and became fascinated with the story of St Thérèse of Lisieux. In 1946, at the age of eighteen, she joined the Sisters of St Joseph in her home town.[17] *The Story of a Soul*, St Thérèse's autobiography, also inspired Mary Agnes Baudo to join a contemplative branch of the Dominicans and devote her life to "praying for priests."[18] And it was the starting point too for Sister Mary Jean, a San Francisco native and convert from the Episcopal Church, who entered the Sisters of St Joseph in California.[19] *The Story of a Soul* was a religious bestseller and made Thérèse one of the more popular saints among young women. In it she recounted how she obtained a papal dispensation to join the Carmelites at the age of fifteen, enabling her to flee "the false glitter of earthly pleasures."[20] Considering its simple and engaging style, it is not difficult to understand the book's appeal as a recruitment instrument, although the saint's preoccupation with suffering and death may have discouraged at least some readers.[21]

Quite apart from religion classes and other areas of instruction where the merits of the religious life could be advanced, teaching sisters were never slow to "put in a plug for vocations," as Father Poage suggested. Catherine Whitney recalled the uncontainable joy of her teacher, Sister Martina, in 1963 when Hollywood star Dolores Hart, the first woman to kiss Elvis Presley on screen, abandoned the glamour of Tinseltown to become a Benedictine nun. Here was proof of God's power, according to Sister Martina; even Elvis could not compete with Jesus.[22]

Teaching sisters did much more than simply extol the virtues of religious life, whether in casual remarks or in structured teaching situations. They also sought to identify girls who were "convent material," lavishing on them special attention and privileges. In interventions of this sort, sisters were acting as "scouts for Christ," in the manner of a football coach, as one school principal put it.[23] In a survey of former parochial-school students conducted in the late 1950s, the subjects were asked if anyone had tried to talk them into a vocation. One-fifth answered affirmatively and identified the teaching sisters as those responsible for the persuasion.[24]

Father Vincent McCorry, in acknowledging this practice, added a critical note: "The plain fact is that where vocations are few, nuns are apt to fly into a panic of desperation when they think of the future of their congregation; and the measures of the desperate are usually desperate." "Girls are even assured, no doubt with merry laughter," he observed, "that their room in the novitiate has already been assigned to them." He attributed these aggressive tactics to "a certain currency among nuns" that if you led another to religion, your own salvation was assured.[25]

Two of those who recalled the circumstances of their recruitment to author Marie Therese Gass provide us with examples of solicitous nuns and their interventions. Doris remembered it this way:

> You bet I was persuaded. We had moved to another school in my 8th grade and the nun-principal acted like she liked me somewhat, but I shied back when she told me that she had a gift from God to be able to tell if a girl had a Vocation, and I had one, period. I was shocked ... But my fear of hell (what would happen to me if I didn't follow a true Vocation) was so great that I hung around this nun as much as possible trying to talk her out of this notion. She kept it up, and within two years it dawned on me that I was wasting my time unless I wanted to go to hell, so I gave up and got it over with.[26]

For Theresa, the standard arguments in favour of a life in religion proved persuasive: "I was urged to enter by my senior religion teacher, who convinced me that if I really loved God, I could sacrifice. I was told that religious life was 'nobler' than motherhood. I wanted to be the best I could be. I wanted to please God and my dad. I hoped in the convent I would find peace, community, and friendship."[27]

Mary Ann Cahill grew up in Bemet, a small town in central Illinois, where she was the only Catholic in her elementary-school classroom. She decided to spend her high-school years at St Mary's Academy, an all-girls boarding institution run by Benedictine Sisters in Nauvoo, on the western boundary of the state. According to the sociology of vocations, it was the ideal setting in which to entice girls into the religious life. And that's what happened. At St Mary's, Cahill came under the influence of Sister Joann, the friendly business teacher and dormitory prefect, who nudged her gently and constantly in the direction of the religious life without ever revealing what it was really like to experience it. One day in her senior year, Sister Joann slipped a prayer card into her hand on which was inscribed: "To whomsoever much is given, of her much is required." The message struck a chord with Cahill, and she became a postulant in the community upon graduation in 1953. A year later she was received as a novice and went on to spend twenty years as a Benedictine.[28]

Sister M. Maura was an eighteen-year-old New Yorker who was developing a relationship with a man named Paul when she was invited one evening to the convent of the sisters who had taught her in grade school. The Sister Superior's message was blunt: "You know you have a religious vocation ... If you do not give yourself to God now, you will begin to think you have met the right man." The revelation had its intended effect. Maura began to spend a lot of time in church, broke up with Paul, and joined the School Sisters of Notre Dame.[29]

Patricia Grueninger's experience was similar. Sister Andrew, her music teacher, asked repeatedly if she was going to stop denying her vocation and suggested more than once that she could go to Hell if she refused God's call. Grueninger loved music and dancing, planned to go to art school, and even had a boyfriend. But she was worn down eventually by her teacher's pressure and began to give a career in religion serious thought. When she inquired, however, into the nature of convent life, Sister Andrew was evasive: "Pat, put aside your fears. Just know that the God who loves you so much, who has given you the wonderful gift of a vocation, will be with you every step along the way. Trust in Divine Providence and God will reward your trust. Now tell me, what have you decided?" Grueninger gave in and in September 1955 entered the postulancy of the Daughters of Charity of St Vincent de Paul in Baltimore, Maryland, the congregation that conducted her school.[30]

Keeping the nature of religious life hidden from public gaze served the recruitment agenda. When Katherine Hulme's book *The Nun's Story* appeared in 1956, with its graphic descriptions of the world behind convent walls, it alarmed many congregations, who felt it would undermine their attempts to attract new recruits. And when the book was released as a major Hollywood movie in 1959, under the same name and starring Audrey Hepburn as the protagonist, Sister Luke, the alarm was even more pronounced.[31] The convent was no longer a *terra incognita*.

While it was generally agreed that priests, brothers, and nuns were all recruiters, it was clear that not all were particularly gifted in the role. As Father Poage pointed out in his extensive writings, recruiting did not come naturally; it required knowledge of applied psychology, public relations, advertising, and an aptitude for interpersonal skills.[32] It was with this realization that dioceses and congregations began to appoint full-time vocations recruiters. As early as 1944 Father William J. Ferrer was urging that every religious province have a "director of vocations" in place.[33] In 1945 there were 34 of these professionals in the country; by 1955 the number had risen to 319.[34] By the 1960s, the Sisters of Mercy had a vocational director for each of its nine provinces and a coordinator at the national level.[35]

The recruitment professionals were busy people. They delivered vocational talks to young people; they produced and distributed vocational literature and films; and they organized vocational clubs in schools and parishes. These activities will be examined in some detail later. A key to the professional's success was her ability to relate to young people on their own terms. She needed a ready smile, a clever joke, and knowledge of the latest songs, teen idols, and sports results – all allowing for easy integration in the social world of the young. She had to avoid negative judgment of any kind, while providing a sympathetic ear to girls perplexed by life's choices. Her plan was to persuade them to seek God's guidance in deciding their future, a point at which at least some could be steered towards the convent door.[36]

As the professionals experimented with different strategies, they shared the results with one another at conferences, in books, and in articles. At the Vocational Institute held at the University of Notre Dame in July 1948, delegates were asked to formulate a "vocational plan" that could be implemented in any diocese, and to return a year later with their ideas. The Institute of 1949 was attended by more than four hundred priests, brothers, and sisters, with around sixty congregations of women religious represented. The comprehensive plan they developed envisioned a series of complementary strategies involving the following: talks, literature, clubs, campaigns, retreats, confession, and spiritual counselling, all of which would be examined in practice later.[37] When the NCEA met for its annual conference in Philadelphia in April 1949, it established a

Vocations Committee to serve as a nationwide coordinating group
for the distribution of ideas and information.[38] The committee was
central to the vocations knowledge network, and its sessions at the
conference became an important forum for the exchange of recruitment strategies.

How should the advantages of religious life be pitched to young
women? What evidence or argumentation should be presented,
either in written or oral form? For the recruitment professionals,
these were central concerns. While there was some disagreement
respecting emphasis, on the general themes there was consensus,
and all agreed that the moral superiority of service to the Church
over worldly pursuits should always be to the fore.

Describing the religious life as the "state of perfection" and most
pleasing to God conveyed the less-than-subtle message that the laity
were deficient in some way. The perfection of religion, it was said,
could be traced to the advice of Jesus to the wealthy young man in
Matthew 19:2: "If thou wilt be perfect, go sell what thou hadst, and
give to the poor ... and come, follow me." In answering the divine
call and in renouncing possessions, physical pleasure, and free will
by their vows, the religious achieved perfection.[39] Jude Senieur put
it this way: "The religious life is the higher state of life because it is
the perfect proof of love. And the proof of our love for God is the
very purpose of life." When asked if a woman who sacrificed herself
for her children was as equally meritorious as a nun, his reply was
an emphatic "no." A married woman, he pointed out, chose human
love and only sacrificed herself for a dozen people or so. A nun, on
the other hand, put the love of God first and sacrificed herself for
thousands; there could be no equal weight in the "spiritual value"
of their relative sacrifices.[40] Senieur was theologically correct. Those
who espoused the spiritual equality of marriage and the religious
life were guilty of the Jovinian heresy, although the penalties for
such a belief were much less serious than they would have been
some centuries earlier.[41]

Since matrimony was a sacrament, the recruiters had to be cautious in how it was portrayed. They were able to evade the problem
in part by noting that nuns, too, got married, but to "the most wonderful of persons, Jesus." Teenage girls were presented not so much
with the choice between marriage and the single state (although
this did happen), but rather between marriage to Jesus or to a mere

human. Father Poage urged his fellow recruiters to explain to their young audiences that sacrificing "visible affection and visible companionship" was indeed a worthy trade for the "deeper love and never-ending companionship of a heavenly spouse."[42]

Besides, marriage for Catholic women was a more complicated undertaking than for women of other faiths. The Church's prohibition on divorce and the difficulty of obtaining annulments meant that marriage could not be entered into lightly. The further prohibition on birth control meant that Catholic women were expected to have many children – and childbirth was still something to be feared. And in postwar Catholic literature, married women were often portrayed as the moral bulwark of the family – raising lots of children while reining in their shiftless, dissolute husbands in the true spirit of sacrifice and virtue.[43] Under the circumstances, the image of the convent as a place of simple tranquility, as seen in the quotation from Sister M. Claudette that opened this chapter, could be irresistible.

Sister Florence, a nun who advised Poage on the matter of recruiting schoolgirls, said it was best to stress the rewards of religious life and to avoid the unappealing vows of poverty, chastity, and obedience. The ultimate reward, of course, was in the next life, since Jesus would hardly reject his own spouses: "the most important thing to stress is the sense of security that we enjoy in the religious life. Every woman is tormented by a desire for certainty in the matter of her eternal salvation. We hate risk and long with a deep instinct of our natures for security. In the convent we have the greatest security possible ... and that reward has a very strong appeal."[44]

In other words, become a nun and eternal salvation was virtually assured. As Poage put it, while the life of a nun was hard, she was motivated to keep going by the knowledge that one day "sister and her Lover (were) going to meet." And what would that meeting be like? Here is his description: "And then in one blinding flash of everlasting, infinite joy, all the years of hardship and all the dark, comfortless hours will be swept away forever. Jesus will enfold her to His heart, and in the happiness of that embrace sister will not take a hundred worlds or a thousand pleasure-filled lifetimes."[45]

Poage was well aware that constant reference to sacrifice and hard work, combined with the somewhat grim image of convents in the popular imagination, might hamper recruitment. He admitted that girls would not be attracted to religious life if they thought that nuns spent all their free time embroidering vestments. Recruiters, in his opinion, had to represent convent life in more positive terms and to show that nuns did have fun:

> However, regardless of the spirituality of our appeal, let us not neglect to tell also of the more human things that make convents ring with gay laughter and keep smiles playing on a sister's lips. Sisters know which end of a tennis racket to use, and some have a batting average well over .300. A few hold private croquet championships, and the habit doesn't keep others off ice skates and bobsleds.[46]

While the religious life did lead to happiness in Heaven – and this was virtually guaranteed – it was also important to convey that it provided happiness on earth. A religious could choose the security and tranquility of the convent – and they usually had beautiful gardens – and this was the appeal of the contemplative congregations. But at the other extreme, she could choose the adventure of working in foreign missions, bringing faith and salvation to "the millions living in the darkness of idolatry and paganism."[47] The recruiters agreed that the apostolate or professional work conducted by a congregation – whether missions, teaching, nursing, and the like – was what attracted girls under fifteen to the convent, and publicity campaigns were encouraged to highlight such career opportunities.[48]

In summary, then, girls were advised that God looked more favourably on nuns than on married women, that it was infinitely preferable to choose Jesus over a mere human spouse, and that the rewards of such a choice were happiness after death and even before it.

In what forms were these messages conveyed to the young? It is best to categorize them along the lines suggested by the Vocational Institute at the University of Notre Dame in 1949.

VOCATIONAL TALKS

The most common strategy, and the principal activity of recruitment professionals, was the vocational talk delivered to students in

Catholic schools. The recruiter was usually from the congregation that conducted the school, but opportunities were also provided to other congregations, and especially those whose apostolate did not include teaching and were consequently disadvantaged in their access to the young. The captive audiences of teenagers were likely to be apathetic, the experienced Father Poage warned his fellow recruiters, so it was important to avoid being ponderous or long-winded. It was better, he advised, to try to break through to them with a dramatic opening assertion, such as: "Some of you are going to be surprised to learn how God will pick you for the greatest job on earth." This should be followed by discussion of the signs of a vocation and vivid descriptions of "hospitals understaffed, schools unmanned, and missions ... nearly abandoned." The lives of saints was always an inspiring topic, he suggested, since it might lead to a desire for emulation. Another theme might be a human-interest story to which adolescent girls could relate, such as that of Helen Horton, who abandoned her successful career as a nightclub singer to become a Sister of Charity,[49] or that of Stella Consigli, who quit the Ice Follies to join a Dominican convent.[50] Archbishop Richard Cushing of Boston added his own unique touch to these talks by asking those who wished to become a religious to stand, and then invited everyone else to applaud them.[51]

At St Luke's, the pseudonymous typical parochial school studied by Joseph Fichter in the mid-1950s, a mix of both male and female religious communities made vocational presentations to the Grade 5, 6, 7, and 8 students during the course of the academic year. The speakers, "youthful and dynamic," were adept at dramatic descriptions of foreign mission work and illustrated their talks with high-quality technicolour films.[52]

The Sisters of St Joseph of Cleveland, Ohio, took the idea of vocational talks to a new level in the early 1950s with a unique presentation that circulated among their schools. The Symposium on the Religious Life, as it was termed, consisted of three pep talks – one each by a postulant, novice, and professed sister. Betty McCafferty, a postulant, spoke first. She recalled how, in her senior year in school, as her mother made plans for her to attend college, she began to spend a lot of time with a nun whom she admired and who gave her "all the help and guidance" she needed to decide on a life in religion. Upon entering as a postulant, she told of her surprise at all the recreation available in the convent: basketball, volleyball, tennis, dancing, and card games. Following a brief description of the daily routine of prayer, study, work, and recreation, she concluded with: "I only hope and pray that I may be a worthy daughter of St Joseph, as are those who have gone before, setting such a heroic example of faith, courage, piety, and charity."

Sister Thomas More, the novice, was the next to speak. She too described how she had been drawn into the religious life. It had happened during her senior-year retreat, when the subject of vocations was before the students. Sister Thomas was intrigued and, in a conversation with a sister about it later, decided to enter. Her description of convent routines was realistic, and while she admitted that every day seemed the same, she insisted that the days were different – but in ways that she could not explain. She confessed to having had misgivings about forsaking dances, friends, and family upon entering because of her impression that religious life was "rather dreary." But once inside she had found a happiness and joy beyond her wildest dreams. Here is her description: "And after all, why shouldn't a nun be happy? She receives God Himself in Holy Communion every morning. God lives in her very own home – she is separated from Him by only a thin partition. And she knows that if some sunny day, as she is walking up the path, someone drops an H-bomb on Cleveland, Ohio, she will not die; she will only be drawn to a new life – a life with the same Divine Master she had tried to love and serve while on earth."

Sister Agnes Joseph, who had been a professed sister for almost twenty-five years, spoke last. Like Sister Thomas, she emphasized the happiness to be found in the convent, saying that nuns had "the most beautiful life to which one could be called." Her principal theme was the special satisfaction sisters found in teaching "God's little ones," and she regaled her listeners with amusing tales from the classroom by way of illustration. She was careful to point out, however, that the rewards of teaching were much greater for sisters than for seculars, since the former were, above all else, "spiritual mothers" to their students. She concluded with a stirring appeal: "Is there any life greater than ours? If civilization is to triumph, it will be the result in great measure of the work religious teachers are doing for Christ. Isn't that a challenge?"[53]

The young captive audiences to whom the symposium was presented learned that convents were filled with happy nuns upon whose work civilization depended and who were completely free from fears and worry.

Mary Gilligan recalled the steady stream of sister recruiters that addressed her class while she was in Grades 7 and 8 in Peoria, Illinois, in 1955 and 1956. They were young and attractive, in contrast to the nuns who taught her, and they talked of how they had once been "red-blooded American girls" and had loved clothes and dating. This opening message, designed to establish rapport with their audience, was usually followed by something like this: "But then I began to discover that worldly pleasures left me empty and unsatisfied ... Only giving myself completely to God has brought me peace and happiness." Gilligan was intrigued, but remained troubled by the thought of not having children should she choose to enter the convent. When she raised her concern with one of the recruiters, she was assured that nuns had lots of children and that "the spiritual motherhood they experienced in the classroom was every bit as satisfying as physical motherhood."

On one occasion a recruiter from the Sisters of Providence (St Mary-of-the-Woods) captivated Gilligan in extolling the glories of serving God and the possibilities of changing the world in doing so. The recruiter assured her listeners that they would not have to hear a voice in order to know if God was calling them, but rather would have a sense of being drawn towards the life. And if any of them felt that this was so, she advised them to put it to the test by completing their education in her congregation's juniorate or aspirancy (see Chapter 5), which was but a short distance away. She ended her talk by asking her listeners to pray for vocations: "The modern urge for riches, comfort, and pleasure is preventing many young men and women from following vocations. Pray with me that more young people will find within themselves the generosity and the idealism to join Christ in His important work." Gilligan found the idea appealing and secured her parents' consent to attend the aspirancy.[54]

Before leaving such talks, students were asked to complete "vocational interest cards" on which they indicated their interest or lack of interest in the religious life. A third choice was also presented: "Would like more information." In addition to the basic question, they were asked to supply their names, addresses, schools, dates of birth, and grades in which they were enrolled. They might also be asked if they had discussed their vocation with their parents.[55] The cards were the "little black book" of the recruiter; they were the database with which she operated to establish a list of "prospects" to be contacted for further discussion about their vocations. The database was kept up to date by winnowing out those who were merely "suspects" and unlikely to sign up.[56]

LITERATURE

Vocational pamphlets and brochures were an important component of recruitment campaigns and were widely distributed through Catholic schools and churches. Recruiters always had an abundance of them at hand when delivering vocational talks or when engaged in related tasks. Illustrated with either photographs or drawings, and about four to six pages in length, the pamphlets sought to convey their message in short, punchy paragraphs and dramatic language.[57]

"Could I Measure Up?" a brochure produced by the Sisters of Charity of Providence (Seattle) in 1957, was a bit longer than normal, in that it featured twenty pages of text and line drawings. Written in the first person, it purported to tell the story of how the writer had joined that particular congregation. First, she had weighed in her mind the advantages of the religious life before concluding that they were significant: "I could have a greater capacity to praise God in Heaven, in proportion to increased grace, merited by a life lived just for Him ... I could answer Christ's invitation to the thrilling adventure of saving souls and serving others." She then confided in her local priest, who assured her that she had all the qualifications. In casting about for a suitable congregation, she discerned that the Sisters of Charity of Providence provided unique opportunities to "do something heroic for Christ." A visit to their convent followed, where she met people "just like me." As she chatted with a friendly postulant she noticed: "the arrival of a group of novices with tennis rackets. Signs of good times, I thought. But I wasn't just imagining things. They were happy. It wasn't just the cheery smiles that convinced me of that. There was a deep serenity, and joyous anticipation on the faces of those novices." Her mind was made up and her parents were "thrilled" with her decision.[58]

"The Story of YOU," a pamphlet produced by the Sisters of Providence (St Mary-of-the-Woods) in 1964, also emphasized heroism and happiness. The cover featured a photograph of Marilyn Marschall, taken in 1955 just before she entered religion as Sister Peter, who was portrayed as "Miss Average American Girl." The congregation was looking for girls of average intelligence and ordinary health and who had a generosity of spirit, by which was meant a "willingness to be expendable for Christ." There were references to nobility, heroism, and the great career opportunities open to Sisters of Providence. Pictures of smiling postulants, novices, and junior professed sisters adorned the pages, and the pamphlet concluded with a stirring appeal: "There is a place for you as a Sister of Providence. Christ is paying you the greatest compliment a girl can receive: He wants you for His own. What will be your decision? On that depends the Happy Ending for the most important narrative in (and OF) your life – THE STORY OF YOU!"[59]

The pamphlets may not always have been as effective as their originators assumed. Mary Jane Masterson recalled that her high-school companions in Cleveland who were identified by "hopeful nuns" as likely candidates for their congregation were showered with "nun literature" but laughed secretly at it.[60] Father Poage was quite critical of some of the pamphlets, especially those featuring forbidding convent buildings, stained-glass windows, and lists of the old-fashioned clothes that postulants were required to purchase. He suggested the use of more "action shots" that appealed to youngsters, "pictures of the sisters at prayer, at work, or at play."[61]

The "nuns having fun" approach did not meet with universal approval. At a Vocational Institute at Notre Dame University, Bishop Fulton Sheen showed a brochure featuring young sisters playing tennis. We should recruit with the cross, not the tennis racket, he said disapprovingly. Don't emphasize pleasures and security, he advised his listeners, but rather appeal to the idealism and heroism of youth.[62] Sheen's view was echoed by Father Joseph Fichter when he observed that some vocational literature distributed in schools depicted novitiates as sports camps, with "postulants shooting baskets and Sisters umpiring baseball games."[63]

The debate about pamphlets and their contents reflected the influence of Madison Avenue and the slick sophistication it was bringing to the world of advertising at the time. The Advertising Research Foundation, in place since 1936, had achieved new momentum after the Second World War in investigating the most effective strategies with which to manipulate taste and influence behaviour. Although the Church in general disapproved of the materialism and worldliness inherent in the propaganda of consumerism, the techniques of those whom Vance Packard called "the hidden persuaders," appealed to vocational recruiters.[64] This improbable partnership could be seen when advertising executive Dennis O'Neill was invited to address the Notre Dame Vocational Institute in 1949. O'Neill advised his listeners to make their "brand" – religious life – resonate with American youth by targeting the right audience with the right message and being willing to spend money in doing so.[65]

Picking up on this idea, Sister Berchmans of Mary chose an elaborate promotional campaign in order to boost the intake of postulants to her congregation, the Sisters of Notre Dame de Namur. Launched over a two-year period in the early 1950s, the campaign had as its key feature the printing and distribution of forty thousand vocational pamphlets for an expenditure of $2,400. The result: twenty-eight new postulants, each one costing $86 when the recruitment budget was averaged out.[66]

There was another form of vocation literature that appealed even more to the recruitment professionals, since it could be placed in school libraries without an overt admission of its intention – which was rather obvious in the case of pamphlets. Two short books published in the 1950s stand out in this respect. Although quite different in format, they both conveyed the idea that becoming a nun and living the religious life were experiences of intense joy and fulfillment.

Sister Mary Paul Reilly's *What Must I Do?* (1950) was written in the hope that more teenage girls would ask unreservedly of Christ, "Master ... what must I do?" Written in language readily accessible to its target high-school audience, the text followed the experiences of ten fictional young women from the beginning of their religious formation to the moment they took their vows. "You," the reader, was asked to imagine herself as one of them and accordingly "you" became "Sister Mary Michael." All the challenges of adjusting to convent routines were minimized and life within the cloister was portrayed as safe, simple, and filled with good companionship and blissful moments with Jesus. Was this the life for you? Sister Reilly strongly suggested that it was and provided a long list of motivations and indications, any of which might persuade a reader to reply in the affirmative. And then, in common with the pamphlet literature, she appealed for courage and a willingness to put Christ before selfish concerns: "Respond to his demands with a courageous heart, making a clean break with whatever you must renounce to follow Christ. Accept the future with all that it may hold, saying not, 'Will I be happy?' but, 'Whatever you will, Lord. My life is Yours.' Then your vocation will be a joyous and untroubled quest of Him and your perseverance is assured."[67]

Bernie Becomes a Nun (1956) presented a similar message, but did so primarily through the medium of a photographic essay that followed Bernadette Lynch from her home in Brooklyn to the completion of her training as a Maryknoll Sister. A text by Sister Maria Del Rey Danforth accompanied the photographs, explaining the various stages of religious formation and recording Sister Bernie's thoughts as she experienced them. Bernie was pictured in prayerful contemplation, working joyfully on domestic chores, and playing games with her companions. In one instance, while still a postulant, she was captured sitting among day-lilies following a day's work in the garden, gazing skyward with a glow of radiant happiness on her face. The caption revealing her thoughts went: "This is the hundred-fold, dear Lord, which you promised to all who follow You. This joy in simple things; this deep peace; this serene enjoyment of You and of the world You have made." The final image showed Bernie and three other Maryknolls smiling and waving from the deck of a ship that was about to take them on a mission to Bolivia. In her text, Sister Maria said that community life had "the joy of a happy family," which summed up the central message of the book.[68]

What Must I Do? and *Bernie Becomes a Nun* were but two among several books appearing in the 1950s and 1960s either extolling the virtues of the convent or partly satisfying public curiosity about a "walled-in world."[69] Rebecca Sullivan argues persuasively that vocational literature portrayed religious life as normal, in the sense that it replicated in language and imagery the ideal of bourgeois domesticity in which many teenage girls were socialized in the postwar era. The path to religious vows paralleled that to a conventional wedding, in that it featured gifts, trousseaux, going-away parties, and white dresses. The metaphor of the family was employed too: congregations were caring families presided over by a mother. And while there were hints of independence in the careers open to nuns, the independence was always tempered by the priority assigned to common goals.[70]

VOCATIONAL CLUBS

Clubs devoted to chess, debating, school newspapers, and other special interests were common features of the extracurricular programs available in public high schools. The clubs served to cultivate social skills deemed useful in the modern economy.[71] Catholic high schools had similar programs, and some provided an additional offering that was unique to that milieu and that served a special purpose: the vocational club.

An influential model of the vocational club was developed by the Passionist Fathers in 1938 for Catholic boys' schools: Bosco Clubs. Adapted for convent schools as Our Lady of Good Counsel Clubs, they were quickly established in institutions run by the Sisters of Charity of Nazareth, the Ursulines, the Loretto Sisters, and the Sisters of Mercy. By 1954 there were 1,172 Good Counsel Clubs in the United States.[72]

What were the clubs expected to accomplish and how? Father Senieur was concerned that many girls in Grades 7 and 8 who were inclined towards serving God were being diverted by the "tinselled glamour" of teen social life. He felt that vocational clubs could help by bringing such girls together until they were "strong enough to withstand the attraction of the world."[73] He was also aware of the many complaints about sisters who talked excessively about vocations to "prospects" and at awkward and inappropriate moments. Vocational clubs would address this concern, he felt, by providing a setting in which to convey information to interested girls but "without cornering them in the corridor."[74] One club moderator claimed that the most important club function was "to give the sister an opening to talk to girls privately about the religious life."[75]

Father Poage agreed. He advised his readers that club moderators had clear mandates to talk about vocations at any time and that the presence of a club made a school more "vocation conscious" by bringing the subject out in the open. And when girls joined a club and talked about it at home, it gradually prepared parents for the possibility of a vocation in the family and made it more difficult for them to object later when a decision to enter was announced.[76]

A more general aim of the clubs was educational. The idea was to inform members about the nature of religious life and to counter the "erroneous ideas" that were sometimes circulating. According to Mother Mary Wulston of Holy Child High School, Waukegan, Illinois, club members learned that religious led "rich full lives" rather than "dull and uninteresting" ones.[77]

Clubs were organized at the school level, or they might open membership to students from a number of smaller schools that were not too distant from one another. They were also organized at the parish level, where an attempt could be made to sign up Catholics attending public schools. Boys' and girls' clubs, it goes without saying, always met separately. Meetings were usually held twice a month – once during school hours, and once in the evenings or on weekends.[78] At Nazareth Academy in the Chicago suburb of La Grange Park, the monthly club meetings were scheduled during morning class periods, and non-members were sent to the auditorium for supervised study.[79]

Prospective members were told they would be introduced to "all the wonderful things about the life of a sister," but they didn't have to become one. The rules, however, made little pretense about the true purpose. Members were obliged to say a daily prayer to know God's will about their vocation; to receive Holy Communion once a week, and more frequently if possible; and to offer Mass and Holy Communion for fellow members on the first Sunday of the month.[80]

Meetings opened with a prayer to "Mary, Queen of Vocations," and there followed a "rousing talk" by the club moderator. Members learned about different aspects of the religious life, including the various apostolates that were available, how to apply for admission to a congregation, and how to answer objections to one's vocation from parents and friends. They also visited a number of convents, sometimes playing games with postulants.[81] At Nazareth Academy, newly-admitted postulants and novices with the Sisters of St Joseph made an annual visit to the club for informal chats with members about life in the novitiate. It was one of the highlights of the year, according to Sister Mary Joanne: "We have found that the students are always deeply impressed by the fervent spirit of these young sisters, by their happy laughter over the ups, and their generosity in the downs of their first years in religion."[82]

The vocational club at Archbishop Walsh High School, Irvington, New Jersey, got parents involved. On the first Friday of every month the pastor conducted a Holy Hour with the club members and their parents. Sister Mary Blaise explained the initiative: "it is in the true Catholic home where prayerful parents unite with their children daily in the recitation of the rosary and where obedience and respect are demanded, that the seeds of a religious vocation are sown." The results were gratifying, she added. In 1955 no less than twelve of the Grade 8 girls wrote seeking admission to the aspirancy of the School Sisters of Notre Dame, the congregation that conducted the school.[83]

During the mid-1940s the Good Counsel Clubs of Chicago organized a vocational congress to which representatives of thirty-five different communities were invited to display their wares. Sister Mary Corona of Providence High School was initially dubious about it, since she was hesitant "to risk passing our girls around as subjects to other congregations." But she eventually came around to the idea upon realizing that everyone benefited from the prayers of nuns, irrespective of the convent they chose to join.[84]

Father Senieur advised club moderators to use "every legitimate means to encourage the girls to consider the religious life." Just as publishers put appealing covers on books to boost sales, he observed, so too could the convent be presented in a positive way: "There is no harm done in turning the attractive side of religious life to the young mind as a 'come-on' for considering the total sacrifice of love."[85] Father Poage too felt that club moderators had unique circumstances in which to provide the young with a "systematic indoctrination" in all aspects of the religious life as well as "private counselling and regular spiritual direction." As habits of "piety and devotion" took root, he said, moderators could dispose a member "to the supreme act of religion; namely giving herself completely to God."[86]

By Poage's estimation, no more than 20 to 30 per cent of students in a school or parish could be expected to join a vocational club. Of those who did so, perhaps 9 per cent would enter the convent. The other 91 per cent would not have been wasting their time, he surmised, since they would be "wiser and better for the training." And perhaps one day they would have children of their own and be favourable to their pursuing careers in religion.[87] Sister Mary Joanne agreed and even predicted that, within ten to fifteen years, there would be a sharp increase in vocations, since former club members who had become mothers would be "deeply convinced of the tremendous value of the religious life."[88]

VOCATIONAL CAMPAIGNS

The recruitment efforts of the clubs were supplemented by vocational campaigns that were organized either by a diocese or an individual school. In fact, in 1944 the NCEA selected the month of March to promote vocations in parochial schools. March was ideal, it was thought, since final exams were still some time away and the month either preceded or included Easter – a time of elaborate religious rituals and pageantry. During the month, teachers and invited speakers addressed such issues as the nature and signs of a vocation, how to overcome difficulties, the various apostolates that were available, and the need for "prayerful examination of one's own inclinations." Programs culminated with the students composing essays on the topic: "Why I Would (or Would Not) Like to Become a Priest, Brother, or Sister." The essays were examined to identify "prospects," who were then encouraged to write for more information to the seminary or convent of their choice. It was even suggested that their essays might accompany their letters of inquiry.[89]

The Serra Club, a lay organization founded in Seattle in 1935 to promote vocations to the religious life, sponsored an essay contest during vocation month for all the parochial-school Grade 8 students in the Midwestern city in which Fichter's St Luke's was located. The topic was: "What I would like to do for God if I had a religious vocation." The local bishop invited the winners to dinner and used the occasion to deliver a talk on vocations.[90]

When campaigns were conducted by the diocese, a special effort was made to ensure that all Catholic youth aged twelve and over who were enrolled in public schools (the majority, in fact) were able to attend at least one talk on vocations and sign an interest card. Further information about the families and academic performance of those who were interested was then compiled and passed on to recruitment professionals.[91]

Catherine Whitney, in recalling her elementary schooling with the Dominican Sisters in Seattle, noted that recruitment efforts by the nuns were constant from the earliest grades, but during March, which was designated "vocation month," the efforts intensified. In Grade 5 she was chosen to participate in the diocesan vocation pageant in which boys and girls were dressed respectively as priests and nuns. The bishop informed the children so attired that God had a plan for them and that being selected for the pageant might well be a special sign from him.[92] Some retailers of Catholic paraphernalia actually sold miniature replicas of nuns' habits to be worn by children during pageants.[93]

RETREATS

The religious retreat was one of the most powerful strategies in securing recruits.[94] Retreats were usually weekend affairs conducted by religious orders specializing in the work. The Passionist Fathers, for example, built retreat centres wherever they operated. They provided participants with intense religious experiences with much meditation on the suffering of Christ and harangues against the sinfulness of the world.[95] Two of the Sisters of Charity interviewed by historian Heidi MacDonald, for instance, turned to the religious life following retreats.[96] And it was likewise for four of the Dominican nuns who recorded their experiences in *Vocation in Black and White*.[97] Rosa Bruno-Jofré, in her study of the Missionary Oblate Sisters, noted the role played by retreats in attracting recruits.[98] During the 1950s, Mother M. Walburga, SSJ, organized a retreat for ninety-five hand-picked girls from her congregation's schools and from recent graduates. Ten of the participants entered the novitiate that fall and eleven more did so the following year.[99]

While attending a retreat as a Grade 9 student, Mary Jane Masterson was stunned to hear the presiding priest declare: "You, too, can be a nun." The words struck her like a hurtling rock, and she realized that she was being called by God.[100] Joanne Howe had a similar experience. In April 1953, as she was completing her education at a Catholic high school, she was persuaded by friends to attend a retreat with the Sisters of St Joseph in Baden, Pennsylvania. She prayed fervently throughout the weekend and was strongly encouraged by the postulants who were present to join their ranks. And she did.[101] The four retreats attended by Mary Griffin while a high-school student in Chicago affected her profoundly. The retreats were conducted by "persuasive Jesuits," who convinced her to choose the "higher path." In August 1939, she became a postulant with the Sisters of Charity of the Blessed Virgin Mary in Dubuque, Iowa.[102] Karen Leahy grew up in Canton, Ohio, and was educated by the Sisters of the Humility of Mary, who told her on many an occasion that she would make a good nun. Six months before she completed Grade 12, the sisters persuaded her to attend a retreat at their mother house in nearby Villa Maria, Pennsylvania, so that she might better understand if she had a religious vocation. Leahy had always been intrigued by nuns and their lives and throughout the retreat felt that she was being carried by an irresistible tide into the convent. On 15 October 1959, a few months after graduation, she returned to the mother house as a postulant.[103]

CONFESSION

The Catholic school was not the only arena in which active recruitment could be practised. Fathers Poage and Senieur agreed that the confession box presented opportunities that were underemployed in identifying "prospects" and directing them to the cloister. The advantage of the confessional was that it allowed the priest to see "the youthful heart laid open." If a girl seemed like "a solidly pious person," he could "prudently suggest an interest in religious life."[104]

Father John P. Kennelly, vocational director in the Archdiocese of Chicago, used this strategy to great success and addressed the

Vocational Institute of Notre Dame in 1948 on the subject, urging others to emulate him. When they identified a girl making regular Confession (a favourable omen, unless she was a serious sinner) he suggested saying to her in the confessional: "When was the last time you thought about the religious life?" Any form of affirmative response should be followed with: "Well, when we find good ... girls like you, naturally we want you to attain the highest degree of sacrifice and sanctity and perfection possible." Further questions might be: "Are you praying for your vocation?" "Do you ever ask God to make you a ... sister?" Before leaving the confessional, the girl should be persuaded to promise to talk to a priest about her vocation – just to clear up any questions in her mind. Over a twenty-five-year period, Father Kennelly's Confession strategy allegedly "helped over 300 girls to convents around the Mid West." When asked how many had come to him voluntarily, he replied: "Only seven percent came to me of their own accord or were sent by others. The rest I had to go after."[105]

At a meeting of the NCEA Vocations Committee in 1949 Father V.J. Campbell claimed that the confessional had been his "greatest single source" of vocations. Within the previous decade he boasted of having recruited thirty-two candidates for fifteen different sisterhoods through advice he had dispensed in Confession, followed by weekly counselling for up to a year in each case.[106]

SPIRITUAL COUNSELLING

All of the strategies used to identify and influence suitable recruits to the convent ultimately led to a series of personal interviews with an experienced vocations expert. The interviews were described as spiritual or vocational counselling. Recruiters were advised to proceed slowly, to probe into the prospect's personal life. What sort of literature did she read? How were her evenings spent? Was she involved with Catholic organizations such as the Legion of Mary? The Maryknoll Sisters were very much concerned with patterns of dating: "We advise a normal social life but no steady dating. Find out how frequently she dates and how often and with the same boy. This is important."[107] Having a steady boyfriend was seen as a bad sign – a harbinger of trouble ahead.

If the prospect met the requirements as "convent material," the interviewer was encouraged to put her at her ease, using chocolates or cigarettes if necessary, and ultimately, through Socratic questioning, to lead her to believe that the decision to enter a convent was hers alone. If the prospect was wavering between marriage and the religious life, the astute recruiter would point out that marriage was an irrevocable decision (at least for Catholics), whereas the lengthy postulancy and novitiate that led to religious vows gave many opportunities for a change of heart. Therefore, in the event of indecision, it was best to try the religious life first.[108]

It was precisely that line of reasoning that convinced Rachel Ethier to enter. During her final year at a boarding school in Maine run by the Daughters of Wisdom, she was unable to decide between college – favoured by her mother – and the convent. A teaching sister in whom she confided urged her to try the convent first, since college would distract her from thinking about a religious vocation. On 2 August 1957, she became a postulant with the Daughters of Wisdom at their Mary Immaculate Novitiate near Litchfield, Connecticut. At the time, she had only a vague notion of what religious life was like; she stayed until 30 December 1967.[109]

If a prospect simply had doubts about her vocation, she should be encouraged to voice them, advised Father Poage. And he suggested that recruiters use the following line of argument to combat the doubts: "Who put this idea of a vocation in your mind? Where did it come from? Did it come from the devil? No! Do you think the devil wants you to be a leader in Christ's army? Of course not! The inspiration, then, must be from God, and if He has chosen you, He doesn't demand anything beyond your strength. He simply offers you an invitation. You can accept or reject. What will it be?"[110]

Invoking the spectre of the Devil was a standard strategy to stiffen the resolve of those wracked by doubts. In fact, Satan was held responsible for all sorts of obstacles and distractions that might derail vocations. What if, for example, a prospect were tempted by a "rebellion of the flesh"? The temptation should be attributed to the Devil, was Poage's advice, since when Satan saw someone entering religion, he renewed his assaults all the more fiercely. Mortification and prayer would, however, quickly deal with the problem. The role of recruiters and spiritual directors, then, was to fortify a prospect in the conviction that she had a vocation. She should be trained from the beginning to keep asking herself: "What am I here for? Is it not for God? I expect to suffer like Christ. The more I can take for Him, the more generously I can give in return."[111]

Once a "prospect" had made the commitment to enter a convent, she was considered a candidate. How should she now behave? According to the recruitment professionals, she could continue to enjoy the company of her female friends, but should stay away from the opposite sex or what one nun called "entangling alliances and allurements."[112] The idea of "one last fling" was, in Senieur's word's, "the devil's most potent weapon" and was to be avoided at all cost.[113] Instead, the candidate should become more acquainted with her future spouse by talking to him in prayer and by receiving him daily in Holy Communion.[114] She should also come under the direction of a spiritual director – a local priest who would "condition" her for possible difficulties, such as homesickness, in the convent. The director's role was not just to explain what she was about to experience, but to encourage her to pursue her vocation "no matter what sacrifices were entailed."[115]

What was the relative effectiveness, it might be asked, of the various strategies employed by the recruitment professionals? This is a question that cannot really be answered, since girls attending Catholic schools probably experienced most of them in differing combinations and degrees of intensity. It was the steady and persistent advocacy that ultimately won them over, and particularly if the message were conveyed by a friendly nun who exuded a "spirit of joy," as the sociology of vocations had discovered.

Even so, we can say with some confidence that the practitioners of these strategies were convinced of their utility. We can see this in the actual number of recruits claimed by Sister Berchmans of Mary with her pamphlet distribution, Sister Mary Blaise with her vocational club, Mother Walburga with her retreats, and Fathers Campbell and Kennelly with their use of the confessional. The fact that the total number of nuns in the United States rose steadily every year until 1965 is a further indicator that systematic recruitment was working. It meant that those lost annually through death and defection were being more than replaced by new arrivals.

If we examine the number of novices entering a specific congregation, we can see the success of recruitment more clearly. In the four-year period 1952 to 1955, the Maryknoll Sisters had an average annual intake of fifty-nine novices. In the subsequent four-year period, 1956 to 1959, ninety-one new novices were received every year. And that number rose to ninety-seven between 1960 and 1963.[116] The congregation was in a confident, expansionist mood after the war. A new novitiate was built in 1947 in Valley Park, Missouri, and another in Topsfield, Massachusetts, in 1953. Known as Ladycrest, the latter institution was designed to house the canonical novices who had completed their postulancy at the mother house in Ossining, New York. By 1961 new construction gave Ladycrest a capacity for 120 novices – a number that was anticipated but never realized.[117]

CONCLUSION

To what, then, may we attribute the success of the Catholic Church in attracting thousands of young American women annually to religious sisterhoods? It would be difficult to argue with any conviction that all the teenagers in question were making informed choices, were fully aware of alternatives, and arrived at their decisions after mature reflection and a modicum of diverse experience. Nor is it plausible to claim that they were simply responding to an unmistakable call from God, since the Church itself advised prospective candidates not to expect disembodied voices, pillars of fire, the appearance of an angel, or being knocked from a horse.

In truth, the Church needed nuns – large numbers of them – to staff its various institutions, and especially its schools, at minimum cost. And it was determined to recruit them actively, rather than wait for volunteers to come forward. The Catholic school was the key institution in the recruitment process. Teaching sisters constructed educational experiences for their students that steered them into one of two possibilities in life: religious vows or marriage. The religious life was presented as by far the most desirable choice, while its disadvantages were downplayed or ignored.

And while every teaching sister was a recruiter, the Church took the matter further by engaging professional vocations directors charged with the task of discovering and applying the most effect-ive recruitment strategies. The professionals shared their techniques and experiences with one another at conferences and in literature, so that seeking candidates for the religious life took on the appear-ance of a nationwide marketing campaign.

It is well to remember, however, that there were always girls and young women for whom a life in religion held an irresistible appeal and who needed little encouragement to pursue it. Systematic re-cruitment accomplished an expansion and diversification of the pool of candidates to include not only those who were convinced of their calling, but many who were unsure about it and were not quite certain what was expected of them.

. . . .

CHAPTER 4

What If

Parents

Objected?

Now Mother and Dad must be consulted ...
If you are from a staunch Catholic home,
the news will be matter for great rejoicing
and pride that God has so singled you out.
Just to be realistic, however, most future
nuns will receive no such enthusiastic
reception. You will probably have to face
shocked surprise at the least, or maybe even
a storm of disapproval.[1]
Sister Mary Paul Reilly (1950)

For me it is hard to understand how many
good Catholic parents, outstanding for
their charity toward everyone, can fail to be
just as magnanimous toward God. Gladly
will they give any number of their children
to creatures in marriage. Why do they
object so strenuously to giving even one
to God, the Creator?[2]
Mother Catherine Thomas (1955)

IN *TAKING THE VEIL*, Marta Danylewycz's study of nineteenth-century Quebec convents, she claimed that Catholic families were honoured to have children in the religious life, believing that it improved their own chances of salvation.[3] Margaret McGuinness made a similar point in reference to American families in the period following the Second World War. She argued that parents "usually supported" a daughter's decision to enter a convent in the belief that "God was bestowing a special blessing on them."[4]

The truth is a bit more complicated. As early as 1933 Sister Josephine, OSB, identified parental objections as a major factor in discouraging young women from joining religious sisterhoods: "However, when at length the decision to accept [the invitation from the Divine Spouse] is made known, how frequently it happens that much opposition is met, possibly from the very ones who should uphold, or even encourage the decision."[5] Pope Pius XI, in the encyclical *Ad Catholici Sacerdodii* (1935), acknowledged the problem: "It must be confessed with sadness that only too often parents seem to be unable to resign themselves to the priestly or religious vocations of their children. Such parents have no scruple in opposing the divine will with objections of all kinds; they even have recourse to means which can imperil not only the vocation to a more perfect state, but also the very conscience and the eternal salvation of those souls they ought to hold dear."[6]

In Father Godfrey Poage's recruitment work in the 1950s, he discovered that two-thirds of parents voiced some objections to the religious life when their daughters expressed an interest.[7] Sister Mary of the Angels Garland found that 53 per cent of the nuns in her 1951 survey had experienced opposition to their vocations from one or both parents.[8]

Writing in the summer of 1952, Father Martin Stevens complained that in his own parish over a six-week period "seven sincere youngsters [had] been persuaded, threatened, or forced by their parents to give up all thought of religious life." He referred specifically to two girls who had wanted to enter a preparatory school or aspirancy. The father of one of them had flown into a rage, refused to let his daughter "bury herself alive," and forbade her mentioning religious life until she was twenty-one years old. The mother of the second girl said: "Betty is only a baby – she's only fourteen ... Why, she's never been out with a boy, and doesn't know what to say to them when I make her go to parties. How can she give up something she doesn't even know?" Stevens described these cases as "a tragic pattern" that was causing vocations to drop, while sisters exhausted themselves "in heroic struggle trying to do work calling for five times their number."[9]

A year later, lay Catholic activist Catherine de Hueck, addressed the problem in urgent tones: "The main point I wanted to make in this letter is that you have to face the fact, as has the Church, as have we all, that many vocations are stifled and lost – incredible as it seems, *in Catholic homes* – and that something *must* be done about it soon. If not, the wrath of God will fall on all of us."[10]

In his pamphlet, "Parents and Vocations" (1958), Ben Palmer, Minneapolis lawyer and Catholic philosopher,[11] had this to say: "Practically all authorities agree that one of the principal obstacles to entrance into a religious life is to be found in parental objections." And he concluded that "every year thousands of young people are deterred from entering seminaries or novitiates because of the objections of parents."[12] Brother André, writing in 1951, calculated that about 50 per cent of potential vocations were lost regularly due to "parents' refusal to the requests of their children."[13]

In her interviews with former nuns, Marie Gass found that nine of her informants came from families opposed to their vocations, eight had supportive parents, and in four cases the family was either neutral or divided on the question. The remarks of some of those with uncooperative parents give a sense of the conflict a daughter's vocation could provoke. Julia, who spent seven years in a convent, remembered it this way: "My parents did not understand at all what I was doing. My mother accepted my decision reluctantly – she didn't cut me out of her life. My father, on the other hand, was totally without understanding." He refused to contact her while she was a nun and never read her letters home. The families of two others reacted with equal vigour. Casey had this to say: "My parents were very sad at my entering and opposed it. After I entered, I was encouraged to be rigid and distant from them. My parents mentioned that I was 'holier-than-thou.'" Cherry recalled that: "My parents had thrown such an absolute fit when my older sister wished to go into a convent, so I knew that it would be difficult. It was a royal battle and ended up in my being totally ostracized ... It totally tore up the family. My entering the convent had made our family totally dysfunctional."[14]

There is no shortage of individual testimony on the matter, and a few examples will suffice by way of illustration. One well-known case was that of Pat Drydyk, who battled her parents for five years prior to becoming a Franciscan nun – and her mother rarely spoke to her afterwards.[15] Sister Mary Jean Dorcy, OP, recalled that her family dismissed her decision to take the veil as just another of her passing enthusiasms. "Good heavens, are they that hard up for nuns?" said one of them. But she persisted and "stubbornly resisted" all their arguments.[16]

There were many instances of parents acquiescing in their daughters' career choice, but with great sadness and reluctance. In *The Calling*, Catherine Whitney records the arrival of Barbara, an attractive blonde from Portland, Oregon, at the Dominican Sisters' novitiate in Seattle to begin her postulancy in 1954: "delivered by her parents, who seemed very unhappy to see their only daughter – their beautiful child – swallowed up by the convent. Although they were devout Catholics, Barbara's parents nevertheless agonized over the loss of their daughter. There would be no wedding bells, no babies, no nighttime chats around the kitchen table. Their daughter would never belong to them again."[17]

"You don't know what you're talking about," was Beryl Bissell's mother's reaction when told of her daughter's intention of joining the Poor Clares, a contemplative congregation, in the spring of 1957. The parents maintained their opposition in the months that followed, throwing parties and encouraging their daughter to go to college. But Beryl, backed by her adviser, Mother Columba, who warned that college was "the graveyard of religious vocations," held her resolve. In August, her parents finally gave their consent.[18]

Shirley Dyckes graduated in 1951 from an exclusive private school in Miami, Florida. While studying at St Mary's College, South Bend, Indiana, she became intrigued by the work of the Holy Cross Sisters in the slums of Chicago and decided to join that congregation. When she arrived home for Christmas vacation, she informed her parents, who were dismayed at her decision. But by Christmas morning her father declared that the mourning should end, since Shirley's resolve was unwavering, and that it was best to enjoy her company in the short time they had left together.[19]

How did the Church account for parental objections in the first place? A recurring explanation was that parents were too fond of their children and were unwilling to part with them, especially if they were still quite young.[20] Some writers blamed the "religious indifference" and secular/materialistic values that prevailed in America – values that affected even sincere Catholic families.[21] Father Stevens put it this way:

> Secularism is creeping rot. It works in secret, and is usually far advanced before there is an outward sign. It creeps into the men and women who are pillars of the Church, and they remain handsome pillars to others (and, unfortunately, to themselves) until the test comes. Then they crumble. Parents who do not rejoice at the signs of a vocation in a child are parents who are becoming paganized from the inside out. They have accepted worldly standards; they measure and evaluate all things in worldly terms.[22]

In the case of daughters, secularism/paganism fostered the belief that marrying a man of wealth or potential wealth was the surest path to happiness: "These are the attractions of a socially advantageous marriage, the prospects of connections of social and financial value. Great is the pressure on the parents to see to it that their daughter is married as advantageously as the daughters of their friends,"[23] as Ben Palmer put it. At the end of the 1950s, Father Joseph Fichter, in noting that parental objections to their daughters' vocations were on the increase, agreed that the phenomenon was linked to the social ambitions of Catholic families. It was all about upward mobility.[24]

The Devil was said to play a role in discouraging vocations among the young by causing "his agents to act, who, in this case, are often one's own relatives, friends and companions."[25] The idea that one's family could be an agent of the Devil seems to have originated with St Jean Baptiste de la Salle, the seventeenth-century French priest who founded the Brothers of the Christian Schools. It was an extreme position and perhaps more than anything illustrates the degree of aggravation that parental opposition provoked.

Parents were accused of hindering vocations in the following ways: by refusing permission; by promoting alternative careers; by giving wrong advice and information; by making discouraging remarks; by causing unnecessary delays; and by trying to "test the vocation."[26] The aggravation is further illustrated by frequent recourse in the recruitment literature to biblical quotations denigrating family. These passages, attributed to Jesus of Nazareth, were the ones most often cited:[27]

> For I have come to set a man at variance with his father, and a daughter with her mother, and a daughter-in-law with her mother-in-law; and a man's enemies will be those of his own household. He who loves father or mother more than me is not worthy of me; and he who loves son or daughter more than me is not worthy of me. And he who does not take up his cross and follow me, is not worthy of me. Matthew 10:35–8.

> If anyone comes to me and does not hate his father and mother, and wife and children, and brothers and sisters, yes, and even his own life, he cannot be my disciple. Luke 14:26.

The recruitment literature of the postwar period acknowledged the problem of negative parental attitudes, but also outlined a series of strategies to overcome it. The strategies fall under the following classifications: prayer, persuasion, intimidation, and defiance. We will examine each of these in turn.

PRAYER

Sister Mary Paul Reilly, in her short book *What Must I Do?* (1950), encouraging high-school girls to enter the convent, advised her young readers to turn to prayer if they encountered uncooperative parents. "It certainly can be a bitter trial," she said, "but unwavering calmness and trusting prayer will almost always turn the trick for you where there is a background of faith in the family."[28] Moreover, she suggested St Joseph as the personage most likely to assist under the circumstances. And she even provided the words: "Kind St. Joseph, I have always come to you when there's work to be done, and you never let me down. For the sake of Jesus and Mary help me out again. Make my parents look on my vocation as God's will and be happy with it. Make it possible for me to enter as soon as I have planned. See that everything goes smoothly, St. Joseph, for I'm counting on you."[29]

There were prayers too for parents and expectant parents designed to predispose them to the idea of a career in religion for their children. Here is a sample from a lengthy piece in a brochure published by the Sisters of Charity of Providence (Seattle). The first part addressed Jesus directly:

O Jesus ... How happy we would be if You would make us the parents of a priest or religious. We know that we often offend You and are not worthy of so high a privilege. But, dear God, do not think of our many sins. Think, rather, of the great needs of Your Church ... Remember ... the great number of boys and girls who must be taught in our Catholic schools how to know You, and to love You, and to serve You ... We ask nothing for our selves. We desire only Your glory and the salvation of souls. We offer You in advance the child You may give us. We dedicate that child entirely to Your service, to the saving of souls for You.

A short concluding paragraph addressed Mary in a similar manner, suggesting her intercession: "Mary, Mother of Jesus, and the Queen of Vocations, your Son was the first Priest. God gave you that privilege. Please put in a good word for us so that we, too, may become the parents of a priest, a brother, or a sister. Amen."[30]

While it is impossible to estimate how many parents, if any, actually recited this prayer, its intention was fairly clear. Upon learning that a child of theirs wished to enter religion, parents would feel especially blessed or privileged and therefore less likely to oppose the decision.

The idea that a couple should offer a child in its infancy, or even unborn, to the service of Jesus had a decidedly medieval ring to it, but instances of such an offering in twentieth-century America were not completely unknown. Madeline DeFrees (born 1919) attended St Mary's Academy, Portland, Oregon. She admired her teachers, the Sisters of the Holy Names of Jesus and Mary, for the happiness they radiated and for "the simplicity of their lives and the zeal of their teaching." At the age of sixteen she decided to join the congregation. Her mother was delighted with the news and disclosed that when Madeline had been a sickly infant she had promised God that she would give her a Catholic schooling and would encourage her to pursue a religious vocation if she didn't die.[31]

PERSUASION

In the event that recalcitrant parents were not swayed by the response to prayer, more down-to-earth approaches were called for, the most important of which was persuasion.

Persuasion took place on a number of fronts. Arguments were presented in print, usually in the form of articles in religious periodicals or in pamphlets distributed in churches and schools. Vocational clubs were often responsible for disseminating these materials and at times they were the publishers as well.[32] "Information for Parents," a brochure produced by the Sisters of Charity of Providence (Seattle), was typical of the genre. It was written in the words of a father and mother who were musing to themselves about their daughter's decision to join the congregation: "God has chosen one of our children, our own flesh and blood, to be consecrated to Him for the service of the family of God. Are we to stand in her way as she seeks to find happiness in her life? She has heard and understood, perhaps, in a way that we never did, the words of Christ, 'If thou wilt be perfect ... come follow Me.' There is something personal between our child and God." The parents then went on to acknowledge that sisters worked hard, but observed that God rewarded them with longevity – a life expectancy of seventy-five years. They admitted to worrying about losing their daughter, but had recently been assured by a sister that she would draw closer to them in religious life, since she would not have a family of her own. They then turned to the advantages their girl would have in the convent: educational opportunities and work that she enjoyed. And they, too, would benefit: "We shall feel quite secure when our time of judgment comes, for our daughter loved and worked for Him."[33]

The recruitment professionals hoped that at least some parents would put aside objections to their children's vocations upon reading the mix of reasoned argument and emotional appeal featured in the literature. Prominent recruiters were convinced, however, that the most effective antidote to family opposition was a personal interview with parents in their homes, provided the interviewer was skilled, personally charming, and adept at both logic and psychology.

Well-known Passionist retreat master, Father Howard Ralenkotter (1910–2003), observed that some religious constitutions prevented nuns making home visits but suggested that perhaps mother superiors would find a way to "manoeuvre" around it. If that proved impossible, it was best to invite parents to the convent. Ralenkotter felt it would be wise to find out beforehand which parent would be more supportive of their daughter entering religion, and to use this information to "divide and conquer." His advice was: "Divide the opposition and win out. After you have one of the parents on the child's side, the other parent will gradually weaken."[34]

In *Vocational Replies* (1954), Father Jude Senieur advised recruiters to maintain a pleasant atmosphere above all when interviewing parents in their homes. He suggested a subtle approach, such as pretending that the visit was a purely social affair. It was unwise, he warned, to raise the question of a daughter's vocation immediately. It was far better to seek out an "approachable spot," where it could be addressed almost naturally while conversing on mundane matters of interest to the parents. He gave the following examples:

If Dad is a painter, express genuine interest in the problem of painting. Perhaps you have a chapel that needs painting and you wonder what would be the best way to paint it. You ask him about his painting work. When did he first get interested in painting? If it was early in life, you have an opening for extolling the value of getting an early start on a vocation.

If the father is interested in baseball, perhaps you can talk baseball for a while and explain that the postulancy and novitiate are like the minor leagues where young girls are sent to prove their qualification for the major leagues.

Recruiters needed to convey the message that they were just as interested in the child's happiness as the parents, according to Senieur. It would do them no good, he advised, "to moan every time the father or mother suggest[ed] the possibility of the daughter's getting married." An open mind to marriage on the part of recruiters was more likely to foster the same openness to the religious life among parents.[35]

In his *Secrets of Successful Recruiting* (1961), Father Poage provided his fellow recruiters detailed instructions on how to interview parents with the aim of overcoming opposition. His approach was a little more direct than Senieur's, at least in the initial part of the conversation, but he, too, advocated a careful, preplanned strategy to steer parents towards consent. He suggested that the home visit be arranged beforehand to ensure the presence of both parents and lots of time for the discussion to evolve to a satisfactory conclusion. There was no point in being evasive, he advised; it was best to declare a sincere interest in the youngster and in her family. "I just had to meet you," was a line that might be used. There was a danger, he admitted, that sociable and hospitable parents might distract the recruiter with convivial chatter. It was essential, therefore, to keep focused on where the conversation was leading: securing approval for the child's vocation.[36]

Poage had been reading psychology books and was impressed with the potential of what he called the "way of suggestion." He proposed that the recruiter begin by explaining the nature of the religious life and conclude with remarks such as: "That's really a wonderful life, isn't it?" or "What will give you greater happiness at the end of your life than knowing your daughter is a nun?" This was more effective than simply refuting parental objections with reasoned argument, he said, an approach that risked provoking the kind of stubborn resistance Dale Carnegie had warned about in *How to Win Friends and Influence People*.

Poage's preferred strategy was for the recruiter to keep emphasizing agreement with parents. For example, recruiter and parent have the same objective – the happiness of the child. By taking this as a starting point, he advised, it was possible to structure the discussion along affirmative lines, until parents found themselves cornered logically into consent. He even presented a model dialogue, illustrating how this might transpire. This was his strategy to win over parents "without a fight."[37]

Poage and other recruitment professionals were well aware that reasoned refutations of parental objections should also be part of their repertoire of persuasion. Indeed, the literature on recruitment clearly catalogued typical objections and suggested arguments that could be used to counter them – while not annoying parents, of course. Let us examine some of these.

My child is too young to know her own mind. This objection was most often heard when a teenager was being pressed to enter an aspirancy. Several writers challenged the immaturity objection on the grounds that most young people began contemplating their careers while in their early teens.[38] Father Stevens argued that, if children from the age of twelve onwards were ready for studies, responsibilities, entertainment, sports, and exposures to temptations, then surely they were ready for God. And he added: "God usually calls His chosen ones early, when hearts are still unencrusted with worldly careers and ambitions." Besides, the Church demanded that "budding vocations be protected and nurtured throughout high school years in preparatory seminaries and juniorates." He suggested that parents be reminded "that Mary was not too young at sixteen to give her full consent to God, nor was Christ too young at twelve to be about His Father's business."[39]

Sister Reilly advised the teenagers she was trying to recruit on how to respond to parents who claimed that they could not know their own minds. There were two answers, she said:

1 A vocation is from God, and he should know when you are able to follow him.
2 There are thousands of happy nuns in the country who entered convents at an early age. Just ask them if they regret it.[40]

The first answer put perplexed parents in the position of questioning God's wisdom; the second was simply rhetorical, since the average father or mother could hardly be expected to conduct a survey on the happiness of American nuns.

Father Senieur was ready to admit that a thirteen-year-old was too young to know her own mind. But, he argued, if she showed an interest in the religious life, why not put her in circumstances where she would ultimately come to know it? If she entered an aspirancy or preparatory school, she would acquire "a healthy view" of both life in religion and life in the world and would "really be in a position to make an intelligent choice." Enrolling in such a school was not a decision either way, he said, but rather it enabled her to "find out for sure" if she had a vocation: "And here, in a well-balanced schedule of prayer, study and recreation, they acquire a true outlook on life that enables them to make a mature and intelligent decision."[41]

Wait a while. This type of response followed logically from parents who felt that their children were too young to enter aspirancies or novitiates. The delaying tactic annoyed recruiters, who argued that it risked the loss of a vocation by fostering parental attachment to their children while at the same time exposing the young to habits inimical to religious life. Ben Palmer summed up the recruiters' frustration: "The longer departure from home is postponed, the harder it is to sever the connection between parent and child. And so the most conscientious Catholic parents may rationalize, and unconscious of a submerged selfishness, place obstacles in the way of entrance into training for the religious life and delay such entrance. Sometimes, of course, the delay continues so long that the child never enters the novitiate or seminary. This is a risk of delay."[42]

The admission that entering a convent meant their child would be severed from them can hardly have been encouraging to parents. The recruitment literature, however, provided a reassurance that the love between them would not suffer because of early separation. In fact, Father Senieur confidently asserted that novices delighted in their families "more than ever before." "True love for others," he claimed, "has a strange and marvelous way of increasing in quality and intensity, the closer you get to Christ."[43]

Let the child see something of the world first. This was a further extension of the "too young" and "wait a while" arguments, and the recruiters were quick to dismiss it. Sister Reilly advised her young readers that it was not really necessary to see the world before "you wall yourself up." Her reasoning was: "You don't have to have an experience to reject it for a higher good."[44] Father Senieur wondered what part of the world parents wanted their children to see. Surely it was not the "evil" and "filthy" side of life on display in bars and clubs, he said. If parents meant the "innocent pleasures of the world," they had nothing to worry about, since such pleasures were readily available in preparatory schools and novitiates in abundance.[45]

Palmer, paraphrasing the passage in Matthew 4:8–11 in which Jesus was tempted by Satan, asked rhetorically if parents wanted to take their child to a mountaintop to see all the kingdoms of the world and be tempted by "the prospect of a life's banquet of all the world's delicacies, the allurement of all the senses, the concupiscences of mind and body ... all the treasures of books and music and art and travel and the companionship of secular associations, sports, the prospects of power, and the gratifications of ambition and pride." He asked parents why they would give preference to the world. Since children already knew something about secular life, but little about religious life, it was only fair to give the latter a chance by a spell in a preparatory school or novitiate. He warned that by exposing the child "to the attractions and allurements of the secular world you may be loading the dice against the religious life and not holding the scales even."[46]

The child should know the facts of life before deciding. The concern of parents who expressed this objection can be readily understood, since a young woman taking a vow of chastity should presumably have some understanding of what she was renouncing. The objection was a difficult one for the recruiters, since the Church was adamant in its opposition to sex education. In *Divini Illius Magistri* (1929), Pope Pius XI had denounced sex education as a foolhardy premise advanced by those who refused "to recognize the innate weakness of humanity."[47] His successor, Pius XII, was equally opposed to instruction on reproduction in schools, but urged Christian parents "carefully and tactfully to lift the veil of the truth, to the degree that appears necessary," while preserving in their children "their natural and particular instinct of shame whereby Providence wills to restrain them from being too easily misled by their passions."[48] The "Pope of Purity," as some of his admirers called him, also objected to instructional manuals on sexuality, even if they were intended for couples about to be married, on the grounds that such literature "greatly exaggerate[d] the importance and scope of the sexual element in life."[49]

The recruiters were well aware that the vast majority of parents were uncomfortable in lifting "the veil of the truth" themselves, but somehow wanted their daughters to be fully aware of the implications of chastity before embracing it for life. Fathers Senieur and Poage were quick to assure such parents that their children would not enter religion in ignorance, but would become "acquainted with the facts of life and the true meaning of sex-life" during their novitiate. Their children would be innocent, said Senieur, but it would be "an informed innocence that makes their decision not only an intelligent one, but a very meritorious choice."[50] Poage, in addressing his fellow recruiters, had this advice: "All you need to do is point out how in the seminary or convent their youngsters will get the whole truth about human love and sex – but from God's viewpoint. The only thing they don't get is a sordid or prejudiced approach. All seminarians or novices are better informed before their vows than most couples on the verge of matrimony."[51]

It is difficult to fathom exactly what was meant by "the true meaning of sex-life" or "God's viewpoint" on it. It is not unreasonable to assume, however, that these assertions were at the very least misleading. There is little evidence that either novices or nuns were well informed about sexuality, and considerable evidence to the contrary. This will be examined in some detail in Chapter 7.

The religious life is too hard and would not make my child happy. The recruiters attributed this objection to popular myths and misconceptions about convents. Parents who felt this way, according to Senieur, believed that convent life was a "living death" filled with "peculiar penances and morbid mortifications," and that nuns were "queer individuals with sanctimonious natures who wanted to get away from the world." A major challenge for recruiters, he said, was to combat the bleak image. "Once parents realize that the austere walls of the convent are used to contain happiness and not keep it out, they will begin to soften their objections," he predicted. One of his suggestions to this end was to encourage parents to visit convents where young nuns were in training and where they would see "wholesome, normal American youth, full of the joy and fun typical of Americans." Moreover, since such youngsters had "caught the secret of real happiness," they would be "bubbling over with a peace and joy that the world was still looking for."[52]

Stevens used similar language when describing postulants and novices and urged parents to visit convents to "investigate and see for themselves the happiness that radiates from every face."[53] The recruiters were at pains to point out that many parents mistakenly believed that material and worldly achievements were the keys to a fulfilled life for their children. Not so, said Palmer, and buttressed his claim by citing Church fathers and medieval saints who had written of the joys of religious life. This quotation from St Augustine is representative: "Happy is he who knowest thee; and the happy life is this – to rejoice unto thee, in thee, and for thee; this is it; there is no other."[54]

Some of the recruitment literature played down the "bubbling with joy" image of religious life and acknowledged that nuns worked hard and had few luxuries. Poage advised recruiters to explain to parents that, while religious might live in plain quarters, they had every necessity of life and more than the average lay person. The argument could be turned against them if necessary, he said, by asking if marriage was devoid of unhappiness and disappointment. And while it could be admitted that religious worked long hours, "what mother can say she has time on her hands?"[55]

Poage was not alone in casting doubts on the presumed advantages of married life in order to combat the unhappiness objection. Palmer warned parents that they might be mistaken in judging the character of the man their daughter was marrying. And since marriage was irrevocable, the wrong choice could ruin a child's happiness. But in selecting a life with God, there could be no such mistake, he said, since God would never change or disappoint.[56] Popular Catholic magazines such as the *Messenger of the Sacred Heart* occasionally featured stories of women who had married under parental pressure rather than follow their vocations, only to find themselves in unhappy relationships with worthless, abusive husbands.[57] Bishop Joseph Schrembs of Cleveland[58] was sometimes quoted in order to contrast the relative probability of happiness in marriage and religion: "How often are the lives of parents blighted and their hearts broken by the unhappy state of their married children in the world? But those who have consecrated themselves to God will never cause them to worry nor grieve them in any way. They are happy and contented, and will pray for them during life and after death."[59]

The child's talents will be wasted in the convent. In responding to this objection, the recruiters were able to claim with some justification that the Church needed people in many demanding professions, especially in the fields of education and nursing. Moreover, nuns had access to advanced studies and career-development possibilities that were less readily available to laywomen.[60] In fact, Palmer suggested that recruiters imitate the enlistment campaigns of the armed forces by stressing the occupational and travel opportunities open to religious. And he added that the Church had an advantage over the military in its "supernatural appeal."[61] He failed to point out, however, and it was not indicated anywhere in the recruitment literature, that while nuns had careers open to them, the work was for little or no remuneration.

INTIMIDATION

If parents were not swayed by persuasion, recruiters were encouraged to resort to threats and intimidation. A favourite quotation to this end that was used widely in the literature came from the pen of Saint Alfonso di Ligouri, founder of the Redemptorist Fathers: "Parents who, without a just and certain cause, prevent their children from entering the Religious state, cannot be excused from mortal sin; and not only parents, but also anyone else who unlawfully prevents another from following a religious vocation sins mortally."[62]

Poage urged his readers to remind recalcitrant parents that, at its twenty-fifth session, the Council of Trent had anathemized "those who shall in any way and without just cause impede the holy wish of virgins or other women to take the veil or pronounce vows." He confidently asserted that most parents would acquiesce when informed that they were "theologically in error" and in "danger of sin" in opposing their children's vocations.[63]

Stevens took the argument further by asserting that recalcitrant parents were infringing on God's rightful prerogatives: "Do they [parents] understand that their children are merely entrusted to their care by God, and that they violate this trust when they refuse to give to God what was His from the beginning?" And he added for good measure that their actions might "indict them on the Day of Judgment."[64]

In his booklet *Shall My Daughter Be a Nun?* prolific Jesuit author Daniel A. Lord put similar arguments in the mouth of a fictional "Father Brooks" as he tried to dissuade a "Mrs Hutton" from obstructing her daughter Jane's entry to a convent: "If Christ were sitting here where I sit and asking for your daughter, what would you say? After all, it is considerate of Him to ask you. He is God. He gave her to you in the first place. He might have refused to allow you a child. He might have left you a childless wife." He then reiterated the same threat as Stevens: "And the mothers who have thwarted their daughters' vocations – I pity them when Christ questions them on judgment day."[65]

Some of the literature implied that divine retribution might not be that far off. A booklet on vocations produced by the Brothers of the Christian Schools had this to say: "Even in this life, parents may be punished for having hindered or prevented the higher vocation of their children. It often happens that after having thus thwarted God's design, these parents may be punished for their unjust opposition by some unexpected misfortune such as: the early death, the reckless life, or the unworthy conduct of their unhappy children."[66]

Lest this be dismissed as an extreme and unrepresentative example, consider the following from the novice diary of Sister Catherine Frederic, in which she addressed Jesus: "If the parents refuse to part with their child for a life devoted to Your service, You sometimes take that loved one in death."[67] Father Lord's "Father Brooks" used the same line in his interview with "Mrs Hutton": "He (Jesus) could, you know, so easily stoop down and pluck for the gardens of heaven the lovely flower He has lent you ... He has taken pure souls like Jane's just to keep them from being sullied with the stains of earth."[68]

When Joyce Zemba was a Grade 8 student with the School Sisters of St Francis in 1950s Milwaukee, the nuns tried to pressure her to continue her education in the congregation's aspirancy, with a view to recruiting her to their ranks. Her mother wouldn't hear of it and was told by one of the nuns that God would take Joyce with an illness if she wouldn't let her go. The mother capitulated.[69] Threats of this kind had the potential to be seriously disturbing to Catholic parents.

In some cases, the intimidation could take the form of humiliating harangues. Jann, one of the ex-nuns interviewed by Gass, recalled that she had been persuaded to enter the convent by a nun who had lavished special attention on her – a common enough occurrence. Then came the parental opposition: "My mother wanted me to wait a year, then the priest delivered a sermon against her. She was furious and humiliated."[70]

DEFIANCE

When prayers, persuasion, and threats did not produce consent, the Church had one more card to play: encourage defiance of parents. In justifying this policy, St Jerome was sometimes quoted. The Church father had advised Heliodorus to push aside family and friends who might impede his entrance into the religious life:

> Effeminate soldier! What are you doing under the paternal roof? Even though your nephew entwine his arms around your neck; even were your mother, with streaming hair, to show you, through her rent garments, the breast that nurtured you; even though your father were to throw himself across the threshold of your house, step over the obstacle and, with unquivering eye, rush to take your place beneath the standard of the cross. Lo, your sister presses you in her arms; your attendants, your grandmother, your tutor exclaim: "Wait a while until we are dead, bury us before you go"; love of God and fear of hell easily break all chains.[71]

A more contemporary version of this doctrine was provided by Father Winfrid Herbst, SDS, in the *Ecclesiastical Review*: "In this matter [vocations] the parental will is not a manifestation of the will of God, so permission of the parents is not strictly necessary. If the son or daughter is of the required age, say at least fourteen or fifteen years old, he or she is quite justified, after consultation with others who are able prudently to advise, in disregarding the parental wishes when they are opposed to the manifest call of God."[72] Although fourteen- and fifteen-year-olds were minors and under the legal guardianship of their parents, the recruiters were prepared to undermine that authority in the matter of religious vocations.

In a booklet on vocations, "A Redemptorist Father" argued that the problem of parental objections was so commonplace and difficult that it was best to enter religion without telling anyone – a slightly different angle on defiance. He cited the examples of Saints Thomas Aquinas, Francis Xavier, Philip Neri, and Louis Bertrand, who, as soon as they felt the divine call, "set off quite unknown to their families." And St Alphonso di Ligouri's endorsement of such action was quoted:

> if the Lord sends you an inspiration to quit the world, be careful not to manifest it to your parents; be satisfied that God alone blesses you, and manage to follow your vocation as soon as possible, and without their knowledge, if you do not wish to run great risk of losing it. For the same reason, be on your guard against revealing your vocation to your friends, for they would make no scruple of turning you aside from it, or at least would disclose your secret, which might thus come to the ears of your parents.[73]

CONCLUSION

Promotional literature is problematic as a historical source, since it is difficult to assess its impact with much confidence. Nonetheless, it can provide insight into the nature of a problem or of a perceived problem and can reveal the thinking of those who sought to solve it. The problem in this instance was the obstructionist attitude of many American Catholic parents upon learning of a daughter's religious vocation. In fact, the recruitment professionals identified family pressure as their most persistent obstacle in replenishing and expanding the ranks of religious sisterhoods. Moreover, and in keeping with the increasingly sophisticated nature of recruitment, they developed a strategic plan to combat the problem. Their strategies represented much more than a list of suggestions; they were rooted in an understanding of psychology, sociology, and marketing, and appeared in the literature as a progressive continuum – if prayer did not work, then try persuasion, and so forth. Father Poage was probably right in advising that it was best to get parents on side "without a fight." But the recruiters were quite prepared to invoke more aggressive measures if necessary – and did so when the circumstances warranted.

In some cases, as we have seen, parents were not so much objecting to their daughters entering convents upon high-school graduation, but rather to completing their secondary studies in aspirancies or preparatory schools that would steer them towards lives in religion. Aspirancies were unique institutions in that they served both as instruments of recruitment and as an initial formation stage. They deserve our attention.

CHAPTER 5

. . . .

Aspirants:

Secluded from

the World

In the early years of grade school children
are very impressionable, and their young
hearts are quite innocent and generous. It is
then easy for a recruiter to implant in them
the idea of becoming a priest or religious
... and God, according to the needs of
His Church, will bring these seeds of a
vocation to fruition.[1]
Godfrey Poage (1950)

Why doesn't it seem propitious for a girl
who wants to go running off with God to
learn at an early age the secrets of leaning
on His Heart? ... Most firmly do I believe
that God supplies for all deficiencies in
those who go unto His Altar in their youth –
economic immaturity, sex immaturity, and
social immaturity. These children He
touches; to them He puts forth His Hand.[2]
Sister Mary Alene, SSND (1957)

ST BRIGID'S MISSIONARY SCHOOL in Callan, County Kilkenny, Ireland, was a unique institution. Founded by the Sisters of Mercy in 1884, it provided a few years of secondary schooling to girls who showed an interest in becoming nuns and serving as teachers in Catholic schools in foreign parts. Since the students were too young to enter religion, they were known as aspirants – those aspiring to the religious life, but their socialization in St Brigid's prepared them well for the routines of the convent. Once they were old enough, they were sent abroad to become postulants and novices in places of Irish settlement or missionary activity. Australia and New Zealand were the most popular destinations for these young recruits, but at least 256 of them went to the United States before the school closed its doors in 1958.[3]

Could an institution such as St Brigid's thrive on American soil? The Church was well aware that much could go wrong in the world of an adolescent before she was old enough to enter the religious life. With this understanding, and perhaps with the example of St Brigid's before them, a number of congregations established specialized boarding institutions to provide secondary schooling for those who, at the age of thirteen to fourteen, showed the right inclinations and dispositions. The institutions were known variously as apostolic schools, juniorates, juvénats, scholasticates, preparatory schools, religious guidance schools, or aspirancies, and since the last of these terms was the one most commonly used, it will be employed here for the sake of clarity and consistency. The schools were the female equivalent of the minor seminaries in which boys destined for the priesthood often received their second-level education.

This educational experiment began as early as the 1920s, and some of the more enduring institutions in the genre trace their origins to that decade. For example, Ancilla Domini High School was established in 1921 by the Poor Handmaids of Jesus Christ as part of their convent complex near Donaldson, Indiana, and it continued to operate as an aspirancy until the mid-1970s.[4] And when the Franciscan Sisters of St Joseph[5] established their mother house in Hamburg, New York, in 1928, part of the building was designated Immaculata Academy, which eventually evolved beyond its aspirancy role to become an exclusive private school for girls.[6]

While it is difficult to establish the exact number of aspirancies operating during our period of inquiry, we can be certain that it was not significant as a proportion of the total number of Catholic secondary schools. A survey conducted by the Sisters of St Joseph of Concordia, Kansas, in 1953–54 found that there were at least fifty in existence at the time, but their size and effectiveness varied enormously.[7] Another survey of 1958 found seventy-nine of them operating. According to Father Joseph Fichter, the rise in the number of apirancies in the postwar period was attributable to the general expansion of the Catholic adolescent population, but also to "increased activity of vocational promotion."[8]

Most congregations, however, did not take this route in cultivating vocations, and even the congregations that did so found many of their postulants coming to them via "ordinary" Catholic day and boarding schools. Aspirancies, nonetheless, deserve our attention, since their advocates and sponsors remained firm in their conviction that the vocations of girls thus educated were proportionately greater in number and less likely to be later abandoned for what the world had to offer.[9]

As a form of schooling, it was not for everyone; in fact, there were strict requirements for admission. Aspirancy directors sought to attract girls of "a docile and amiable disposition," and who demonstrated "a desire and aptitude for the religious life." The girls were also required to be healthy, free of hereditary diseases, of irreproachable character, of legitimate birth, and from respectable Catholic families.[10] Where were such girls to be found? Since the program of studies typically began with Grade 9, girls in Grade 8 in parochial schools were targeted for recruitment. If the parochial school were conducted by the same congregation as the aspirancy, active cooperation in identifying and signing up suitable candidates could be expected. But it was not always easy going, especially in the early years before aspirancies established their reputations for academic excellence.

In 1930, when the Sisters of Providence (St Mary-of-the-Woods) opened Providence Juniorate, the superior, Mother Mary Raphael, wrote to the sister principals of the congregation's parochial schools seeking cooperation in finding the first students. The principals responded enthusiastically to the idea, because, as Sister Emmanuel of St Patrick's Convent, Stoneham, Massachusetts, observed, once girls left school, started making money, and discovered worldly pleasures, the religious life lost its appeal for them. None of the respondents, however, could promise to send students that year. Sister Francis Lucille, of St Anselm's Convent, Chicago, was able to identify a number of suitable eighth graders, but noted that their parents considered them "too young to go away from home."[11]

The aspirancies, then, had growing pains, and more systematic recruitment campaigns were required before they could attract strong cohorts of "freshmen," as Grade 9 students were called. It meant dispatching recruitment professionals to parochial schools armed with enticing brochures and prepared to negotiate with dubious parents.[12] An early brochure promoting the Providence Juniorate boasted of small class sizes, an excellent library, cultural experiences, and beautiful surroundings that were "conducive to mental and bodily fitness." Moreover, there was access to daily Mass, Communion, and Benediction. "Nowhere," it was claimed, "can you find a happier, more contented group of young girls than the Candidates of Providence Juniorate." There was no attempt to disguise the fact that the school was directing its students towards the convent novitiate. Another Providence brochure, with the title "Our Lady's Cadets," made its pitch for the religious life unequivocally to its young readers: "What cause more worthy than the cause of Christ? To labor for Him, thousands of young girls have given up worldly ideas, plans, and pleasures. They have offered themselves gladly, and have never regretted it ... Why? BECAUSE THEY LOVE CHRIST AND THEY LOVE SOULS." And the reward for a life in religion was spelled out clearly in a brochure called "My child, give Me thy heart." Such a life, it was said, was the "simplest, surest, shortest way to heaven."[13]

Aspirancies were boarding schools, and this fact alone meant that they were expensive to operate. Fees were charged to defray the costs, and this presented a further recruitment dilemma. Parents were not only being asked to send away their thirteen- to fourteen-year-olds to an educational experience designed to steer them towards the convent door, but also to pay for it. It put parents in a strong bargaining position. For example, in September 1945 Mrs

Glenn Whitten agreed to enrol two of her daughters in Ancilla Domini for a monthly fee of $10 for one and $25 for the other.[14] The fee of $25, or $225 for the nine-month school year, was considered the full payment, but few parents actually paid it. There were forty-three students enrolled in Ancilla Domini that year, nine of whom paid the full fee. Most parents paid only $45 in total – one fifth of the actual cost.[15] In other words, the congregation was heavily subsidizing the aspirancy in the belief that its novitiate would thereby be filled. Fee negotiations revolved around two considerations: the ability of the parents to pay and the desirability of the student as "convent material."

The congregations were able to reduce costs by requiring students to do much of the domestic work around the institutions, regardless of what their parents had paid. At Providence Juniorate, seniors directed groups of younger students in what were called "employments," the most disliked of which was cleaning up in the kitchen.[16]

The students were called aspirants, since they aspired to the religious life but were as yet too young to be part of it. They were also known as candidates or by the more colloquial term, prepsters. Their clothes – long dark-blue or black dress of poplin or serge, with starched white Peter Pan collar and cuffs, long stockings, and sensible shoes – gave them a distinctive appearance. Joanne Howe, who entered the aspirancy conducted by the Sisters of St Francis[17] at Mt Alvernia, Millvale, Pennsylvania, in September 1949, recalled grimacing when first presented with the clothing requirements and found the uniform cumbersome to wear.[18] Joyce Zemba was seventeen in 1958 when she decided to complete her high school as an aspirant at St Joseph's Convent, Milwaukee, an establishment of the School Sisters of St Francis.[19] She strongly disliked the heavy black uniform, which she found unbearably hot.[20] The dark colours and simple styles of the uniforms – which were increasingly common in Catholic schools from the 1920s onwards – projected modesty above all else, and even bore a resemblance to religious habits. The required attire cultivated a collective identity and restrained impulses towards self-display and flamboyance.[21] By the 1950s the uniforms had modernized and were less religious in appearance. Dark pinafores over white, long-sleeved blouses were now the norm.[22] The modification signalled a concession to contemporary practice, rather than an indicator of any change in institutional purpose.

In vocations talks with Grade 7 and 8 parochial school girls, recruiting agents from congregations with established aspirancies invariably encouraged their listeners to try that route if they thought they might have a vocation. It was in response to such a talk that Mary Gilligan entered the Providence Juniorate on 15 September 1957.[23] Aspirants with the Sisters of Divine Providence (San Antonio, Texas)[24] sometimes accompanied nuns from the order when they went on recruitment drives to the congregation's schools in order to answer any questions students might have. They also assisted with the week-long "vocation camp" held in the summer for students in Grades 8 and higher.[25]

Shortly after entering Mt Alvernia, Joanne Howe and the thirty other "freshie" aspirants were lectured on the advantages of their institution. The director advised them that the religious atmosphere of the school, combined with careful supervision, would "preserve, protect, and foster" the vocation they had been privileged to receive. Removed from the world's distractions, they would be better placed to "listen to the voice of God."[26]

One of the main purposes of the aspirancy, then, was to create an environment that shielded the religiously-inclined but impressionable teenager from the "detrimental influences of newspapers, magazines, movies, radio, and bad companions."[27] While bad companions could be either male or female, the recruitment professionals were convinced that all young men, no matter how moral or well-disposed, fell into the category. The reasoning was that young men were a powerful temptation whose very presence could derail an incipient vocation, and they were best kept out of sight if aspirants were ever to become postulants and novices, and ultimately nuns. Father Jude Senieur explained the Church's position with the following analogy: "When a teenage girl decides to give up ice cream and cake for the sake of her physical figure, she doesn't spend her evenings sitting in ice cream stores or bakery shops gazing at the objects of her self-imposed restraint. When a girl gives up certain legitimate pleasures for the sake of her spiritual figure, there is no reason why such pleasures should be continually paraded before her eyes."[28]

Sister Mary Alene, who directed the Notre Dame Aspirature in St Louis, Missouri, in the mid-1950s, made a similar argument in response to critics who alleged that the schools limited students' choices in life: "Isn't it equally absurd for a girl who envisions the life of a sister to engage in all the parties and practices which lead girls her own age into the much different joys of wedded life?"[29]

Families, too, were viewed with an element of disapproval, since they were of "the world" and a reminder of its preoccupations. Once a young woman became a nun, in any case, contact with her family was almost completely severed. Aspirants were expected to grow accustomed to separation, and rules were devised accordingly. It was normal practice to allow family visits to the school on the first Sunday of the month.[30] On these occasions the students sometimes provided entertainment for their parents, perhaps to show off their developing talents. When parents turned up at Ancilla Domini on 16 February 1964, they were treated to a "hootenanny," in which the aspirants sang songs by Peter, Paul, and Mary.[31] There were no visits, however, during Lent and Advent, and there was no question of family members dropping by spontaneously. Joyce Zemba recalled that her father knew she would be playing volleyball outdoors in the evenings at St Joseph's, Milwaukee, and he and her sister would sometimes drive up and try to converse with her. If the nuns noticed this contact, they would hustle her indoors with the reminder that she could see her family only once a month.[32]

In all aspirancies, incoming and outgoing mail was strictly censored in order to discourage family closeness and the influence of worldly friends. While the rules varied respecting the quantity of letters, they were generally restricted to between two and four weekly.[33] If letters arrived at St Joseph's from the outside discussing dates and boyfriend issues, they were suppressed, and the director informed the aspirants that they had been in receipt of mail that they could not read.[34] And telephone calls home or to friends were out of the question except in emergencies. Joanne Howe recalled longing for the company of her siblings and for the advice of her mother when she needed it while at Mt Alvernia, but to no avail.[35]

The outside world could pierce the convent walls via radio and television, but only if the content met with the sisters' approval. At Ancilla Domini, students could listen to *The Catholic Hour* – a Sunday radio broadcast conducted by Father Fulton Sheen between

1930 and 1950.[36] By the early 1960s the rules were less restrictive and television viewing became more common, although religious themes continued to dominate. On 5 January 1964, for example, the *Ed Sullivan Show* was watched by all, but mainly because it featured Soeur Sourire, Belgium's singing nun, and her hit, "Dominique," a song about St Dominic. Around the same time, the aspirants watched the 1955 historical drama *Seven Cities of Gold*, a movie that told the parallel stories of Gaspar de Portola's search for fabled wealth in California and Father Junipero Serra's missions to the native peoples of the area.[37] A similar relaxation of the rules respecting television was discernible at Providence Juniorate, especially in the case of events that had significance for Catholics, such as the election of John F. Kennedy to the presidency.[38]

There were, of course, Christmas and summer vacations, during which family life could resume. A number of aspirancies allowed their students home for Easter and Thanksgiving, but many did not.[39] Easter vacations were discontinued in Ancilla Domini when reports of "unbecoming behaviour" at home reached the school.[40] But holiday time for aspirants was not as it was for others. Attendance at daily Mass and Communion remained an expectation, especially if a church were nearby.[41] Before leaving for the summer of 1946, students at Providence Juniorate resolved to add the following prayer to their daily Rosary:

> O my Jesus, forgive us our sins.
> Save us from the fires of Hell.
> Release the souls from Purgatory, especially those whom
>   everyone has forgotten.

This was the prayer of the children of Fatima, which, if recited regularly, would cause Russia to be converted, or so the Virgin Mary had promised.[42]

Dating and wearing makeup were discouraged during vacations and were expressly forbidden for Mt Alvernia students.[43] Those attending Notre Dame Aspirature were "cautioned concerning recreations in mixed company" while at home.[44] When she worked as a lifeguard in the summer of 1960, Mary Gilligan refused a date for fear of losing her vocation. She was aware that several of her companions had quit the aspirancy after summer romances.[45] The idea that an aspirant should test her vocation in mixed social gatherings was anathema to the recruitment professionals. Here is Senieur: "Reasonable social recreation is certainly in place. But dates and dances will do the candidate no good. And, please, they will not 'broaden' her mind; they will merely confuse her judgment. Worldly pleasures as such have never contributed to an intelligent vocational decision."[46]

Aspirancies provided an academically rigorous curriculum of the college-preparatory type. Initially, the full program of studies was not necessarily available, especially in the 1920s and 1930s when girls often entered the postulancy at the ages of fourteen or fifteen. In 1935, Ancilla Domini extended its offerings to four years of study when high-school graduation became a requirement for those wishing to become Poor Handmaids of Jesus Christ.[47] Graduation soon became an aspirancy norm, and especially for congregations whose members were destined for teaching. The curriculum reflected the heavy bias towards the humanities characteristic of traditional female education – English, math, history, Latin, French, and religion. As might be expected, the study of religion was not taken lightly. At the Holy Ghost Academy, the aspirancy of the Missionary Sister Servants of the Holy Ghost[48] at Techny, Illinois, the program had four distinct components: Christian doctrine, Bible study, liturgy, and church history.[49] Science did gain acceptance in time, but in an uneven manner. It was not until the early 1960s, for example, that physics and chemistry were taught at Ancilla Domini.[50]

Mary Gilligan noted the competitive nature of the academic program at Providence Juniorate, with the aspirants striving to outdo one another for high grades. Being a "brain" was not a problem, she recalled.[51] It was also competitive at Mt Alvernia, but due in large measure to a regime of strict surveillance, incentives, and penalties. In her memoir, *A Change of Habit*, Joanne Howe wrote of the three hours of study every day, supervised by older students who were known as "snitches" from their habit of tattling to the director. Grades were carefully monitored, she remembered, with sanctions, such as exclusion from recreation, for those receiving anything less than a "C." The nuns devised an additional form of reward and punishment leveraging the students' love of candy, one of the few pleasures in which they could indulge. Aspirants were given individual candy boxes at entry day, and the boxes were refilled at the end of each month, the refill being proportionate to the grades they had received. Poor grades could mean an empty candy box and no sweet treats until things improved.[52]

Inculcation of discipline and the fostering of character development were the anticipated results of a demanding curriculum. Father Godfrey Poage explained it in these words: "Regularity in study and class helps their intellectual growth, and the practice of obedience strengthens their will. The silence of the study halls, dormitories, and corridors, the restraint at meals, and supervision of recreation – all bring out the best in the candidates and give them self-control and the ability to cope with real problems later on."[53] The "real problems" Poage was referring to was the difficult adjustment to convent life experienced by many postulants and novices, especially those who had not graduated from an aspirancy.

The arts were an important part of aspirant education. Both at Ancilla Domini and Providence Juniorate the students learned musical instruments and formed themselves into orchestras, although the results in the former institution were evidently less pleasing to the ear.[54] Mother Théodore Guérin, who had led the Sisters of Providence to Indiana in the 1840s, was a highly educated Frenchwoman, and insisted on the central role of the arts in her congregation's schools.[55] At Providence Juniorate there were occasional lectures and performances by prominent artists, although the arts often took on a peculiarly Catholic flavour.[56]

With only restricted access to the products of Hollywood and Tin Pan Alley, aspirants looked to their own talents and resources for entertainment. Much effort went into writing songs, poems, and skits, and into the staging of plays.[57] The preponderance of religious themes in these works brings out clearly the ethos of the aspirancy and its distinct purpose. For example, in 1944, those at Providence Juniorate compiled a booklet of their favourite songs – compositions with "local words" sung to well-known tunes. One of them reads:

Dear Woodland Home, where reigns our Spouse supreme,
Were we not here, how dark the world would seem,

Soon by His grace, Novitiate joys we'll share,
Soon the veil and chaplet, long-desired, we'll wear.[58]

There were aspirant poems as well, many of which found their way into student newspapers and magazines. Joan O'B. composed this one in 1946:

We start each day with Holy Mass,
To ask God's blessing on every class,
On every hour of every day,
Whether we're at work or play

We've seen the weeks pass day by day,
The first of September 'till last of May,
And in our minds the one thought runs,
That we're among His chosen ones.[59]

Student newspapers and magazines are tainted prisms through which to view school life, and must be approached with caution. The publications were carefully monitored and controlled by the nuns, and only items that reflected the purpose of the institution appeared in print. What we can take from this nonetheless is that some aspirants embraced the destiny set out for them with enthusiasm. As we shall see later, others had serious doubts about their vocations, but student newspapers provided no outlet for such doubts.

Ample provision for sports and physical activity also characterized aspirancies, since candidates for religion were to be in good health and able to work hard. At the Holy Ghost Academy, for example, aspirants were kept "on the go" with tennis, baseball, skating, and bowling.[60] A variety of sports was also available at Providence Juniorate, as well as a daily walk around campus supervised by a sister to ensure that order always prevailed.[61] At Ancilla Domini, volleyball was the game of choice, and the school was divided into intramural teams – the Birds, the Dynamics, the Jolly Green Giants, and so forth.[62]

Much of what has been described so far would not have been out of place in a typical Catholic boarding school, but the aspirancy was different in fundamental ways. Aspirants, after all, had a particular destiny chosen for them, and so the school aimed "to develop the character and personality suitable for life in a religious community," which required "the virtue of obedience and respect for religious authority."[63] Sister Rose Thering summarized what was unique about the experience:

> In their companionship with girls of the same ideals, the aspirants not only are sources of encouragement to each other but they develop the virtue of community spirit which is so necessary in convent life. In an Aspirancy the girl may not have an opportunity to meet many people, but she has the greater opportunity of knowing herself, which is a very fundamental step in the development of personality.[64]

Chastity was one of the religious vows, or evangelical counsels, to which aspirants were introduced. Severing contact with young men or attempting to do so, as alluded to, was part of this learning. Senieur argued that, while placing a barrier between the sexes was a laudable strategy, something more systematic in terms of instruction was required: "They [aspirants] should be made to understand the nature of the human conflict; the conflict between the lower and the higher self; between the passions and the will; and what to do about it and how to go about doing it."[65]

Keeping males at a distance did not completely remove threats to chastity, since there was always the possibility of a same-sex relationship. Mary Gilligan recalled lectures about the dangers of "particular friendships" while at Providence Juniorate, but the nature of these dangers was never actually spelled out. There were rules, nonetheless, to keep matters in check. It was forbidden, for example, to spend too much time with one person, to keep one's bedroom door closed, or, strangely enough, to sit on the edge of a bed.[66]

While relationships with others were off-limits, there was one exception: Jesus. In fact, one of the roles of the directors of aspirants was to introduce their charges "to the Person of Jesus and through a personal acquaintance with Him learn to fall deeply in love with their Divine Bridegroom."[67] The manner in which this was accomplished could sometimes take a surprising form. On St Valentine's

Day in 1958, the aspirants at Providence Juniorate selected a representative of their cohort who was then attired in a long white bridal gown and led in procession to the refectory, where she sat next to a statue of Jesus. At that moment, the director addressed the aspirants as follows: "Just as in the world a boy asks a girl for a date, in the same way Jesus, the Divine Lover, beckons you from his lonely tabernacle to come be his date. How he longs for you to come visit him there, to whisper little words of love and offer little caresses of mortification."[68]

To further cement the relationship with Jesus, the aspirants were obliged to keep a crucifix on their pillows during the day and to kiss it before going to sleep.[69] A crucifix was much more than a cross; it was a cross with a figure of Jesus attached to it, complete with nails, a crown of thorns, and bloody wounds. The habits of most congregations featured silver crucifixes suspended around the neck, and the presence of this most Catholic of symbols reminded the aspirants that they too would likely wear it one day.

The strict daily routine of the school was modelled on that of the convent, and it socialized aspirants for what they might expect as postulants, novices, and ultimately, professed nuns. The day began early: the awakening bell at Providence Juniorate sounded at 5:45 a.m. There were thirty minutes to dress, make beds, and visit the bathroom before Mass began.[70] Taking Communion daily was expected; it was believed to be beneficial in encouraging piety, but it also signalled that one was free from sin or in a "state of grace." Breakfast, domestic chores, classes, and recreation followed, all according to a rigid schedule. And there were very specific rules governing such apparently mundane matters as bed making, table setting, cleaning, and hair grooming.[71] At St Joseph's, Milwaukee, if a bed were not made according to the exacting standards in place, the director would tear it apart and require that it be redone properly.[72] Following dinner there might be a study period or recreation, depending on the institution. It was common practice, however, to impose "profound silence" from the end of recreation until breakfast was finished the following day. Silence was part of convent culture, and the director of aspirants at Providence Juniorate explained it this way: "You should use the time to reflect on your sins and shortcomings of the day and to formulate resolutions for the next day so as to not repeat those faults. Most important, you should spend time preparing a place inside for the Divine Guest who will come to you in Holy Communion tomorrow morning."[73]

Subduing the boisterous exuberance of teenagers was no easy task and yet it was essential to the behavioural agenda of aspirancies. At Ancilla Domini a persistent problem was noted with the younger aspirants, who were inclined to run through the hallways when going from one part of their daily routine to the next. The seniors, who had been well socialized into acceptable nun-like behaviour, took turns in patrolling the spaces where this was likely to happen, with a view to imposing appropriate conformity.[74] A well-trained aspirant was expected to be self-controlled at all times, and even to adopt nun-like modes of expression. She was encouraged to address her companions and teachers with "Praised be Jesus and Mary" rather than the customary greetings of the secular world.[75]

The socialization into the rhythms and behaviour of convent life tested the suitability and sincerity of aspirants, while preparing them for what to expect were they to enter. One noteworthy element in the socialization was the prevalence of what are known as popular devotions. Unlike the sacraments, which constitute the official liturgy of the Church and are conducted by the priesthood, devotions are informal pious practices involving prayer that can secure divine favour. In convents, they were very much part of the events that filled the day.

The Rosary is one of the best-known examples of a popular devotion. It originated, according to tradition, when the Virgin Mary suggested it to St Dominic as a weapon in his fight against the Albigensian heresy.[76] It consists of a sequence of Hail Marys organized into groups of ten, interspersed with Our Fathers (Lord's Prayers) and Glory Be to the Fathers that are recited while counting them out on a set of chained beads. Aspirants quickly became accustomed to the Rosary, saying it as part of morning or evening prayers, or both. The Feast of the Holy Rosary, fixed for 7 October by Pope Pius X, became a special day at Providence Juniorate. To honour the feast, the aspirants presented a "living Rosary." Gathering round a shrine erected for the occasion, they arranged themselves in the form of Rosary beads, with the Hail Marys wearing white veils while the Our Fathers/Glorias wore black. They then recited the prayers in proper sequence, according to the colour of their veils.[77]

The Forty Hours, or Quarant' Ore (Quarantore), was another devotion to which aspirants were introduced. Like many of these practices, its origins are obscure, but it is often attributed to St Charles Borromeo in sixteenth-century Milano. The devotion involved exposing the Eucharist in a monstrance on the altar for forty hours – the length of time between Christ's death on the cross and his resurrection. But the Blessed Sacrament could not be left alone during this time; a certain number of people always had to be present in the church adoring it. The Jesuits became great champions of this devotion, and promoted it as an antidote to the sins of the world.[78] It was for this purpose that it became popular at Providence Juniorate. One of the aspirants explained its importance during Mardi Gras: "We all know what injuries are done to God at these carnivals, and we try to make up for these injuries by adoring and loving Him in the Blessed Sacrament."[79] This idea was known as the "Carnival Sanctified," and was enshrined in the constitutions of some congregations as an annual ritual "to make an honourable reparation for all the sins caused by the profane pleasures to which worldlings abandon themselves at the approach of Lent."[80]

On 27 May 1947, the Providence aspirants were presented with the Brown Scapular of Our Lady of Mount Carmel – two small squares of cloth attached by strings to be worn around the neck. Those who wore the scapular, said certain prayers, and remained free from mortal sin were assured that, on the Saturday following their death, the Virgin Mary would descend personally into Purgatory and lead them straight to Heaven. Pope John XXII claimed that the "Sabbatine Privilege" associated with this devotion was revealed to him by the Virgin Mary in 1322.[81]

Every day on the calendar is assigned to one or more saints as their special feast. Throughout the school year, these feast days were accorded much greater significance as occasions of celebration than were aspirants' individual birthdays. January 21, for example, was the feast of St Agnes, and the literary and artistic heritage arising from her story became the subject of study at Providence Juniorate.[82] The feast of Our Lady of Lourdes followed on 11 February, and on that date in 1943 the junior French class enacted a series of episodes from the life of Bernadette in honour of the occasion.[83] On 17 March it was St Patrick's turn, and in 1944 the Providence aspirants stepped on the stage to enact "Brigid from Ireland" on his

118 · *Into Silence and Servitude*

feast day. The play told the story of Brigid, who came to New York in order to attend college, but in the end joined a convent novitiate.[84] The seniors had St Catherine of Alexandria as their patron, and a special celebration was held on her feast day, 25 November.[85] There is little historical evidence, however, that either St Agnes or St Catherine ever existed.

There have been several references to the director of aspirants. She was, in effect, the principal of the school. According to Senieur, the ideal incumbent should be "cheerful and approachable," have a "spirit of Christlike joy," and be able to "apply kind and helpful correction" to the teenagers subject to her control. Another key figure in the institution was the chaplain. This was the priest who said the daily Mass and provided ready access to Confession. Moreover, he was always available to dispense a form of "spiritual guidance" that was "far more direct and detailed and intimate" than anything available in ordinary schools.[86]

In fulfilling their various roles, the director and chaplain remained focused on two overarching concerns: expelling aspirants whom they felt were unsuited to religious life and encouraging the others to complete the program of studies so that they might enter the postulancy. The strict routines and social isolation of the aspirancy could be discouraging to teenagers accustomed to much greater freedoms, and it was deemed necessary to issue frequent admonitions on the importance of perseverance. Shortly after arrival at Providence Juniorate, Mary Gilligan and her cohort of aspirants were warned by the director that the Devil would tempt them to leave by afflicting them with homesickness. And to reinforce the message she told of the misfortunes that had befallen those who had turned their backs on Christ's call. Some had brought forth stillborn children, she said, while others had died of cancer or in traffic accidents.[87]

Senieur advised directors to give special attention to aspirants who were unhappy or wavering in their commitment. If they found the rigours of the aspirancy challenging, he observed, then the much more demanding regimen of the postulancy and novitiate would be too much for them. Nonetheless, it was best to challenge such aspirants to persevere, and he suggested that directors try the following line of argument: "God is calling you to a higher life. The fact that you are here creates a presumption that He wants you here. That call requires certain sacrifices ... It is up to you to make the choice ... You cannot fashion a dainty little cross to suit your shoulders; you must suit your shoulders to the cross of Christ."[88]

By the time aspirants entered their senior year, they were reasonably acquainted with the cloistered life and came under intense pressure to answer "that big question": would they enter the postulancy? The Ancilla Domini graduating class of 1964 experienced it like this. Towards the end of February, the director, Sister Julienne, scheduled individual conferences with each aspirant to determine her intentions. On 1 March three postulants arrived at the school for a question-and-answer session with the seniors. The postulants would play a similar role a few months later, urging others to emulate them.

The Ides of March fell on a Sunday that year and a good part of it was given over to a vocational assembly. At this event the seniors presented a play called "Career Angel Returns." The story line involved an angel of vocations appearing to assist aspirants in making their career choices. Sister Evamarie had written a poem for the occasion and had set it to a choral arrangement. As the poem was being sung, students acted the roles of a postulant receiving her veil and a novice making her vows.

On 7 May the seniors were interrupted in study hall by Sister Julienne, who presented them with their entrance papers. They were then invited outside for a picnic with the postulants, who described for them what their first weeks in the postulancy would be like.[89]

While practices varied from one institution to the next, what has been described for Ancilla Domini was fairly typical of the attention focused on "that big question" for seniors in convent aspirancies. The congregations invested heavily in these schools, and results were an understandable concern. The issue was: How many aspirants went on to become postulants and ultimately nuns?

The question is best addressed in a circuitous manner. Aspirancy enrolments followed a unique pattern that demands detailed description. A typical class of freshmen lost many of its members as it progressed towards the senior grade. We can chart this pattern at Ancilla Domini and Providence Juniorate in Tables 5.1 and 5.2.[90]

The numbers were not as stable and predictable as the charts suggest, since it was always possible to enter a program in the upper grades, and there were always a few who did so. Nonetheless, the

TABLE 5.1 · ANCILLA DOMINI HIGH SCHOOL

Average beginning enrolment in each grade between 1949–50 and 1959–60

Freshman	20
Sophomores	17
Juniors	13
Seniors	9

TABLE 5.2 PROVIDENCE JUNIORATE

Average beginning enrolment in each grade between 1955–56 and 1964–65

Freshman	30
Sophomores	24
Juniors	18
Seniors	9

pattern of declining numbers for each successive grade was remarkably consistent at both institutions. It meant that on average the initial enrolment for a class of seniors was about one-half of the size it had been upon entrance three years earlier. Why was this so? A combination of dismissals and voluntary withdrawals is the simple answer. But if we look closely at the class of freshmen that entered Providence Juniorate in September 1934, we can discover the reasons for these individual decisions.

There were forty-six aspirants in the cohort in question, twenty-five of whom were not in the sophomore class twelve months later. Of this twenty-five, four were sent home during the academic year and another eight were told not to return after the summer holidays. Almost half of the non-returnees, then, were expelled by the institution. The sisters had their reasons. Mary H. and Florence M. were dismissed at Christmas when it was discovered that their parents were divorced; aspirants had to be of respectable Catholic families, it will be recalled. Three were expelled for poor health, and another three on suspicion of stealing. Regina O'B. was asked to leave on account of laziness. Irene G. was also lazy, but – and this was much more serious – her correspondence revealed a fondness for boys. Ruth S. was labelled "very queer" by the sisters, and hence unacceptable. And Katherine K. was "odd" and inclined to be critical of everything.

Of the thirteen who left of their own accord, eight remained until the end of the freshman year, while five departed at earlier dates. In the majority of these cases, the aspirants came to the conclusion that they had no vocation. The sisters often regretted the departures, especially when the aspirants were considered "good children." But some of the voluntary withdrawals were welcomed, and it seems that dismissal was almost inevitable in these cases. For example, Ethel T., who left in January 1935, was "vain and attracted to boys." Eleanor M. and Catherine C. were "very worldly," but stayed until the first year of studies was completed.[91]

The pattern of expulsions and voluntary departures continued throughout the history of the institution. In the early 1960s, Gilligan recalled two of her classmates being expelled, one for smoking, another for smuggling out love letters to a boyfriend. The departures were not announced; those who left simply disappeared, and their names were erased from all signs and lists.[92]

The sisters made it quite clear that only those who were "convent material" were welcome to stay and complete the program. Conduct or attitude that indicated unsuitability for the cloister or that might adversely affect other aspirants was simply not tolerated: "If, in the judgment of the directress, a candidate is exerting a harmful influence in the Juniorate, she may be dismissed without any special act of insubordination on her part."[93]

Let us now return to the question: How many went on to become postulants and ultimately nuns after the unsuitable were screened out? We have accurate figures for Providence Juniorate between 1933 and 1954.

Total number of aspirants admitted: 397.
Aspirants who left or did not enter the postulancy: 233, or 59 per cent.
Aspirants who became postulants: 164, or 41 per cent.
Aspirants who became professed nuns: 118, or 30 per cent.[94]

The figures were impressive, but aspirancies were a potential source of controversy for the Church. Some alleged that young people were being subjected to undue pressure to become religious by a segregation that limited their knowledge of the world and their ability to make informed choices about their lives. And, as we saw in Chapter 4, many parents wondered if their children were experienced enough at thirteen or fourteen to make important career decisions. Furthermore, aspirancies, by their very nature, found themselves in opposition to a number of pronounced trends in postwar America: the preference for educating children in day schools rather than in boarding schools; the idea that career choice should be postponed until at least after high-school graduation; and the idea that an occupation should be freely chosen.[95]

Writing in 1957, Sister Mary Alene dismissed the criticism of aspirancies. She admitted that adolescent girls were indeed immature and restless, but pointed out that this was true whether they were in an aspirancy or not. And since restlessness was inevitable until we find God, and an aspirancy was a school focused on God, then surely it was the best place to be.[96]

Criticism plagued the aspirancies throughout their existence, however, and by the early 1960s new conditions and the winds of change fanned by the Second Vatican Council made the sponsoring congregations more circumspect on the matter. In 1963 the Sisters of Providence (St Mary-of-the-Woods) observed that former aspirants were defecting from the ranks of their novices and junior professed sisters in greater numbers than previously. Moreover, institutional fees were not even covering the costs of the meals provided, let alone the educational and cultural advantages conferred. And the Sisters were now ready to acknowledge the disadvantages of the sheltered lives aspirants were leading "where associations are limited and where they might not mature normally as they might do in the home atmosphere, especially if the home atmosphere is wholesome and the vocation genuine."[97]

The liberal critique of the seclusion approach to recruitment can be seen in an address to the NCEA convention in 1966 by a member of the Maryknoll congregation. Sister Rita Anne Forbes pointedly challenged the continuing relevance of aspirancies in the context of the Church's renewal following the council: "*Experience* also is acquired best in open society, where the girl is free to meet others of both sexes, of all ages, of all religions, and of all social classes. From this experience in adolescence flows the *self-assurance*, and ultimately the *self-acceptance*, so necessary for the unselfconscious openness to others in religious life and in the apostolate."[98]

Declining enrolment, rising costs, disappointing results, and the persistence of criticism led to the closing of Providence Juniorate in the summer of 1966.[99] It marked the symbolic end to a unique chapter in professionalized recruitment to religious sisterhoods.

CONCLUSION

An aspirant was presumed to have a religious vocation, even if there were elements of uncertainty in her young mind. Cultivating the vocation and protecting it from worldly distractions was central to the purpose of the rules and protocols that governed the institutions that educated them. Isolation was a consistent theme – isolation from seculars (and particularly from young men), from families, and from all of the popular entertainments so readily available in American life. Convent walls formed a defensive cocoon against the wiles of Satan, who was believed to subject nuns and those training to become nuns to greater temptations than ordinary women.[100]

With the pleasures of the world held at bay, experiences were structured to strengthen the will, so that aspirants might more readily embrace that most essential of evangelical counsels: obedience. An obedient nun was a good nun and it was never too early to start practising. The strict daily schedule of religious rites and devotions, domestic chores, and study, coupled with a culture of restraint, silence, and constant surveillance, ensured that those with the appropriate deference and dispositions were identified and encouraged to move forward to the postulancy, the next stage of religious formation. Conversely, those of an independent or questioning mind, or those given to indolence, slovenliness, sensuality, or a love of comfort, were singled out and, if corrective measures proved ineffective, were asked to leave. In many cases, of course, they simply left of their own accord upon realizing that the constraints of convent life were not for them.

CHAPTER 6

. . . .

Postulants:

"Moving Backward

in Time"

The night I entered the novitiate of the
Sisters of Charity of the Blessed Virgin Mary
I felt that I was moving backward in time to
some magic country where nothing would
ever change. In a certain sense I felt that my
life was ending. I knew that there would be
work. I knew that there would be prayer.
I'd been told there would be austerity and
discipline and an inevitable loneliness
as one sought to unite oneself perfectly
to the will of God.[1]
Mary Griffin (postulant in 1939)

The sisters should be simple in their manners, their speech, and their demeanor.
Artificial manners, affected speech, boastful
and arrogant demeanor, a passion for display of elegance; in fact, all that is pompous
or vain is not becoming to a Poor Hand-
maid of Jesus Christ ... The more unaffected

and artless a Sister conducts herself, the
more pleasing she is, the more acceptable
she is to God and man.[2]
Rule of the Poor Handmaids of Jesus Christ

ENTERING RELIGION MEANT apprenticing to a unique and distinctive way of life, and the first stage of the learning process was
known as the postulancy. Unlike the aspirancy, which never accounted for more than a minority of those who became nuns, the
postulancy was a requirement. The Code of Canon Law, as revised
in 1917, specified that it last for at least six months in religious institutes of women with perpetual vows. A congregation's rules could
extend this period for up to another six months, but the normal
duration of this phase of formation was nine months. If all went
well, the postulant was accepted into the novitiate. Since canon law
ruled that a girl could not take her temporary religious vows until
she had reached her sixteenth birthday, a novice could be as young
as fifteen, and a postulant could be fourteen or even younger.[3] The
rules of some congregations prescribed high-school graduation as
an entrance requirement, especially for those destined for careers in
teaching. It was also customary to specify an upper age limit; it was
usually thirty, but exceptions were always possible.[4]

The postulancy, sometimes known as the postulate, then, was the
first official stage of religious formation. The term was derived from
the Latin verb *postulare*, meaning "to ask." In effect, a postulant was
asking a congregation to admit her to its ranks upon judging her
suitability over the six to twelve months of the program. And, as the
recruitment professionals were always pointing out, the postulant
was also deciding if a life in religion was what she really wanted for
herself. Both parties to the experience were testing each other to see
if there was a mutual fit.

Sister Mary Paul Reilly, however, cautioned her teenage readers
against too casual an attitude, saying that it was best not to enter
the postulancy with the idea that you could leave at any time. It
was better, she advised, to pray right from the start for the grace to
persevere and to resolve to "burn your bridges" and abandon your
old life.[5] In a similar vein, the priest presiding at the first Mass for
postulants with the Sisters of Charity of the Blessed Virgin Mary

(Dubuque, Iowa) in the summer of 1960 assured his listeners that their acceptance by the community was sufficient proof of their vocations. He urged them to cast aside their doubts and to stand by their "generous decision" to give themselves completely "to the religious life and to Christ."[6]

On admission day, a postulant arrived at her chosen convent in the company of her parents and perhaps other siblings. The main convent building, the mother house, was not her destination, since that was the residence of the professed nuns with whom she would have little contact. She went instead to the novitiate, a separate building that housed both postulants and novices.[7] Here the family was ushered into the parlour, while a "guardian angel" took charge of the postulant. The angel was usually a novice, and her role was to orient the new arrival to the physical layout of the premises and to some of the rules and routines that she would need to know right away.

The first stop was the dormitory, where the postulant was shown the bed that had already been selected for her. Madeline DeFrees, upon becoming a postulant with the Sisters of the Holy Names of Jesus and Mary (Marylhurst, Oregon) in 1936, recalled her initial astonishment at the order, simplicity, and cleanliness of everything – rows of perfectly made beds, small chests of drawers, and straight-backed chairs, all arranged in a geometrically perfect pattern.[8]

Dormitory beds had curtains around them to be drawn when dressing and undressing, and these safeguards to modesty were immediately deployed as the postulant changed into her uniform. Although the design of the uniform varied a little depending on the congregation, there was one consistent theme: the preponderance of the colour black. In fact, at the Dominican convent in Seattle in the 1950s, postulants were known as the "black crows."[9] There were black stockings, black shoes, a long black dress, a black cap to which was affixed a black veil, and in some cases a black cape that snapped around the neck.[10] If she were skilled at needlework, the postulant may have made the uniform herself according to the community's specifications, or she may have had the assistance of her mother or of the nun who recruited her in high school. There were also manufacturers of religious apparel that would do the job for you.[11] The uniform was part of a trousseau families were expected to provide, as well as a dowry.[12] For DeFrees, the uniform was her first encounter with the restrictions of religious life. She realized that it would now be more difficult to ascend stairs two steps at a time, to climb fences, and to ride bicycles – assuming such activities were even allowed.[13] Once suitably attired, the postulant returned to the parlour to be greeted by her family.

It was now time for a brief initiation ceremony, which was conducted in private. Postulants with the Sisters of Charity of St Elizabeth (Convent Station, New Jersey) were asked to kneel in turn before their mistress of postulants and answer three questions: Do you wish to become a Sister of Charity? Are you here of your own free will? Do you intend to follow our rules and practices? If they answered affirmatively, they were welcomed into the community.[14] Or they might be led to the chapel by the Mother Superior, where the chaplain invested them through an "Act of Consecration to the Blessed Virgin." They recited words something to this effect: "Jesus, I'm here. Help me stay always." They also asked for a blessing for their parents, many of whom may have had serious misgivings about the enterprise.[15]

There was some time with families afterwards, before separating from them. Patricia O'Donnell, who became a postulant with the Dominican Sisters, Adrian, Michigan, in 1963, recalled that many of her companions were crying as they bade farewell to their loved ones, and some were still hysterical as they ate their supper later.[16]

At entry, each postulant was assigned a number that she retained until the end of her novitiate. The number was usually determined by the date of her application. It served as a sort of seniority system and established such matters as her place in chapel or dining hall or in the single-file processions in which the postulants walked from one locale or activity to the next.[17]

The mistress of postulants now took charge of their lives. She reminded them that the postulancy was a time of prayer, self-sacrifice, and a character formation that led to subjugation of the will.[18] Sister Ann Joseph Wagner, the mistress with the Sisters of Divine Providence (San Antonio, Texas) in the 1940s and 1950s, emphasized doing "the right thing at the right time."[19] There could be no room for individualism, or "singularity," as it was termed. In recalling her time as a postulant, DeFrees concluded that community life could not prosper unless nuns, and especially new recruits to the system, learned to regulate "independence of thought and action; intellectual and social ambition; self-assertiveness."[20]

Obedience was everything, since, after all, nuns were "special servants of the Lord," and being a servant meant that you had to obey.[21] And because God's will was manifested in that of the mistress, there was no ambiguity in what was required. In Sister Reilly's description of the postulancy, the mistress spelled out the essence of the relationship:

> You have come to seek God – to draw nearer to Him, to be with Him always, to belong to Him. You are going to effect that by performing the work that will be assigned to you for His love; by being silent so that He may speak to you; by talking to Him often in prayer; and by constantly sacrificing your own comfort and desires in the performance of His will. You will always know what He wants. His will for religious is contained in the order of the day and the commands of superiors. You can never go wrong.[22]

Mother Gertrude, mistress with the Sisters of St Mary of the Presentation (Valley City, North Dakota) in the 1940s, was unambiguous on the matter as she addressed her postulants: "You must be obedient as your formation begins. You are not to question my directions or the rules ... You must look forward to strict discipline that is meant to weed out your obstinacy and willfulness."[23] The mistress with the Sisters of St Joseph (Cleveland, Ohio) in 1946 promoted obedience by reading from Father Alfonsus Rodriquez's three-volume work, *Christian Perfection*. One of her favourite stories from the book was that of a young monk who was ordered by his novice master to water a stick stuck in the monastery ground. Although the monk could not understand the logic of the command, he did so anyway, and passed the obedience test.[24]

Mother Mary Rogers (1882–1955), founder of the Maryknoll Sisters (Ossining, New York), liked to surprise her postulants with an occasional homily. On the question of obedience, she advised them in this way: "The bell is for us the voice of God. When the bell rings at any time, that is God calling to us. He has an appointment with us at that particular moment and if we don't answer the bell, we are simply saying, 'I have something more interesting than keeping an appointment with You.'"[25]

Learning to obey, then, was central to the postulancy experience. Obedience was, of course, one of the vows or evangelical counsels to which nuns pledged themselves at the time of profession, and writers on the subject considered it the most vital. An obedient nun, it was often said, would have no problems with the chastity and poverty requirements. In fact, several congregations specified in their recruitment literature that they were seeking girls of a "docile" disposition.[26] Others sought girls with "a pliant will" or a "submissive spirit."[27]

The vow of chastity did not receive much attention during the postulancy, probably because most of those in the program were young, presumed to be fairly innocent, and not yet members of the community. The mistress with the Missionary Sisters of the Holy Rosary (Bryn Mawr, Pennsylvania) in the early 1960s did, however, issue some cautionary advice. She suggested that her postulants sleep on their backs with rosary beads in their hands in order to protect chastity.[28] Occasional warnings about "particular friendships" – a major taboo in convent protocol – were sometimes issued. This was so with Carmen and Michelle, who attended the Dominican Sisters' boarding school in Seattle, and who were, in the words of Catherine Whitney, "shielded from the normal teenage experience of going to dances and movies and having dates." When they joined the congregation upon graduating in 1954 they remained close and were reprimanded for doing so by Sister Karen, the mistress of postulants. "Believe me when I tell you that terrible sins have been committed in the name of friendship," was Karen's warning. But the absence of details perplexed the two young women. Whitney explains: "they hadn't the slightest clue what kind of sin Sister Karen might be talking about. They were unworldly, naïve girls – innocents. They were unfamiliar with sexual matters of any kind. So the underlying fear of lesbianism contained in the concept of 'particular friendship' completely eluded them."[29]

A postulant's life was one of strict rules, rituals, and schedules. Many of the rules seemed quite arbitrary, and perhaps capricious, and may have been devised to test a willingness to obey. At the Dominican convent in Seattle, postulants were forbidden to look out the window. Nor were they allowed to eat fruit on a Saturday, in honour of the Blessed Virgin.[30] At the Sisters of St Joseph (Philadelphia), permission to leave or enter a room was required of the person in charge – and there was always somebody in charge. Lateness for anything brought an instant reprimand and required pleading for forgiveness.[31] Postulants with the Sisters of the Immaculate Heart of Mary (Hollywood, California) were warned never to discuss their past lives with one another.[32] A similar rule was in force with the Sisters of St Joseph (Cleveland) lest "the sin of pride" be committed.[33] The Sisters of Charity of the Blessed Virgin Mary (Dubuque, Iowa) forbade smoking and laughing – fairly common prohibitions.[34] The Daughters of Wisdom (Litchfield, Connecticut) prohibited smelling the flowers in the convent gardens as a means to mortification of the senses.[35]

For some postulants, the myriad rules made them feel that they had returned to childhood. Most frustrating in this respect was the need to seek permission for the most trivial of acts. What had once been spontaneous now required prior approval, whether it was washing your hair or going to the toilet. In the event of the call of nature, postulants with the Sisters of St Joseph (Cleveland) had to ask, "May I go upstairs?" This was the officially sanctioned euphemism, since nuns would never utter the word "bathroom," let alone "toilet."[36] If a postulant with the Dominicans of Adrian, Michigan, needed toothpaste, for example, she knelt before the mistress and made the request. When permission was granted, she said, "Blessed be God and His Gifts."[37]

While some rules were explained and justified, many were not. Postulants and novices shared chapel with the professed nuns of their community, but social contact between them was off limits.[38] Nobody knew why. During her postulancy with the Sisters of St Joseph (Cleveland), Mary Jane Masterson speculated that the still-worldly habits of those who had yet to take their vows might disturb those who had already done so. The bad influence could work in reverse too, she thought. If professed nuns showed any dissatisfaction with the religious life, might it not discourage postulants and novices from pursuing their vocations?[39]

One universal convent rule was the code of silence. There were, in fact, two kinds of silence. During the day, ordinary silence prevailed. It meant that, as postulants went about their assigned tasks, there could be no casual conversation or unnecessary noise. They had to walk with a light step and close doors quietly. There could be no clatter or clamour. Obviously, the rule against talking did not apply during classes, recreation, and Confession, but otherwise, the convent was supposed to be a place of quiet solitude. After evening prayers, profound or sacred silence was imposed until morning bell. It was a time to prepare for welcoming Jesus in Holy Communion.[40] O'Donnell worried that her habit of sometimes talking in her sleep broke this rule.[41]

Instant conformity to the protocols of convent culture was rarely achieved; teenage exuberance was just not that easy to subdue. Postulants with the Sisters of Charity of the Blessed Virgin Mary could not deny themselves a good laugh, and some even ran "giddily through the house." Silence was often broken, and this violation was rarely detected at night.[42] Grace Stolz became good friends with two of her fellow postulants while with the Sisters of Mary of the Presentation (Valley City, North Dakota) in 1945 and found occasions to chat with them during silence. She even found opportunities to run up and down stairs just for the fun of it.[43]

Rule-breakers were punished if caught or betrayed by an overzealous companion. And punishment was not just a corrective or deterrent measure; it was considered essential to spiritual growth and therefore valuable in itself.[44] A postulant who broke a rule found herself kneeling before the mistress, requesting a penance. The penances were usually public, and their intensity varied with the gravity of the violation. Talking in chapel, for example, was much more serious than doing so in the laundry. Punishments could take the form of extra housework, saying prayers with arms outstretched, exclusion from recreation, or – and this was the most humiliating – eating your meal while kneeling on the refectory floor.[45]

How did postulants respond all of this? Mary Gilligan felt completely boxed in by the rules imposed by the Sisters of Providence (St Mary-of-the-Woods, Indiana). She had little peace of mind and a feeling of constant inadequacy as she wondered if she had been negligent in any way in submitting to expectations.[46] Midge Turk (1930–2012) accepted the constraints as necessities in striving for perfection during her postulancy with the Sisters of the Immaculate Conception (Hollywood, California) in 1948. But she observed: "The minutiae of convent living were overwhelming. One was able to cope only by constantly thinking that in the eyes of God, nothing, but absolutely nothing, was trivial."[47] Masterson also resigned herself to the rules, in spite of some misgivings: "Penances, reprimands, and put-downs were all part of the way to the mystical intimacy with which a true bride of Christ would be gifted. Some of the penances, rules, and regulations seemed senseless, but I usually embraced them willingly because I believed that these were acts of humility to be offered to Jesus."[48]

The strict and unwavering rhythm of convent life shocked newly arrived postulants, although those who had been through an aspirancy found it less strange and demanding. Many communities allowed for a few weeks of adjustment before imposing the full force of the normal schedule. Postulants were permitted to sleep until as late as 6:30 or even 7:00 a.m., for example.[49]

How did a typical day begin once the regular schedule was in place? At 5:00 a.m. the dormitory supervisor rang a loud bell that shook the postulants from their sleep. They were expected to imagine their beds on fire and to leap instantly from them. Falling on their knees, they kissed the floor in gratitude for their vocation while saying aloud: "Glory be to Jesus and Mary."[50] There were twenty minutes to dress, make their beds, and perform morning ablutions – often without a mirror in which to look.[51] This was a bit of a challenge to the uninitiated and was further complicated by having to recite prayers in unison while so engaged: "My Lord and my God, when shall I be entirely Thine and when shall I be entirely to Thy heart."[52] It was an early-morning reminder that perfection was still a long way off.

The first formal part of the day was at chapel, where the entire community gathered. Thirty minutes were devoted to meditation, or silent prayer. Masterson recalled nodding off during meditation more than once. A number of her fellow postulants did likewise, one of them even falling from her pew into the aisle.[53] Falling asleep during meditation or during any other activity was one of the many faults that had to be accounted for.

The Divine Office or the Little Office of Our Lady followed. This was a series of prayers prescribed in the rules of the congregation and was chanted by the choir sisters in Latin. Then came the Rosary, which was said by all and in the vernacular. Sister Reilly described the sound of so many voices in unison as "like a low humming of a great dynamo generating power for thousands."[54] And finally, there was Mass and Holy Communion.

By the time it was all over it was almost 8:00 a.m. and time for the first meal of the day. Breakfast was eaten in the refectory and, like all aspects of convent life, was carefully orchestrated and choreographed. Taking their assigned places at large oilcloth-covered communal tables, the postulants were expected to eat everything placed before them and to do so in silence. Gestures and nods were permitted if you needed something passed to you.[55]

Spiritual reading accompanied the meal. While the reading usually fell to the mistress, postulants were also compelled to take turns at the lectern. It was all part of their training. Many dreaded the experience, since stumbling over a phrase or mispronouncing a word could bring an instant reprimand, and perhaps a penalty.[56] What was read? Thomas à Kempis's *The Imitation of Christ* was used extensively, although it was not to everyone's liking. Turk described it as akin to "so many medieval helpful hints for old-time monks."[57] Butler's *Lives of the Saints* was favoured too, since it was organized into brief biographies, allowing a different saint to be presented on his or her feast day. Many of the early saints ended their lives in martyrdom, and the details of their trials were sometimes featured as breakfast proceeded. The readings reminded all that, whatever inconveniences and discomforts came their way, nothing compared with the sufferings of saintly martyrs.[58] The other meals of the day followed a similar pattern, with silence and more spiritual readings.

Convents were complex institutions, requiring much physical labour to keep everything humming along with the order, predictability, and cleanliness for which they were renowned. Communities of Canadian and European origin usually had lay sisters in charge of kitchens, gardens, laundries, and the like. There was no question, however, of bringing in paid workers. In fact, there was no need. The postulants quickly discovered that, because they occupied the lowest rung in the organizational hierarchy, they were "the help."

Domestic chores were variously described as "charges," "obediences," "offices," or "ménages," and were usually undertaken by the postulants after breakfast, unless they had been assigned to preparing that meal or serving it to the professed sisters.[59] Work details were allocated arbitrarily, which often seemed unfair, since certain tasks – in the kitchen, laundry, and toilets – were deemed particularly disagreeable.[60] Sweeping hallways and stairs was a more desirable assignment, even if it resulted in only "a meagre store of dust." All work was inspected to ensure that exacting convent standards were met.[61]

What did postulants make of it all? Mary Griffin (1916–1998), a postulant with the Sisters of Charity of the Blessed Virgin Mary (Dubuque, Iowa) in 1939, provided this description: "Our fingers reddened and cracked, peeling their way through a thousand bushels of green apples, new potatoes, carrots. Our tender knees sprouted protective scabs as they shifted from scrubbing pad to wooden kneeler in an already boring rhythm."[62] Some resented what they considered menial labour. Others were prepared to endure it on the understanding that one day they would be professed sisters and freed from such servitude. And there were those who believed that the work was payment for their education.[63]

How much education did postulants actually receive? Was there a program of study or a curriculum that had to be mastered? The Code of Canon Law was silent on the matter, and even the rules of diverse congregations were not very helpful. There was a good reason for the ambiguity: postulants could enter a program between the ages of fourteen and thirty, meaning that their academic preparation could range from Grade 8 to university graduation or beyond. What was learned, therefore, varied greatly with the individual and with the specific needs and purposes of the congregation.[64] It is possible, however, to make some generalizations. "Instruction," as it was called, which occupied much of the mornings and afternoons, fell into two categories: the sacred and the profane.

The sacred, which was considered the most important, was the responsibility of the mistress. Since praying occupied a major part of a nun's day, it was central to a postulant's program of study. Some prayers were recited daily; others were reserved for special occasions. They all had to be memorized, whether in the vernacular or in Latin. The Divine Office/Little Office of Our Lady was in the latter language and, although postulants were not permitted to chant it in chapel, they had to make a start on learning it. It was a serious challenge to the many who had no acquaintance with Latin.[65]

Memorizing the words, even if their meaning remained a mystery, was only part of it. It was also necessary to learn *how to* pray and meditate. Some congregations distributed excerpts from *The Art of Praying* by influential European theologian Romano Guardini.[66] Postulants were told that it was all about talking to God, telling him that you adored him, were sorry for your sins, and were prepared to put his will before your own. O'Donnell and Deborah Larsen (a postulant with the Sisters of Charity of the Blessed Virgin Mary in 1960) were assured that, if it was done properly, they would hear the voice of God. Try as they might, they never heard it.[67] Masterson was more successful. Her fondest memory of the postulancy was the opportunity "to be still and to listen to God in a beautiful sacred place." The highlight of each week for her was the intimacy she felt with Jesus during the exposition of the Blessed Sacrament at the chapel of the mother house on Fridays. The hour spent in this devotion was never enough for her.[68]

Meditation was praying in another form – in absolute silence. Sister Martin, mistress of postulants with the Sisters of Charity of Providence (Seattle) between 1907 and 1947, gave specific instructions to her charges on how they might proceed. She suggested beginning by addressing God as follows: "What am I, O My Creator, that I should dare to present myself before Thee? Alas, I am nothing and what is worse, nothing as I am, I have rebelled against Thee." Once a proper relationship of deference was established, the postulant could continue in that mode with these utterances or variations on them:

My God, I love Thee! I am sorry for having offended Thee.
O Jesus, inflame my heart with Thy love.
O Sacred Heart of Jesus, I put all my trust in thee.

O my God, be merciful to me, a sinner.
My God, I have sinned too much during my life.[69]

Church history, Gregorian chant, the Bible, and the spiritual life were other components of the sacred curriculum. Father Adolphe Tanqueray's *The Spiritual Life: A Treatise on Ascetical and Mystical Theology* (1930) was employed as a text in places.[70] It was typical of the manual approach to theology that was popular before the Second Vatican Council and was widely used in seminaries for priests. Relying heavily on St Thomas Aquinas, St Teresa of Avila, and St John of the Cross, Tanqueray addressed such issues as mystical phenomena, dark nights of the soul, and the problems arising from human passions. Many of the obstacles on the road to perfection were attributed to "diabolical temptation," and several remedies were proposed. One suggestion was to invoke the assistance of St Michael the Archangel, who had once defeated Satan in battle.[71]

Profane knowledge was part of the program, but it lacked consistency. It was sometimes possible to earn high-school credits during the postulancy, sometimes not. And even when it was possible, there were cases where the subjects were taught poorly. When Grace Stolz entered the postulancy of the Sisters of St Mary of the Presentation (Valley City, North Dakota) in 1945 she was only fifteen years of age. At the time the congregation was extremely short of teachers and was determined to produce them with a maximum efficiency. Stolz and her cohort advanced quickly and were given credit for subjects they never studied properly. Cleaning the convent, for example, became a credit in home economics, while reciting prayers in French became a credit in that language. There was no opportunity to do science, math, English, or social studies. Stolz did not challenge these practices at the time, since she was trained to obey and not to question.[72]

There were several instances, however, where postulants took university courses if they happened to be available in a college located on the convent grounds. The range of programs could be limited, and sometimes the mistress even prescribed the courses to be taken in order to meet the professional needs of the congregation. When postulants found themselves in the company of female lay students in the classroom, they were forbidden to communicate with them.[73]

Their black uniforms, in any case, would likely have encouraged social segregation.

Nonetheless, Father Senieur perceived danger in even allowing postulants in the same classroom as seculars, since it meant contact with the outside world during a period of formation that ought ideally to be nothing but "religious training." "By sending the postulant to school with the other girls," he said, "you are putting the seedling of a religious vocation to an immature test." He acknowledged that congregations were paying more attention to the academic preparation of their teachers because of "the mad scramble in our Catholic schools to simulate the expensive set up in the public schools." The problem with that approach, he surmised, was that sisters could mistakenly come to believe that their real vocation was teaching: "That is not really true. The vocation to the sisterhood is a vocation to the religious life. Teaching is the Sister's job. Once again, she is not a teacher who is also a religious, but a religious who is also a teacher."[74]

Senieur was touching on two interrelated problems connected with religious formation. The first had to do with the idea, so often articulated in the recruitment literature, that a vocation was a delicate flower that needed protection from the seductive pleasures of the world if it were to survive and flourish. Isolation behind convent walls and exposure to knowledge and values that were religious rather than secular were seen as the kinds of protection that vocations required. But secular knowledge had to be accommodated in some way if nuns were expected to become competent teachers, and historically they had often been able to do so with some degree of balance and compromise. The second problem was that, in the 1950s, there was increasing pressure on congregations to improve the academic credentials of their members through the Sister Formation Conference, and Senieur sensed that this trend threatened to undermine the essence of the postulancy and perhaps expose postulants to influences inimical to their vocations.[75]

An important part of a postulant's education was learning convent decorum and the deportment appropriate to the religious state. She had to practise behaving like a nun in order to become, in Turk's memorable phrase, "one of those serene gliding creatures."[76] Posture was important. A nun stood erect and never slouched or leaned against a wall. When sitting down she did not cross her legs. Her hands were kept hidden from view beneath voluminous garments – unless deployed usefully in some way. And she never stretched in the presence of others. Moving about was subject to similar strictures. A nun walked but never ran. She walked purposefully but without haste. She made as little noise as possible while doing so, and kept her eyes cast downwards. "Custody of the eyes" was an essential and hard-won skill; there could be no looking around, no smiles or nods of recognition for a friend, and no humming or whistling. Father Charles J. Mullaly explained it this way: "Custody of the eyes curbs worldly curiosity and is a sign of the humility that goes with the Religious state. It should be easy for a Sister to guard her eyes. She is unlike the woman of the world whose eyes ever seek new sights and new objects to feed a frivolous soul sated with the things of earth. A Sister will only see what will lift her thoughts to God."[77] The story was often told of St Clare's resolve never to fix her gaze on the face of a man. One day during Mass, however, she lifted her eyes to see the consecrated host and found herself looking at the priest's face, an episode that disturbed her greatly.[78]

The manner of personal communication was also regulated. A nun spoke in subdued tones and only when necessary. Casual and spontaneous remarks were out of the question. She did not gesticulate with her hands or crack jokes. She did not look people in the eye or become familiar.[79] Every task was approached with careful deliberation and in accordance with age-old customs. At least two convents even had protocols for eating bananas; they could not be eaten "the monkey way."[80] DeFrees readily accepted the rules on comportment; they were necessary in order to shut out the world and prepare for awareness of the Divine.[81]

A postulant's day was a busy one and, even if instruction occupied much of the morning and afternoon, there were frequent interruptions for devotions such as the Stations of the Cross and the Rosary.[82] Patricia Grueninger, a postulant with the Daughters of Charity of St Vincent de Paul (Baltimore) in 1955 summed it up well when she wrote: "Our daily schedule left no free time, no time to think or be alone, no time to steal remembrances of the past. We had to keep busy praying, working, and learning all there was to learn about our new life."[83]

The day was certainly busy, but an hour was put aside for recreation either late in the afternoon or immediately following supper. Recreation was a time when talking was allowed and, while this was appreciated, the fact that everything was planned for them was resented by some postulants. It was not simply a period of relaxation or free time, and all had to participate in the planned activities. Sports were possible, but rare enough; baseball was sometimes the choice here, since its slow pace did not require removal of the postulant uniform. More often quiet walks were as physical as it got. Indoor activities included card-playing, sewing, knitting, charades, and what one former postulant called "childish games."[84] Masterson recalled dancing the "Hokey Pokey." It was something she disliked, but she did it anyway, since it was required.[85]

Radio, musical recordings, television, movies, and other artifacts of popular culture were not considered appropriate as recreational diversions. When asked if postulants should be allowed to see feature films that appealed to high-school girls, Senieur demurred. He felt that such an experience "would hardly contribute to the development of the religious character." Nor did he see any virtue in listening to "popular mushy love songs."[86] The strict isolation from worldly entertainments, it should be noted, was relaxed somewhat in the 1960s. Sister Barbara Fry recalled that her group of postulants with the Sisters of Divine Providence (San Antonio) was the first that was permitted to listen to selected popular music. The songs of Peter, Paul, and Mary were on the acceptable list.[87]

Life in the convent was routinized and predictable and, at least for some postulants, therein lay its appeal. In the diary in which she recorded her formation years, Sister Frederic noted that "the very simplicity of everything" made her peaceful and contented, since the outside world had always appeared too complex for her. There were, nonetheless, occasions for "joyous outbursts," as when the mistress of postulants produced a box of candy for all to share.[88] Sister Reilly affirmed this impression of the postulancy experience, assuring her readers that the simple pleasures of the convent were far more satisfying than events such as senior prom night. And, lest she encounter skepticism with such a claim, she provided an example of those pleasures: "Just to come down to the refectory after a beautiful feast-day High Mass to find snowy tablecloths covering the oil cloth, flowers at Mother's place, and holy cards or a candy bar at all of yours, makes you genuinely gleeful."[89]

The reference to candy by Sisters Frederic and Reilly is noteworthy here. Convents were known for their food and goodies – one of the few pleasures that were allowed – and the stereotype of the well-fed nun was not without foundation.[90] Indeed Sister Reilly also regaled her young readers with stories of postulants gorging themselves on "mammoth ice cream cones."[91] Food was an acceptable indulgence, which everyone quickly learned. And if a congregation happened to be Belgian in origin – the Ursulines of Long Island, New York, for example – postulants could expect regular helpings of chocolate.[92] Six of the ex-nuns interviewed by Gerelyn Hollingsworth, a writer with the *National Catholic Reporter*, remarked on the abundance of good food placed before them during their postulancies. Several of them gained a considerable amount of weight as a consequence. One mistress urged her postulants to eat up, saying that a robust appetite was a sign of a vocation.[93] Beryl Bissell, while a postulant with the Poor Clares in Bordentown, New Jersey, in 1957 and 1958, grew so immense that the wedding dress she was supposed to wear at her reception ceremony as a novice would not fit. She succeeded in getting into it only by going on a starvation diet during the retreat that preceded the ceremony.[94]

The *sancta simplicitas* of convent life was accentuated by its isolation from the world and its goings-on. In the absence of radio, television, and newspapers, postulants had no idea what was happening outside the walls.[95] Larsen was not terribly bothered by this, since she was sure that they would learn about the most important of events: the end of the world. And she surmised that they might even be among the first to hear the angelic trumpet announcing Christ's return.[96] DeFrees, who felt instantly at home in the convent, considered the outside world shallow and unappealing, since it substituted glamour and dazzle for real love.[97]

For postulants who had gone through an aspirancy, the expectations came as no great surprise, since they represented an intensification of what they had already experienced. Family ties were now severed even more than ever, and photographs of loved ones were confiscated.[98] Letters from home, especially from parents expressing unhappiness at separation from their daughters, were strictly censored.[99] O'Donnell strongly resented receiving letters with words and passages obscured with black marker. When one courageous postulant in her cohort questioned this practice, the mistress explained that it was done for their protection, since families could not be expected to understand the life they had chosen. The letters could be read only once, and then were destroyed. Outgoing letters were also censored. In writing them, postulants were warned to say nothing about loneliness or about such practices as rising at 5:00 a.m. or about having to kneel in order to ask for something. It made writing home awkward.[100]

Families were allowed to visit their daughters one Sunday a month except during Advent (the four weeks prior to Christmas) and Lent (the six weeks prior to Easter). The visits lasted for about two hours and usually took place in the convent parlour. These gatherings could be a challenge for postulants, since they were warned beforehand not to discuss community rules or to inquire into affairs of the world. And just to ensure that such protocols were respected, nuns sometimes hovered around the family groupings or even joined in their conversations. Small talk dominated the visits; O'Donnell recalled watching the clock until it was time for her parents to leave and feeling like a total stranger to them.[101]

Visiting was a one-way street. Postulants were not allowed to return home, even at Christmas.[102] At the Sisters of St Joseph (Cleveland) families could come and see their daughters after Christmas dinner, while at the Sisters of the Immaculate Heart of Mary (Hollywood) they could only phone. The birth of Jesus was a major event in the convent, but it was celebrated with typical restraint. There were decorations, abundant food, a relaxation of the rules, and much singing of hymns. Postulants could receive gifts from their parents – but, in view of the austere life they were preparing for, the list of approved goods was limited. Turk recalled finding darning thread, straight pins, and shoe polish in her stocking. Masterson discovered a black woollen shawl under the tree and, although she gave some thoughts to the celebrations her family were enjoying, she willingly accepted the new reality. Christmas served as a reminder of the world they were leaving behind.[103] As Sister Angela, mistress with the Daughters of Charity of St Vincent de Paul (Baltimore) in the 1950s, explained to her postulants: "If you are sincere in your desire to be Christ's bride one day, you must give all – and that includes pleasant memories that rekindle human love, even the love of parents and siblings ... Jesus must be your only love."[104]

Abandoning all for Jesus was no easy task, and many postulants wavered in their commitment throughout the program. Griffin and Turk recalled seeking some concrete sign from God that they were really among his chosen ones and, when none appeared, their doubts intensified. Sensing their concern, their mistresses assured them that their very presence in the program was a sufficient indication that God wanted them. The mistresses urged that they trust in God and that he would reward them a hundredfold. Time passed and reception day loomed, and Turk's doubts persisted. But she could not walk away, fearing that, if she abandoned her vocation, she would be repaid with "a guilt-ridden, unhappy, and even tragic life."[105] At the Adrian Dominicans, O'Donnell and many of her fellow postulants also wondered about their vocations. Following discussion among themselves, they concluded that it would not be right to renege on their commitment without giving the religious life a fair trial. It was simply easier to carry on: "So, I chose without choosing, but at the time, I didn't think of it quite so clearly. I simply moved forward because moving back to my family right then was still too much like turning my back on God."[106]

The postulancy was a time of exploration and trial in which suitability for religious life was determined. While Bissell, DeFrees, Frederic, Gilligan, Griffin, Grueninger, Larsen, Masterson, O'Donnell, Reilly, Stolz, and Turk persevered and advanced to the novitiate, this was not the case with everyone. Some gave up of their own volition; others were sent away by the mistress.

Sister Frederic recalled that she was only two weeks into her postulancy with the Sisters of the Third Order of St Francis when two of her cohort departed, citing homesickness as the reason.[107] Homesickness was fairly common in other convents as well, and contributed to early departures.[108] The tendency to give up in the first few months was also noted by Gilligan with the Sisters of Providence (St Mary-of-the-Woods). Here it was attributed to the constraints of convent life, which shocked postulants who had entered straight out of high school because of admiration for their sister-teachers.[109] DeFrees was quite critical of those among her fellow Holy Names postulants who went home early, feeling that they had not given the religious life a fair chance. Priding herself on her own perseverance, she admitted to "a little thrill of self-righteousness."[110]

Even when the initial shock wore off, the voluntary departures continued. Rose, a postulant with the Sisters of Charity of St Elizabeth, cohort of 1953, jumped into her parents' car during visiting Sunday and took off with them, still attired in her uniform. Joan, also with the same cohort, walked out one day and headed home on foot. She left a note saying that she couldn't take it anymore.[111]

Expulsions accompanied the voluntary departures, and these too began in the early months of the program. The Sisters of the Immaculate Heart of Mary (Hollywood) expelled eleven of the 1948 cohort within the first few weeks. Some of those sent home were, in Turk's words, "obvious nuts" who began to have visions shortly after arrival. Others were irresponsible, did not take the rules seriously, and behaved as if they were in a fun-filled summer camp. And then there were the particular friendships, some genuinely sexual, some too close for comfort.[112] Illness was another cause for expulsion. Margie, a postulant with the Daughters of Charity of St Vincent de Paul (Baltimore) cohort of 1955 was the first to be sent home when she had an epileptic fit – a condition that would have barred her from entry had it been known at the time of application.[113] Sharon, who entered the postulancy of the Adrian Dominicans in 1963, suffered a severe asthma attack and was encouraged to leave, which she did. Karen, who was in the same cohort, was expelled when the nuns discovered a photograph in her locker of her brother and some of his friends dressed in swimsuits.[114]

As in the aspirancy, departures were secretive and unannounced. One of Gilligan's friends, Bonnie, decided to leave, and her parents had to spirit her away in the middle of the night. There were no goodbyes; she was forbidden to return on a visit, and nobody could communicate with her by mail.[115] And so the question becomes: how many went on to become novices? Table 6.1 gives an average perseverance rate of 77 per cent. Therefore, some 23 per cent decided that the religious life was not for them or were deemed unsuitable by the congregation to which they were seeking admission.[116]

For those who did persevere, it was not always an easy path. Sister Frederic recalled constantly worrying about her imperfections and

TABLE 6.1 · NUMBER OF POSTULANTS WHO BECAME NOVICES

Congregation	Years of Entry	Entered	Persevered
Maryknoll Sisters	1950–65	1,596	1,250
Poor Handmaids of Jesus Christ	1954–64	178	112
Totals		1,774	1,362

praying frequently to Jesus to make her "a docile religious."[117] Masterson, on the other hand, described her postulancy as a beautiful and peaceful time that was "educationally, culturally, and spiritually rich."[118] Towards the end, the postulants were obliged to ask the Mother Superior and the professed sisters if they were worthy of the holy habit. A vote was taken, and those deemed worthy were accepted for admission to the novitiate.[119]

An eight-day retreat followed in preparation for the "day of reception." Retreats were a regular part of religious lives, and they gave postulants a realistic sense of what was to come. They were periods of intense prayer, silence, and meditation, interspersed with lectures on the vows, discipline, penance, charity, and so forth by the retreat master, who was always a priest.[120] Sister Frederic spent much of her retreat reflecting on death and on the state of her soul. Here's how she recorded her thoughts, which were addressed to Jesus:[121] "Oh I beg of You to grant me yet another year in which to do penance, in which to suffer for Your sake, in which to purge my heart and make it a fit dwelling for You. Hold back the avenging hand of death for a little while longer, if it be Your holy will, lest You find me unprepared."

CONCLUSION

Convent life was a mystery to outsiders, and congregations tried to keep it that way. Postulants were introduced to these mysteries, but did not experience them in all their rigour. The black uniforms, for example, may have been dreary and heavy, but they were never as constraining and uncomfortable as those of novices and professed nuns. Contact with families and the outside world was restricted, but the total isolation that would come after entrance it was not. There were strict schedules of prayer, study, work, meals, and recreation, but astute mistresses of postulants showed flexibility in imposing them while resocialization took hold. The mistress had to move her charges forward without unseemly haste, lest the shock of it all provoked mass desertions.

There were desertions, at times early on, especially among those who had had no idea of what to expect and who may have been misled by recruitment professionals. There were expulsions, too, when the mistress judged a postulant unsuitable for the community. News of acceptance into the novitiate was usually a cause for celebration, but for some there were still doubts about their vocations. The doubtful ones often proceeded to the next stage of formation anyway, hoping for greater clarification respecting their calling or in order to give religious life a fair chance.[122]

Those who successfully completed the postulancy and were accepted as novices had learned a lot during their short months in the convent. They had learned how to behave like nuns, how to be docile, to pray a lot, to work hard, to repress the desire for personal intimacy, and generally to sacrifice their own inclinations for a higher purpose. In a word, they were worthy to become brides of Christ and were ready for the reception day that marked the beginning of the novitiate.

CHAPTER 7

. . . .

Novices:

Under the Gaze

of the Zelatrix

My first 18 months in the novitiate were a
special time of growth and deepening. My
Novice Mistress, Sister Anne Roberta, let
me know in no uncertain terms that she saw
undeveloped potential in me, buried under
layers of façade. She chipped and chiseled,
hammered and cut. Sometimes I felt bruised
and bloodied but never broken.[1]
Sister Mary of the Incarnation,
Franciscan novice, 1959

They [novices] will apply themselves
to humiliating practices, considering it
a happiness to be repulsed, ill-treated
and despised in the presence of others,
even for having done well.[2]
Rule of the Sisters of Charity of Providence

THE LATIN FEMALE SUFFIX "trix" appears frequently enough in
religious literature. The Virgin Mary is sometimes described as the
Co-redemptrix or the Reparatrix. A lay sister is a coadjutrix, and a
congregation might employ a procuratrix – financial officer – or a
visitatrix – an inspector of institutions.[3] The term "zelatrix" is a bit
more obscure. The *zelatrix animarum* was literally a female zealot for
souls; in practice, she was an experienced religious responsible for
monitoring and encouraging the zeal of younger ones.[4] Although
the term is medieval in origin, some congregations still used it as
late as the 1960s. In modern times, it was customary to refer to her
as the mistress of novices.[5] We shall meet her shortly.

The transition from postulant to novice was marked by "reception day." While customs varied among congregations, it was
common to include in the sequence of rituals that marked the occasion a wedding ceremony not unlike those conducted in the secular
world. The important difference was that the bridegroom, Jesus,
was not physically present in the church, but rather was "visible
only to the attending angels."[6] Let's follow a typical reception day
through the memories of those who experienced it.

Many congregations maintained a collection of standard white
wedding dresses from which the novices could choose. The dresses
may have been donated by brides "in the world" following their
own ceremony, in the hope that a bride of Christ might one day
wear them – "an exquisite gesture," in the words of Poor Clare
Mother Mary Francis.[7] In some cases parents supplied the dress,
perhaps a family heirloom they had been keeping for a more conventional ceremony. Mary Gilligan's mother sent her sheer nylons,
lacy underwear, and white spike-heeled shoes that she was delighted
to wear after months in the dreary postulant uniform. She and her
cohort with the Sisters of Providence (St Mary-of-the-Woods) had
been provided with small pieces of stationery on which to write
love notes to Jesus; the notes were to be kept in their bras during
the ceremony.[8]

Sister Catherine Frederic, a novice with the Sisters of the Third
Order of St Francis in the late 1940s, recalled her bridal procession
in this way:

What emotion filled my heart as I donned the bridal satin,
and reflected that it was no earthly groom who was to take

me for his spouse, but the heavenly Bridegroom Himself.
At the appointed hour, we entered the chapel to the solemn
strains of the organ, which announced our coming. Slowly
and majestically we moved up the aisle, heads bowed, hands
clasped before us, veils and trains trailing magnificently after
us. We approached the altar and knelt before the officiating
priest.[9]

The brief collective wedding ceremony was conducted by the
priest or bishop, at the conclusion of which he handed the novices their habits. Novices with the Holy Cross Sisters heard the following words as they received their veils: "Receive this White Veil,
bedewed with the heavenly benediction, and wear it as a symbol
of innocence befitting those virgins who are to follow the Spotless
Lamb, to the end that it may withdraw you from the indiscreet gaze
of the world and conceal you in God with Jesus Christ."[10]
Their new names in religion were also revealed at this time. Although novices were permitted to submit a list of suggested names
beforehand, they could never be sure whether their wishes in the
matter would be honoured. The names chosen were almost always
those of a saint, whether male or female. Some anxiety was understandable, since nobody wanted to be named after Gummarus, the
patron saint of cowherds and difficult marriages, Homobonus,
the patron saint of capitalists and shoemakers, or Munchin, the saint
who cursed the Irish city of Limerick. At times the names could be
Latinized female versions of religious phenomena usually, although
not exclusively, associated with the Virgin Mary: Annunciata, As-
sumpta, Concepta, Humiliata, Immaculata, Innocentia, Inviolata.[11]
The choir then sang Palestrina's motet, *Veni Sponsa Christi*, which
went like this:

Veni sponsa Christi (Come, bride of Christ)
Accipe coronam (accept the crown)
Quam tibi Dominus praeparavit in aeternum (that the Lord has
     prepared for you for ever).

A sermon on the nature of the religious life followed, or it might be
an exhortation, such as this one, addressed to Maryknoll novices:

"Most dear sisters, we pray Our Lord Jesus Christ for these His handmaids, who for love of Him hasten to put away the worldly adornment of their heads, that He may give them His Holy Spirit, Who will preserve to them forever the holy Habit of religion and guard their hearts from the snares of the world and from carnal desires."[12]

At this point the novices left the church in procession, carrying their habits. They adjourned to an adjacent room to change from their bridal dresses into their new attire with the assistance of the nun who had been responsible for recruiting them in the first place. Here is Sister Reilly's description of the "clothing":

> You are close to real bliss as you submit to the ministrations
> of Sister Cyril who has been appointed to assist you ... The
> serge robe falls to your feet enveloping you in the spirit of
> the Order ... The cincture, symbol of penance and purity, is
> fastened around you. You feel the linen headdress tighten be-
> neath your chin and thrill as the white veil of virginity, seal of
> His possession, covers your head and shoulders.[13]

But she omitted one important detail that was anything but blissful or thrilling for some participants: the loss of "the worldly adornment of their heads." Before donning the veil – a complex arrangement of pieces of linen and serge held together tightly around the face and head with straight pins – a novice had her hair shorn off with a scissors. Joanne Howe found the experience traumatic, and Mary Gilligan observed several of her cohort in tears as they awaited their turn.[14] A novice who entered the Sisters, Servants of the Immaculate Heart of Mary (Monroe, Michigan) in 1954 was so shocked at the experience that she could not bring herself to touch her shorn scalp. When she saw her shadow on a nearby wall she thought she looked like "someone right out of Auschwitz."[15] Mary Griffin found the snipping difficult to watch, accentuated as it was by the "strangled sobs" of some of her companions. In reflecting on the experience, she observed: "Thus did one separate oneself from the love of things seen and give oneself utterly to the love of things unseen. I fingered my own cropped head and felt that there should have been a death bell tolling."[16] In an unusual gesture, the Poor

Clares placed the shorn hair of each novice in a box, tied it with a ribbon, and presented it to the young woman's mother.[17]

Once suitably attired in their habits and veils, the novices returned to the chapel. Carmelite novices prostrated themselves in the form of a cross on a black cloth laid out on the floor as Mass proceeded – a practice known as shrouding. Sylvia Giem, who went through this ritual in 1961, could hear her mother crying uncontrollably in the audience.[18] Another Carmelite, Mother Catherine Thomas (1907–1988), admitted that this was the saddest moment for families.[19]

For Sister Frederic, the day of reception was one ecstatic moment after another. In her diary, she poured forth her feelings to Jesus: "What happiness can equal mine, for at last I have found the object of my love; my Jesus dear, my King Divine, is come to me from heaven above. What joy!"[20] Mary Jane Masterson also remembered it as a joyous occasion. She was thrilled to be part of a community "leading a sheltered, disciplined life of penance, prayer, and sacrifice in union with Jesus." The loss of her hair did not bother her, and she was pleased with her new name, Sister Mary Judith.[21] Others were not so sure. At the celebration with families following the Mass, Mary Gilligan expressed some misgivings at all she was leaving behind: "As I look around at my brothers and sisters, I realize again the chasm that has grown between us. Forbidden to share my feelings with them, I take refuge in small talk ... Mom and Dad too – I hear the hollow formality in my voice as I speak to them as if I were no longer flesh of their flesh."[22]

Congregations were quite aware of the emotional difficulties attendant on severing family ties, and novices were reminded frequently that the sisters were their new family. Novices were members of the community, unlike postulants who were seeking admission. Their status as insiders was evident in their habits that, in most cases, differed little from those of professed sisters, except for the distinctive white veils. Many novices found the clothing cumbersome to wear.[23] Patricia Grueninger was shocked to learn that her bra had to be discarded in favour of a corset that flattened her breasts. She likened the starched band of linen that encircled her face to "blinders on a horse."[24] Patricia O'Donnell's headgear made it hard for her to move her jaw, and she felt "trussed and all tied up." With her hair gone and her body completely hidden except for hands and face, she mused: "The parts of my body that enabled me to attract a man as well as have children were no longer important, and everything about my new habit reinforced this weakened status of my womanhood."[25]

Novices discovered that the habit was difficult to put on and take off. The complicated array of buttons, snaps, and straight pins holding everything together presented a challenge to newcomers, especially given the limited dressing time after the morning bell.[26] Undressing for bed could be challenging too, but in a different way. A Sister of Providence (St Mary-of-the-Woods), for example, said a prayer as each part of the habit was removed and kissed it before placing it in her cabinet. Nor could any piece of it touch the floor.[27] A Franciscan Sister of Mary Immaculate said the following prayer as she dressed: "Lord Jesus Christ, through your suffering in having the white garment placed on you as a mockery, grant me the grace not to sully the innocence of my soul today."[28]

The uniformity of the habits was a stark reminder that "singularity," or any manifestation of individualism, had no place in community life. In some respects, the wearing of the habit facilitated the protocols of proper nun behaviour that postulants had learned – custody of the eyes, keeping hands hidden from view, and so forth. And a new expectation was now added. Novices had to walk in such a way that the large rosaries suspended from their belts did not swing from side to side.[29]

Trivial as it may seem, it was characteristic of the detailed and comprehensive rules governing religious life. Prescriptions and proscriptions abounded and newcomers were faced with the formidable task of mastering and submitting to them in a relatively short time. The novitiate was the "boot camp" in which this learning took place, and the nun in charge of the program was the mistress of novices, or zelatrix.

The Code of Canon Law required the mistress to be at least thirty-five years old and ten years from first profession.[30] She had two principal tasks: preparing novices for the "profession day" in which they took their vows and expelling those considered unsuitable along the way. To achieve these tasks, she was expected to acquire a thorough knowledge of her novices through private conversations and discreet surveillance.[31] The role called for hauteur and *gravitas*, a solid knowledge of official dogma and ritual, and an aptitude for assessing character. According to the Rule of the Good Shepherd Sisters, the mistress was charged with rooting out as much as possible "all nonsense, tenderness, and weak fancies, of which the minds, principally of persons of the sex, are frequently numbed and weakened, so that, as valiant women, they may perform actions of firm and solid perfection."[32]

Faced with such an agenda, mistresses were often chosen for their unbending wills and toughness of character. Sister Leo, the mistress with the Daughters of Charity of St Vincent de Paul in the mid-1950s, had a reputation for "sternness that bordered on callousness." She made it clear to her novices from the beginning that she would tolerate no levity, incompetence, or carelessness, and that she expected perfection and strict adherence to every rule.[33] Mother Regina, in charge of the Sisters of the Holy Cross novitiate in the early 1950s, was known to be harsh. If a rule were broken, she was always ready to reprimand her wayward novices as they knelt before her.[34] Mother Benedict, mistress with the Missionary Sisters of the Holy Rosary (Bryn Mawr, Pennsylvania) in the early 1960s, instilled fear in her novices with constant corrections – of a word mispronounced, a candlestick slightly out of position, a fingerprint that had evaded the dust mop.[35] Other mistresses were described by their former novices as "chilly," "hard as nails," "large and domineering," "a perfect drill instructor," "a Prussian general," "threatening," and "spooky."[36]

But the harshness was not universal. Sister Adelaide of Jesus, mistress with the Sisters of Charity of Providence (Seattle) between 1937 and 1953, was described by her novices as kind, patient, and a true mother, who was never too busy to listen.[37] Sister Pauline, mistress with the Sisters of St Joseph (Cleveland) in the mid-1940s, was a refined and educated woman who loved history and classical music. She was remembered as "a firm but kind and loving mother."[38]

Sister Ruth, mistress with the Sisters of Charity of St Elizabeth, was elderly and past her prime by the mid-1950s, although she remained on the job. Her strength lay in an uncanny instinct that told her when a rule had been broken. She irritated her novices by beginning her morning instructions, which tended to ramble, with a group recitation of a childish rhyme, such as this one:

Good day my guardian angel
The night is past and gone;
And thou hadst watched before me
At midnight as at dawn

The day is now before me
And as it glides away –
O help me well to make of it
A good and holy day.

Sister Ruth was later replaced by Sister Regina, who better fitted the mistress/zelatrix stereotype, being regal, aloof, and intimidating.[39]

Canon law prescribed that the novitiate last for at least one year and provided guidelines on what should take place during this time of formation.[40] Congregations had some flexibility in interpreting what was to be done in the "canonical year," as it was called, but the pattern of learning tended to be similar. It was common practice to provide a further period of formation – an "apostolic year" – in which novices acquired some of the professional skills and knowledge required to staff their congregation's institutions. We shall focus on the canonical year – the key experience in learning to become a nun.

One of the defining characteristics of the monastic tradition was isolation from secular society. And while the institutional work of active congregations meant compromises in this respect, for a novice's canonical year the isolation was total. The Rule of the Sisters of Charity of Providence (Seattle) described the novitiate as a time of "delightful solitude" from "the pursuits of a seductive world." To profit from the solitude, novices were expected to "renounce all former affections they entertained in the world, to strive to eradicate from their hearts all attachments contrary to divine love, and to so completely change their habits that they [would] no longer be the same when they leave this place of seclusion."[41]

Madeline DeFrees readily accepted the isolation during her novitiate with the Holy Names Sisters. She reasoned that, to fill her mind with things of the spirit, she had to empty it of distractions caused by newspapers and secular books. It appeared to be an extreme measure, she admitted, but was surely worth it when the goal of everlasting happiness was taken into account.[42] Patricia Grueninger, on the other hand, recalled that she and some of her fellow novices with the Daughters of Charity of St Vincent de Paul sometimes inquired about the world outside and were reprimanded for doing so. Only years later did she learn about the civil-rights movement, the birth of rock 'n' roll, and other developments that marked the late 1950s.[43] Rachel Ethier only heard of Sputnik in May 1958 – more than six months after its launch – when a priest mentioned it in passing during a lecture to the Daughters of Wisdom novices.[44] During Giem's novitiate with the Carmelites in Salt Lake City in 1962, news of the death of Marilyn Monroe somehow leaked into the convent, but the novices were told nothing of the Vatican Council that was assembling in Rome.[45] In the same year, when Nancy Sodeman was a novice with the Missionary Sisters of the Holy Rosary (Bryn Mawr, Pennsylvania), she was told by the mistress to pray hard because of a grave situation in world politics, but no details of the Cuban missile crisis were provided.[46]

While postulants had restricted access to their families, novices had none whatsoever. Even when human compassion might have warranted flexibility on the matter, there was none. When Deborah Larsen was a novice with the Sisters of Charity of the Blessed Virgin Mary (Dubuque, Iowa) in the early 1960s, word came that her mother had a brain tumour requiring surgery. She was denied permission to return home and provide assistance.[47] Eileen Nalevanko was completing her canonical year with the Benedictines in Minnesota in the late 1940s when her grandfather died. The mistress of novices, Sister Henrita Osendorf, took her aside and read part of a letter from her mother about the death. Nalevanko felt stunned and disconnected.[48]

The official view was that contact with family members was injurious to the religious spirit, and nuns-in-training had best become accustomed to separation. Saint Teresa of Avila was sometimes quoted as the authority for this policy: "For my part, I cannot conceive what attachment a nun can find in her relatives. By attachment to them she displeases God, and without being able to enjoy their amusements she shares in all their troubles."[49]

The novitiate followed a similar pattern to the postulancy, but was marked by a greater intensity. Each day followed a strict schedule of prayer, physical labour, and study under the watchful eye of the mistress of novices. Mary Gilligan summed up the qualities expected of a novice: eagerness to follow orders, willingness to work to the point of exhaustion, and the ability to apply an even coat of wax.[50] Nuns-in-training spent a considerable part of their waking hours in physical labour – cleaning, cooking, laundering, gardening, and caring for the elderly and sick members of the congregation.[51] Not all "charges," as these tasks were known, were equally desirable. In the novitiate of the Sisters, Servants of the Immaculate Heart of Mary (Monroe, Michigan), anything in the chapel was highly prized. At the other end of the scale, the most dreaded task was removing bags of sanitary towels from the toilets, which could only be done at a prescribed time and by a prescribed route to avoid embarrassing reminders of women's biology.[52] According to Camille D'Arienzo, a novice with the Sisters of Mercy in Syosset, New York, in 1953, chores were made much harder than necessary "with hours spent washing the already clean and polishing the already polished."[53]

The heavy habits, which could not be removed even in hot weather, made matters worse. One novice mistress described the discomfort as an opportunity "to grow in humility and self-abnegation."[54] For Father Daniel Lord, domestic labour was an imitation of the perfect life of the Virgin Mary, who "never ceased to be a queen even when she handled a broom, washed the dishes, set a table, made a bed, cooked a meal."[55]

Religious instruction was the most important element in the novitiate program. Novice mistresses were expected to be thoroughly conversant with Church doctrine and ritual, so that they might impart this knowledge. While the content could vary somewhat with each congregation, it is possible to generalize about what was learned.

The Holy Rule, or constitution, of a congregation formed a core part of the instruction in religion. The constitution was a detailed guide to the governance structures and purpose of a congregation. It defined the responsibilities and powers of those at different ranks in the institutional hierarchy, as well as the codes of conduct expected of all. There were also privileges: a Sister of St Joseph, for instance, was entitled to plenary indulgences on certain feast days and anniversaries. She could accrue them to herself or assign them to a soul languishing in Purgatory.[56]

The prayers and hymns of the Divine Office or the Little Office of Our Lady, to which novices had been introduced when they were postulants, now had to be mastered in their entirety. Since the words were in Latin, this presented an extra challenge. Giem asked for and received special permission to write English translations of parts of the Office on index cards, so that she might understand what she was chanting. The chaplain, unimpressed with her attitude, explained that prayers were more contemplative when you were "in the presence of God in a cloud of unknowing."[57] Sodeman, on the other hand, was exhilarated while singing the Office, imagining herself in a heavenly temple with the saints forming a choir on either side.[58]

Sister Claver, mistress with the Sisters of the Third Order of St Francis (Pittsburgh) in the early 1960s, required her novices to pray while walking through the graveyard. Her explanation for this practice was: "Prayerful thinking about those of the order who lived holy lives and who now rest in the beautiful convent cemetery gives inspiration to the novice for developing in her own self a true spirit of close union with God in prayer."[59]

The Code of Canon Law was part of the curriculum, and in particular the sections that regulated religious orders and congregations. A more general history of monasticism might also be provided. It was normal practice for novices to study the history of their own congregation, and this was presented in the heroic and hagiographic manner.[60] If a member of a congregation had written a book of a spiritual nature, it might be added to the required readings. For example, novices with the Sisters of Charity of St Elizabeth read Sister Miriam Teresa's *Greater Perfection*, a book on how to achieve mystical union with God. The congregation was campaigning for the canonization of the author, a woman of great piety, as manifested in her habit of drinking dirty dishwater.[61]

Following a pattern already established during the postulancy, Thomas à Kempis, St Teresa of Avila, and St John of the Cross were the favourite authors when it came to selecting spiritual readings for novices. The New Testament and the Baltimore Catechism – all 499 questions and answers – were also on this list.[62] During the

1940s, novices with the Sisters, Servants of the Immaculate Heart of Mary (Monroe, Michigan) spent much of their classroom time memorizing passages from Cotel et al., *Catechism of the Vows for the Use of Religious*, a book that presented knowledge in short questions and answers.[63] This instructional approach was also evident elsewhere. In their final examinations on theology and on the New Testament, Maryknoll novices were asked to answer the following questions, among others:

> Can you prove that we are placed on earth to glorify God?
> What is imperfection? Give two examples.
> What are the three kinds of mortification that are most
>   pleasing to God and always free from danger?
> State five new laws promulgated in the Sermon on the Mount.
> Name a miracle showing Our Lord's control over devils,
>   death, nature, and the minds of men.[64]

During the early 1950s the Sisters of Charity of Providence (Seattle) employed the services of Father A. Throckmorton to deliver a course on theology. There were lectures on the sacraments, the nature of Christ's divinity, the end of the world, and on Purgatory and Hell and why people were sent there. Throckmorton informed his novice listeners that while immaterial souls rather than bodies ended up in Hell, they were nonetheless tormented by flames as if they had bodily senses. There was a combative tone to the lectures, and he rarely lost an opportunity to bash Protestantism for its errors. Protestants had no understanding of divine grace, he pointed out, while John Wycliffe (died 1384), a forerunner of the Reformation and a critic of clerical authority, was described as "that slovenly Englishman." Protestants were wrong, he was fond of saying, on the question of Mary, her virginity, and the immaculate conception. His proof for the immaculate conception went like this: "It is repugnant that Christ would live in the womb of a woman who had been in sin." And Mary's statement to the Angel Gabriel in Luke 1:34, "I know not man," was the only evidence needed for the doctrine that she was a virgin "before, during, and after her delivery of Christ."[65]

Novices followed a strict schedule of prayer, physical labour, and study to prepare them for profession day, when they would take the vows of poverty, chastity, and obedience. The behaviours required in the "evangelical counsels" were not to be embraced only after the vows were taken; rather they needed years of practice to ensure that the commitments were not entered into lightly. The novitiate was much more than preparation for the vows; it was a carefully monitored practice of them that built on habits first acquired during the postulancy. There was no question of a "last fling" before profession day.

It was claimed that, in living according to the vows, a nun was imitating the life of Christ and removing impediments to serving him without reserve. Father Felix Kirsch explained it like this: "The vows represent the voluntary giving up of the objects of human desires, and hence remove the three chief obstacles that stand in the way of the perfect reign of love and virtue in our hearts. These obstacles are the greed of gold, the lust of sensual pleasures, and the inordinate attachment to our own will and our own opinion."[66]

The Holy Rule of the Good Shepherd Sisters put it this way: "They [the Sisters] ought to serve Him by most pure chastity, poverty stripped of all things, and obedience founded on perfect abnegation of their own will, since such is the example He has given them."[67]

We shall examine each of the vows to see how novices experienced them, beginning with obedience. Obedience as imitation of Christ was explained to novices in this way: Christ knew that it was God's will that he suffer and die on the cross, and he accepted that fate without questioning. God's will for novices, just as it was for postulants, was a bit different: it was anything that a superior commanded. Novices with the Sisters of Charity of Providence (Seattle) were urged to obey "without knowing why, without reasoning, without murmuring, without examining, without questioning." Obedience, they were told, meant letting themselves "be led by another like a blind person or again to be like the wax or clay in the hands of an artisan."[68]

At an Institute of Spirituality for nuns at the University of Notre Dame in the 1950s, Father Paul Philippe was asked if the mistress of novices should adopt modern methods of teaching in her instructions. He said no, explaining that the modern pedagogy increasingly employed in schools was designed to transform young people into independent adults. But such methods had no place in a religious institute that prepared novices for lifelong dependence on superiors. "Training in initiative could go too far," he said, "and then there would not be training in obedience."[69]

Most novices accepted this reasoning, and they had ample opportunity to practice obedience in submitting to the myriad of rules that marked their days. Being required to ask permission for the most mundane of tasks provided further practice.[70] Deborah Larsen recalled her willingness to clean toilets or teach in Memphis if her superiors so commanded, since it was God's will and could hardly be questioned.[71]

The vow of poverty entailed renouncing the personal ownership of material goods, just as Jesus had done. The Rule of the Sisters of the Immaculate Heart of Mary (Hollywood) explained it as follows: "The virtue of poverty inclines the heart to detach itself from all affection to temporal goods. It is the object of the first of the Beatitudes, as well as the practical imitation of Him Who was born in a stable, Who died naked on a cross, and Who between the crib and the cross often had not whereon to lay His head."[72] Father Daniel Lord provided further clarification: "Money buys opportunities for sin, notably for sins of impurity. Such opportunities are not nearly so easy to find on nothing a year. Shows and magazines and books and movies demand money; the absence of the money has a way of leaving the mind remarkably serene."[73]

However, this did not mean genuine poverty in the sense of being malnourished, homeless, or facing an uncertain future. Many congregations were in fact quite wealthy, but their possessions were held collectively rather than individually. Larsen reasoned that this vow presented few problems, since convents provided all the necessities of life – food, clothing, and shelter – as well as educational and career opportunities and a comfortable retirement home. And a sister wouldn't even have to worry about paying the bills.[74]

Being looked after in this way was one of the attractions of religious life as presented by the recruitment professionals. But there was one potential problem. The Rule of the Sisters of Charity of Providence (Seattle) specified that a sister who left or was dismissed could not "seek compensation for no matter what services she [might] have rendered the Institute."[75] To give this assertion legitimacy if it were ever challenged, newly admitted novices were presented with a form written in legal jargon. In signing this form in front of witnesses, the novice entered into a contract requiring "the first party," or congregation, to furnish room, board, laundry, and health care to the "second party," the novice/nun, in return for work she agreed to perform "free of any charge whatsoever and without compensation from the said first party other than the considerations heretofore recited."[76]

This arrangement was not unique. Shortly after entering the Daughters of Charity of St Vincent de Paul (Baltimore, Maryland), Patricia Grueninger and her fellow novices were asked to sign an agreement relinquishing their right to remuneration for any work they did in the convent if they were ever to leave. It never occurred to Grueninger at the time that her work might be worthy of pay, and when she returned to the world twenty-two years later, she walked away with nothing, not even entitlement to social security.[77]

According to the brief descriptions we have of the life of Jesus, he remained chaste or uninvolved physically with anyone. Father Bernard Mullahy put it this way: "Christ was chaste; born of a Virgin, He lived a life of the most radiant virginity the world has ever seen. It is the desire to imitate the radiance of this purity that draws the religious to make a vow of perpetual chastity."[78] The vow meant that all sensual or sexual intimacy with someone of the opposite or of the same sex, or with yourself, was forbidden. One former nun described it as being "pretty much dead from the neck down."[79] It will be recalled that one of the concerns prompting parents to oppose their daughters' vocations was the fear that they might not understand what they were giving up when taking the vow of chastity. The confident reassurances of Fathers Godfrey Poage and Jude Senieur – that novices would be in full possession of the facts before their vows – were not always convincing. The claim demands examination.

In Marie Gass's interviews with seventy-three ex-nuns, fifty-five answered the question respecting their prior knowledge of sex upon entering the convent. Of those respondents, thirteen confessed to complete ignorance.[80] Of the forty-two who claimed to be informed, many admitted to being vague on details. Fran Fisher's interviews with forty-nine former nuns revealed that very few in the sample had "informed sexual knowledge" when they began their postulancies and novitiates. Many admitted to being afraid of sexuality, because it was unknown and mysterious.[81]

There is further evidence from the autobiographies of former nuns. Deborah Larsen, upon observing two of her fellow novices gazing at one another, noted: "Most of us barely knew how men and women made love, much less – and we didn't want to think about it – women and women."[82] Grace Stolz, a novice at sixteen, recalled that "Our training did not allow us to even admit that sexuality was a normal part of life." When she left religious life after twenty-five years, the urges she had suppressed as a teenager were awakened once again when she met a childhood friend named Dick.[83] Susan Bassler, who became a novice with the Ursulines on Long Island, New York, in 1960, knew nothing about sex, having being sheltered from anything vulgar or erotic during her youth. Here are her words: "I hadn't had a serious boyfriend or a passionate kiss. I didn't consider myself abnormal, because I knew others who were living the same way. I didn't even hear the word 'masturbation' until I was in college. It was alluded to, of course. But I didn't do it. I was 'saving myself.'"[84]

If many or even most novices were "innocents" respecting sexuality, what did they learn about it before making the commitment to chastity? Larsen and her fellow novices were given a book that explained what she called "the hydraulics of sex," with explicit references to penis, vagina, and penetration. In discussing the book, the mistress admitted that sex was "very pleasurable," but since she had never actually experienced it herself, she added that "it would be hard to understand the particulars of the gratification." Furthermore, she had discussed the subject with a married laywoman who had assured her that she "didn't much enjoy sex and that it was something of a nuisance." With this insight at her disposal, Larsen reasoned that the vow of chastity would not be such a hardship after all.[85]

Nancy Sodeman's experience was similar. In a private interview shortly before profession day, the mistress explained the basics of "the marital act" so that she would understand the sacrifice entailed in the vow. In describing the interactions of penis and vagina,

Mother Benedict assured Sodeman that the act was "not very enjoyable" and often painful for the woman, while the man received great pleasure.[86]

The record of novitiate programs in preparing their young women for an informed commitment to chastity was at best mixed, and there were far too many cases in which novices were kept completely in the dark. Margaret Lynch was already a junior professed nun with the Sisters of Charity of St Elizabeth (Convent Station, New Jersey) when she learned how human reproduction worked. Her spiritual director, Sister Caritas, arranged to have a sister who was a registered nurse lecture the juniors on the subject in order to combat ignorance. Lynch learned much from these lectures and, judging by the questions from her fellow juniors, ignorance about sexuality was widespread. Some thought that kissing could cause pregnancy.[87] It is well to remember that these junior professed nuns had already taken the vow of chastity.[88]

A contemporary religious writer, Father John McGoey, readily acknowledged the problem of sexual ignorance among "most religious," and in doing so lent further skepticism to the assertions of Senieur and Poage respecting novices and their preparation for the vow of chastity. Here are his words:

> There is no reasonable excuse for withholding full knowledge of sex from those making the vow of chastity. Yet most religious do not have this knowledge. Any court of the land would consider it illegal to sell something to a client ignorant of what he was getting, with as little knowledge about it as the average religious has about the material of her vow. Lack of sufficient knowledge invalidates the ordinary contract. Yet through ignorance or narrowness, due knowledge is even withheld from many taking the vow of chastity.[89]

McGoey's views were not widely shared, however. Many of his contemporaries held to the idea that ignorance was the best antidote to the problem of sexuality. Father Paulo Provera, for example, conceded that curiosity about "natural processes of which one is ignorant" was not in itself sinful, but attempting to satisfy that curiosity could lead to "a lot of trouble." "In general," he advised," it is dangerous to read books on the subject, for this can be a way of indulging in fancies of the imagination; many begin their perversion in this way."[90]

Perversion may seem like a strong term, but it was used as a generic descriptor for two phenomena that novice mistresses and spiritual advisors believed were poor indicators of success in chastity: particular friendships and solitary vice. Father James Alberione, in a book of advice for mothers superior, warned them to be vigilant for "abnormal sexual attraction towards persons of the same sex" among candidates for the religious life, since it was "very difficult to correct this tendency when it [was] accentuated."[91] And in a collection of conferences for religious, Father Frederick Hoeger reminded his readers that the Devil did not abandon his efforts to stimulate the sexual instinct among those who had dedicated themselves to "spiritual motherhood." In fact, sometimes Satan even tried to "sidetrack it into abnormal outlets."[92] Among the Sisters of Providence (St Mary-of-the-Woods) novices were obliged to draw up lists of the people with whom they had spent time during recreation. The novice mistress examined the lists to see if any patterns of frequent association were developing.[93] Mother Mary Hubert Manion, mistress with the Sisters, Servants of the Immaculate Heart of Mary (Monroe, Michigan) between 1938 and 1956, kept a close eye on novices who got on well with one another, lest the influence of Satan be detected. Her rule governing the number of people socializing together was: "Seldom one, never two, always three or more."[94]

Impediments placed in the way of finding a willing partner were helpful, but there was still the problem of what you could do when you were all alone. Some writers considered masturbation a problem of such magnitude that it constituted a virtual rejection of Christ's call. Here is Father Alberione: "The solitary sin, too, is not easily corrected, yet after a sufficient test, persons once guilty of it can be admitted to religious life. But a long test and sure proof is required; at times it is necessary to wait three years and even more to make sure there are no more falls."[95]

Since the combined postulancy and novitiate typically lasted for almost three years, there was lots of time for "a long test and sure proof." Father Felix Kirsch was equally adamant on this point. He advised an extensive period of probation to ensure that "the habit of mortal sin" was really conquered, especially in cases where there were "overpowering outbursts of nature."[96] Father Philippe acknowledged that his fellow male experts on the subject could not agree on the actual length of the "sufficiently protracted period of complete victory" without a "fall" that a novice was supposed to demonstrate before being admitted to her vows. There was little hope, he surmised, for those who sinned "by themselves with frenzy." But if a novice showed determination to conquer her habit by making small and constant sacrifices, he believed that she should be given a chance, even if it meant, at the discretion of the mistress, extending the novitiate by six months to ensure total "victory."

But how would the mistress know of such delicate matters? Father Philippe suggested that if a mistress gained the complete confidence of her novices, disclosure would be forthcoming. A novice who kept her habit of solitary pleasure a secret, however, would have to admit it in Confession, since it was a mortal sin and a ticket to damnation. The confessor would therefore know all and would advise her to reveal her habit to the mistress. If she refused, the confessor could compel her to inform the mistress that he opposed her admission to the vows, and the right decision would then be taken.[97]

How should the novice combat temptations against chastity? According to Alberione, erotic fantasies should be "banished at once" without thinking about them. "It is in this flight that safety lies," he advised. "The Blessed Virgin is to be invoked and then the mind is to be turned to other things."[98] Hoeger suggested keeping busy, noting that very few religious had much time to spare in any case. He also championed a bit of pain: "Planned mortification, with purity in view, is almost a necessity for the preservation of chastity."[99] René Biot and Pierre Galimard, French doctors who advised the Church on medical matters connected to the religious life, agreed: "It may be opportune with certain subjects to advise corporal penances, and a voluntary privation – even a few strokes of the discipline is often good training."[100] Father Hubert van Zeller, in a 1957 book of advice for monks and nuns, had this to say: "To prevent ourselves from pampering the body we have to chastise it. If we do not chastise it, it will, with its constant demand to be pampered, chastise us. Even when we weaken, listening to our lower nature, we get no peace; our higher nature reproaches us."[101] Writing a few years later, Father John E. Moffatt advised nuns, young and old, against softness, sloth, idle dreaming, and "overindulgence in delicacies," adding: "The occasional sting of mortification is a sine qua non to maintain the soul in a wholesome, healthy state to meet and repulse the assaults made by the foe upon the angelic virtue."[102]

Mortification, or self-inflicted pain, was not unknown among congregations at the time, although it began to fall into disuse in the 1960s. Midge Turk received early instruction from her novice mistress, Mother Regina, on how to make flagellation whips from venetian-blind cords. She and her fellow novices were told only to use the whips on their bare backs, legs, and buttocks in private and at a specified hour on Wednesday and Friday afternoons. They were not supposed to draw blood.[103] The Ursulines of Long Island, New York, had a similar practice when Susan Bassler entered their novitiate in 1960. One of the first recreational activities for the novices was the fashioning of personal whips in five strands from knotted twine. The strands represented the "five holy wounds of Jesus." At bedtime on Fridays, these young women, at a given signal, lifted their nightgowns and lashed themselves while reciting the Lord's Prayer.[104] The Sisters of St Joseph issued whips to their novices in both Baltimore and Cleveland, to be used on their bare flesh as the occasion warranted. The practice made sense to Mary Jane Masterson, since it allowed her to make reparation for her own sins and for those of others.[105]

There was a long tradition of self-imposed physical suffering in Catholic monasticism, and many prominent theologians and doctors of the Church advocated such practices to suppress the annoyance of sensual feelings. An oft-repeated story was that of St Benedict, who threw himself naked into a growth of nettles and thorns to subdue the flesh.[106] In addition to mortification there was always scope for individual novices to strive for perfection by the voluntary rejection of comforts and pleasures to combat the temptations of the world. The following excerpt from St Alphonso di Ligouri's *The True Spouse of Jesus Christ* (1760) serves as an example:

In the lives of the ancient Fathers we read of a large Community of nuns who never tasted fruit or wine. Some of them took food only once every day; others never ate a meal, except after two or three days of rigorous abstinence; all were clothed and even slept in haircloth. I do not require such austerities from religious of the present day; but is it too much for them to take the discipline several times in a week? To wear a chain round some part of the body till the hour of dinner? Not to approach the fire in winter on some day in each week, and during novenas of devotion? To abstain from fruit and sweet meats?[107]

Forms of deprivation and humiliation could also be imposed by the mistress as part of the ritual known as the Chapter of Faults. The Chapter was held every week, every two weeks, or once a month, depending on the congregation. The Rule of the Good Shepherd Sisters, for example, required the mistress to conduct it every Wednesday, during which "she shall correct them, instructing and mortifying them, according to the subjects of them, and afterwards she shall say something general, for their improvement and spiritual profit, as she shall think suitable."[108]

Unlike Confession, which was private and dealt with sins, the Chapter brought a class of novices together in a room where they were required to admit to violations of the rules in the presence of the mistress and of one another. They could also, "in charity," accuse their companions of violations. The faults included breaking silence, laughing, looking at one's reflection in a windowpane, spending too much time with one person, slamming a door, or even feeling lonely or homesick.[109] Grueninger recalled one of her fellow novices admitting that she had addressed a cat that she had encountered while taking out the garbage.[110]

Upon publicly airing their faults, the novices begged for forgiveness and kissed the floor. The mistress then imposed punishments commensurate with the gravity of the faults. The punishment might be longer periods of silence, the cancellation of recreation, saying prayers with arms outstretched, or whatever else was thought to be corrective.[111] Sister Philomena, the mistress with the Oblate Sisters of Providence (Baltimore, Maryland) in the 1950s, liked to inflict silent kneeling in front of a crucifix for an indefinite period on her imperfect novices.[112] At the Ursuline novitiate in Long Island, New York, infractions related to particular friendships, such as spending time alone with another, were punished by having the novice eat a meal while kneeling on the refectory floor.[113] The Daughters of Wisdom (Litchfield, Connecticut) had a uniquely humiliating penance for its disobedient novices: kissing the feet of a fellow sister in public.[114]

Father Philippe advised mistresses to choose punishments with some direct connection to the faults. For example, a habitually untidy novice might be assigned to rearranging library books properly on the shelf, while a novice with muddy footwear might find herself cleaning a fellow novice's shoes for a week.[115] The mistress with the Sisters of St Joseph (Baltimore) in the 1950s reminded her novices that the Chapter was a rehearsal for Judgment Day, when all faults would be revealed and punished.[116] In order to mitigate the unpleasantness of the experience, novices were sometimes reminded that St Gertrude had once had a vision in which she saw the prayers recited in Chapter as pearls falling before the throne of God.[117]

Regular confession, the Chapter, and constant surveillance were the institutional instruments designed to identify and root out inappropriate behaviour and attitudes. The imposition of conformity did not, however, come easily. Sister Paul Miriam, mistress at the Maryknoll mother-house novitiate in the late 1940s and early 1950s, felt overwhelmed by the number of novices under her charge and her consequent inability to get to know each one of them thoroughly. Under the circumstances, discipline was difficult to maintain, a fact noted disapprovingly by Mother M. Columba, the superior. Mother Columba observed a decline in the "sense of religious modesty" among some novices, who went to the bathroom attired in loose kimonos "flowing in the breeze." She urged Sister Paul Miriam to apply a "goodly amount of drilling" on the question of proper decorum.[118]

For many who went through the experience, the novitiate was a time of restrictions and constraints that often seemed petty and unnecessary. Camille D'Arienzo had this to say: "Minor infractions were perceived as indicative of monumental flaws. Psychic energy was expended on trivia and endless hours were wasted on conversations and projects far removed from the reality of our friends and relatives in the real world."[119]

For one of Gerelyn Hollingsworth's informants, the imposition of conformity was a major source of difficulty: "We were not supposed to be intelligent or clever. We were not supposed to be attractive or singular in any way, just good little peas in a pod."[120] Another informant recalled resenting what she felt was a "return to childhood."[121] Grueninger, too, observed that much of what she was expected to do as a novice was "childish" and that her superiors treated her and her companions as children rather than as maturing women.[122]

Similar constraints were evident in the way recreation was conducted. While some novitiates allowed for physical activity in the form of softball or volleyball, far too often recreation was given over to card games, darning tattered garments, or listening to an older nun tell of her life.[123] Talking was allowed, but, as one former novice recalled, it had its limitations: "Since we hardly knew what was going on in the world, we had no topics for conversation. Minor events took on great importance."[124]

Convent life was simple and predictable, and for some, therein lay its appeal. In her fictional account of the novitiate, Sister Reilly provided a glimpse of that simplicity in a brief dialogue between novices during recreation hour: "Sister Denis stops cutting out her angel to remark: 'Look at us, will you? Straight-backed chairs, no radio, same room every night. Yet I don't mind telling you that I'm enjoying myself.' 'Me too,' confirms Sister Cecilia, 'a clear conscience, good company, lots of laughs, no need to make an impression. This is the life.'"[125]

The narrowness and restrictions of it all often had the effect of causing young women who were once spontaneous and fun-loving to become tense, subdued, and incapable of expressing emotion.[126] It could also induce anxieties. Grueninger was plagued with a constant sense of inadequacy during her novitiate. She never felt she could live up to the demanding standards of personal piety that were expected.[127] Sister Frederic had a similar experience and constantly struggled to overcome pride. At monthly retreats she agonized over her shortcomings and pleaded with Jesus for forgiveness and help: "Oh, my God, with what feelings of remorse I write down; remorse for having proved unfaithful to my promises and for having rejected Your love."[128] Mother Catherine Thomas wondered if perfection would elude her: "Will I be able to see, to remember, that my dying to self will bring life to the world? Will I be able to choose suffering and thereby ease the Savior's sorrow and lift the world's cross of sin?"[129]

And there were doubts in the minds of many about the wisdom of completing the novitiate. The doubts never left Stolz, who feared turning into a "sour, crabby, joy-killing nun."[130] After a year in the program, Larsen began to question her vocation. Her friend Tessa had left, and she wondered about the life she was leading out in the world. Whenever these thoughts appeared, she blamed the Devil and banished them from her mind.[131]

A number of Gass's informants had serious doubts about their vocations while in the novitiate. Doris, who entered in 1956, discussed the possibility of leaving with a retreat master, as well as her fear of damnation should she do so. The priest just laughed and said nothing that might assuage her fears. She stayed until 1963. Kathleen and Lorna, who also entered in the mid-1950s, decided to leave, even when pressured by their novice mistresses to stay. Lorna was told that she would never be happy on the outside; Kathleen was warned that she would never be allowed to return. When Donna, who left in 1965, expressed doubts about her vocation to her novice mistress, she was given the usual explanation: demonic temptation. She decided to leave anyway, and her departure was conducted in a punitive manner, perhaps to discourage others who might be of a similar disposition: "I was given the cold shoulder, and the door was slammed on me. I was given no money, goods, or advice – just warnings. I was broken hearted at not being able to say my goodbyes, but happy to leave."[132]

Departures from the novitiate of the Poor Handmaids of Jesus Christ in the 1950s and early 1960s were mainly voluntary, although a small number were considered unsuitable and were asked to leave. Three novices left in 1954. Anna Marie P. had little "real knowledge" of religion. Edith F. was persuaded by her mother to return home. Joan D. "didn't feel she wanted to give up mixed social customs of smoking, drinking, etc." Another three left in 1959, two of whom found the vows challenging. Pauline B. "had difficulty with obedience and proper channelling of affections," while Judith Ann N., a former aspirant, "craved human affection and companionship beyond that proper to religious life." The third novice in this group, Mary Jo T. had spent a few months in the novitiate in 1956 before leaving. Readmitted in August 1958, she remained "unsettled and dissatisfied." When she made her final departure in December 1959, she did so with the encouragement of the congregation, since "her influence on the group was not good."[133]

Among the Maryknoll Sisters, voluntary departures were attributed mainly to homesickness, dissatisfaction with religious life, and attraction to the married state. Rosemary B., who left the Maryknoll novitiate in Valley Park, Missouri, in 1948, found the religious life too hard and needed somebody in her life. That somebody was a former boyfriend, who was still interested in her even though they had not corresponded with one another since her entry.[134]

Around half of those who did not persevere in Valley Park during the 1940s and 1950s left of their own free will. The remainder were young women who were dismissed by the congregation for reasons as varied as: insufficient health, emotional instability, scrupulosity, and "uncorrected character traits which would make life miserable for associates in community life." Among those who did not "measure up" to expectations, we find five novices whose records indicate the kinds of "uncorrected character traits" that led to dismissal. Mary C. was described as highly emotional and burdened with exceptionally poor physical coordination that accentuated her nervousness, especially in sewing class. Mary Katherine M. was gifted academically and talented in the arts. But she lacked fervour and generosity and had not "improved in effort for bettering herself through religious life." Mary Elean N. was good at sewing and cooking, and was friendly and easygoing. Even so, she was a little lazy, could be hot-tempered, and had serious doubts about her vocation. Marilee S. was grateful and loving, but also shy, tense, and lacking in adaptability. Margaret M. was a qualified teacher and had a brother in the priesthood. These eminent qualifications were not enough, however, since she was "impudent, critical, and superficially spiritual."[135]

These remarks indicate the degree of scrutiny to which novices were subjected as they progressed towards the taking of vows. While congregations were keen to swell their ranks with new members, and pressured those who were wavering to stay if they were considered suitable, they were also ready to cull those judged potentially problematic. Dismissal could be swift in cases where behaviour imperilled what was expected in the vows. During Mary Gilligan's novitiate with the Sisters of Providence (St Mary-of-the-Woods), two of her companions struck up a "particular friendship" that they refused to relinquish, in spite of gossip and surveillance. It took only a week or two before they were sent away.[136] Patricia Marks joined the Religious Sisters Filippini novitiate (Morristown, New Jersey) in 1959, only to discover – and she refused to believe it at first – that one of the professed nuns was having "a very, very intense sexual relationship" with one of her fellow novices. The nun and novice left shortly afterwards.[137] When Joanne Howe was with the Sisters of St Joseph, one of her fellow novices "lost it" during chastisement by the assistant mistress and spoke up for herself. Her attitude was considered insufficiently subservient, and she was dismissed.[138] Lack of deference to those in authority or any challenge to the status quo were clearly unacceptable. As Camille D'Arienzo observed the departures from the Sisters of Mercy novitiate, she commented to a friend: "All the beauty, brains, and personality seem to be going home."[139]

What proportion of novices completed the program? Between 1950 and 1965 the Maryknoll Sisters admitted 1,250 novices to their American novitiates. Of these, 752 went on to take their first vows. For this two-year program the perseverance rate was 60 per cent.[140] What if you were expelled or withdrew voluntarily? Could you return? This sometimes happened, but the perseverance rate among returnees to the Maryknoll Sisters was very low. Sister Miriam Anthony, novice mistress at the mother house in the 1960s, opposed readmission except in exceptional circumstances in the belief that those who wished to return had failed to succeed in the world.[141]

In some congregations, novices professed their vows at the completion of their canonical year. It was quite common, however, to extend the novitiate by adding a "scholastic year" – a period of academic study or work, depending on the professional mandate of the congregation. No matter which custom prevailed, the official transition from novice to nun took place on "profession day." We shall follow this day as experienced by Sister Frederic.

The novices were led into the chapel where the profession ceremony was to take place by the Mother Provincial and the mistress of novices. They proceeded to the altar rail and knelt down. The priest addressed them with words from Psalm 45:10 "Harken, O daughter and consider, and incline thine ears; forget thy people and thy father's house, and the King shall desire thy beauty, for He is the Lord your God ... Take upon you the yoke of Jesus Christ, and learn from Him, Who is meek and humble of heart, and you shall find rest to your souls, for He has said: 'My yoke is sweet and my burden light.'"

The priest then asked if they desired to profess the Rule of St Francis, to which they replied: "We do desire it, Father, God assisting us." The choir joined in with the chant, "*Deo gratias*." At this point the novices prostrated themselves before the priest and he ordered them to rise with the following words: "Arise, O daughters, and prepare your lamps; behold the Spouse cometh; go ye forth to meet Him." As they rose, they said: "Behold, we come to Thee, most sweet Jesus, Whom we have always loved, sought, and desired." The prostrating and rising accompanied by the appropriate words took place three times in all. Mass was now celebrated and, just before each novice received Holy Communion, the priest held the host over her head while she proclaimed her vows of obedience, poverty, and chastity. At the conclusion of Mass, the novices made their way to the sanctuary, where the priest presented them with a crucifix, which was part of the Franciscan habit. Following this, the Mother Provincial exchanged their white novice veils for the black veils of professed nuns. They signed their names to a document containing the vows and the ceremony concluded with Benediction back in the chapel.[142]

With profession day, the novitiate was officially at an end and the young women who made their vows were now junior professed sisters or nuns. Their vows were temporary and would require renewal from time to time. About five years later – the actual waiting period depended on the congregation's Holy Rule – they took perpetual vows that committed them to a lifetime in religion, unless, of course, they changed their minds in the interim.

In spite of rules and surveillance, those who negotiated the formation period together did develop deep friendships. It was with some apprehension, therefore, that newly-professed nuns awaited news of their "mission" assignments, knowing that separation from friends was most probable. Shortly after profession with the Adrian Dominicans in August 1965, Patricia O'Donnell and the other sixty-three in her cohort gathered on the lawn of the mother house to learn of their school postings. She hoped to stay in Michigan and close to her novitiate friends, but it was not to be. St Patrick's Elementary School in Joliet, Illinois, was her destination, and she stayed there for three years. Her friends were scattered much further afield – some as far away as Arizona, California, and New Mexico.[143] Dispersals did not bring friendships to an end, however, since it was customary for congregations to reassemble their members at the mother house every summer for recreation and/or further study. Here friends became reacquainted in a setting much less restrained and regimented than the novitiate.[144]

CONCLUSION

The novitiate was a time of trial. It was a time of radical resocialization in preparation for the constraints of religious life. The essence of the experience was coming to understand the evangelical counsels and committing to them personally.

Obedience was the most important of the vows. It meant suppressing personal desires, inclinations, and any tendency to independent thinking, while submitting to the will of God as revealed in every command of the mistress. A novice practiced poverty in exchanging the comforts of modern life for the spartan accommodations of the convent and in agreeing to work without compensation in return for these accommodations. Chastity was the most difficult of the vows for many novices. Mistresses were well aware that stifling the desire for human intimacy never came easily, and they were especially vigilant for signs of weakness in this respect.

A novice learned that the convent was a community apart from the world and that its members were her new family. She had to sever ties with her biological family – to forget her father's house. And it was not just her family she had to renounce, but all unnecessary contact with "seculars" and their concerns. This was the ancient custom of cloister in its purest form. Cutting off the world allowed for exclusive attention to things of the spirit – which was the subject of the instructional program. Novices were being trained as nuns, not as teachers, nurses, or social workers.

The ability and willingness to adjust to the schedules of prayer, work, and study were not equally manifest in all who received the novice's veil. Some doubted if their vocations were genuine and departed voluntarily. Others with similar doubts were persuaded to stay. And watchful novice mistresses were ready to dismiss any they considered unsuitable for community life.

In their studies of convent life in France in the two centuries preceding the Revolution, Elizabeth Rapley and Geneviève Reynes devote entire chapters to the novitiate.[145] What they describe is remarkable for its striking similarity to novitiate programs and practices in twentieth-century America. Very little had changed in the formation of nuns over several centuries. The novitiate was a closed world within a semi-closed world, and novices were not only cut off from seculars and their concerns, but also from most members of the congregation. The asphyxiating regimentation that marked the experience was believed necessary to discipline human weakness; it was nothing less than a fundamental reshaping of mind and body, in which personal inclinations and desires were sacrificed.

The novitiate began with a wedding ceremony, and novices were constantly reminded that they should be worthy brides of their heavenly spouse. Those who persevered and took their first vows had met this test of worthiness.

CHAPTER 8

· ·

Postscript to 1965:

Longing for the

Fleshpots of Egypt?

[W]hen soft living and sensual gratification
have replaced the stark way of the cross,
when personal ambition and selfish desire
motivate all actions ... when grumbling
nuns and dissatisfied monks, whining for
the fleshpots of Egypt, finally fling out cries
of "Non Serviam" – then will the lights of
our monasteries and convents grow dim
and, like their European predecessors,
fade into complete darkness.[1]
Bruno M. Hagspiel, SVD (1957)

Sweet Jesus, grant that I may sincerely
appreciate my vocation, and ... may
never look back and long for the
fleshpots of Egypt.[2]
Sister Catherine Frederic (1953)

IF YOU MAKE YOUR WAY along Haddon Avenue in Camden, New Jersey, pause for a moment at the gothic stone buildings at Number 1500. For over a hundred years this was the address of the Dominican Nuns of the Perpetual Rosary, a cloistered congregation committed, as you may guess, to a continuous recital of the Rosary. It had once been over thirty strong, but by December 2013 death and a dearth of new recruits had reduced that number to four, one of them ninety-two years old. Since their vigil of prayer was no longer sustainable, it was announced that the nuns were to move to the Monastery of Mary the Queen in Elmira, New York, where they would join the eleven Dominicans already resident there. The convent buildings at 1500 Haddon Avenue were to be offered for sale. "We realize," explained a diocesan official, "the lack of vocations to the monastic life made it impossible for this community to continue as is in Camden."[3]

The story is neither exceptional nor unusual. Convent closures are commonplace and are often reported in the media under the headline, "Vanishing Nuns."[4] If you visit a convent that is not boarded up or sold today, it is likely to function as a retirement home for nuns of an advanced age. Postulants and novices, "bubbling over with ... peace and joy," as Jude Senieur put it back in the 1950s, are rarely to be seen. And nearby schools, where the retirees once taught, are shuttered or put to other purposes. Table 8.1 shows this trend playing out at the national level.[5]

The numbers are even more arresting when it is pointed out that the average age of the surviving fifty thousand or so nuns is seventy-four.[6] "We can't be maudlin about this," said Sister Mary Jean Ryan, who retired in 2011 at the age of seventy-three as chief executive of a network of Catholic hospitals. "I mean, yes, we are a dying breed. We are disappearing from the face of the earth and all that."[7] Could it be that American Catholics are also disappearing? Quite the opposite, in fact. Between 1965 and 2014, Catholics increased their numbers from 48.5 million to 76.7 million, a percentage increase of 61. Meanwhile, the nuns declined by 72 per cent.[8]

The figures are astonishing in another way as well: 1964 and 1965 marked the graduation from high school of the first waves of baby boomers – the generation of young Catholics that the nuns had worked so hard to educate. You might have expected the novitiates

TABLE 8.1 · NUMBER OF NUNS IN THE UNITED STATES
(1965 TO 2015)

1965	179,954
1975	135,225
1985	115,386
1995	90,809
2005	68,634
2015	48,546

to be overcrowded, but it was quite the opposite. The graduates were either in college or the workplace.

Clearly something went awry with a system that had been so successful in sustaining and aggrandizing itself for so long. There are two factors to be examined in accounting for this trend: the significant exodus from religious sisterhoods that began around 1965 and the failure of the sisterhoods to recruit and retain new members.[9] A related issue unavoidably demands our attention: how were Catholic schools affected by the virtual disappearance of teaching nuns?

Departures from religious life were rare before the 1960s, but they did happen. For example, 381 professed nuns went "through the narrow gate" in 1950. The overwhelming majority of them were in temporary vows, which is to say that they were in their first five years in religion.[10] Leaving was not easy in a psychological sense, since it was considered shameful and even scandalous. Nobody wanted to be labelled a "spoiled nun" or suspected of some great moral failing.[11] The physical part of it was complicated too, although there was nothing stopping you from just walking out the convent door in your habit. To do so, however, would be a mortal sin for nuns in temporary vows. Nuns in perpetual vows who departed spontaneously would be excommunicated.[12] The officially sanctioned mode of departure required an "indult of secularization" – a permanent release from your vows. It was also possible to request an "indult of exclaustration," a temporary release that could later be upgraded to permanent. Indults were granted either by the Congregation of Religious – the department of the Vatican Curia responsible for religious orders and congregations – or by the local bishop, depending on the canonical status of the congregation.[13] The advantage of following the approved procedure was that your dowry was returned to you and you might also receive a small cash settlement to ease your transition to secular life.[14]

Even by 1965, just as the great exodus was beginning to stir, leaving was not made easy. Mert and Mary, who left that year, described to Marie Gass how they had been grilled and shunned once they revealed their decision. Lilla, who left around the same time for the sake of her mental and physical health, was advised by a priest that her reasons were insufficient. When she refused to be dissuaded, she and two other defectors were removed from their convent early one morning and placed in another congregation's summer home to await their dispensations. "Never tell anyone about the convent life, at the risk of your soul," they were warned before their release.[15]

Why, then, did convent defections turn from a steady drip prior to the 1960s to a major flood during that decade? We shall seek the answer in a complicated constellation of developments connected with the Church's adaptation to the modern world.

It will be recalled that the Sister Formation Conference put measures in place during the 1950s to ensure that nuns received appropriate training before taking up teaching or other professions. Some congregations had their own colleges, making them the logical and convenient places for their members to study. But most nuns were obliged to pursue their higher studies in Catholic or non-Catholic institutions where they found themselves sharing classrooms with seculars, many of whom were not even of their faith. Their courses often challenged them to question and to think for themselves, while bringing them into contact with mainstream American values, such as participatory democracy, freedom of expression, the right to due process, and empiricism – the idea that conclusions should be reached based on reasoning and observed evidence. Moreover, campus life allowed for access to newspapers, radio, and television, and even the simple pleasure of eating in a restaurant. That nuns returning from college to convent found the transition difficult is easy to understand.[16] Their degrees turned out to be more than mere credentials or badges of professional legitimacy; they were windows on a world and way of thinking that were alien to the very culture of the cloister.

By 1960 or thereabouts, many nuns were questioning the constraints on their lives – authoritarianism, impractical habits, isolation from the world, and so forth. The same was true for the new wave of postulants and novices who seemed imbued with the "modern spirit." Girls and young women who only recently had watched television and driven cars could not understand why these were forbidden in the convent. They were independent-minded, rather than docile, to the exasperation of their mistresses.[17]

In 1963 Sister Catherine Fuhrmann was appointed mistress of novices with the Sisters of Divine Providence (San Antonio, Texas), and she immediately detected that something was amiss. She identified the problem as a greater assertiveness on the part of the new generation of novices who "were very vocal" in questioning age-old practices such as enclosure, silence, and restrictions on friendship: "Many times they did not understand a rule and wanted to know why we had it. Sometimes it was difficult to explain it to them. In my formation we did not question the rules, but for them rules were no longer 'the Gospel truth.'"[18]

Something was indeed amiss. Many nuns, and especially younger and better-educated ones, were growing impatient with the status quo. Two academics at Fordham University, in observing the crisis that was beginning to confront the convent system, had this to say: "She [the nun] is not only wrapped in a religious costume as contemporary as a suit of armor; she is entangled in myriad rules and restrictions of staggering pettiness."[19]

But change was in the air, even though few could foretell the form or direction it would take. In November 1960 John F. Kennedy was elected to the presidency, the first Catholic to hold that office. It marked the end of the Church's isolation in America. Catholics were no longer marginalized ethnics, but increasingly assimilated into middle-class suburbia.[20] A year earlier, the newly elected Pope John XXIII had called on his bishops to assemble in Rome for the Second Vatican Council. The council, which ultimately took place between 1962 and 1965, was instructed to adapt Church practices to modern times.

A new open-mindedness was immediately evident in that representatives of Protestant and Orthodox churches were granted observer status at the council, a most unusual departure. It signalled that the Roman Catholic Church was no longer claiming to be the sole avenue to salvation. And one of the documents emerging from the deliberations rejected the allegation that the Jews had been responsible for Christ's death – an idea at the root of two millennia of anti-Semitism. For practising Catholics, a number of modernizations were immediately felt in their weekly routines: the Mass was now celebrated in the vernacular rather than in Latin and penitential practices, such as abstention from meat on Fridays, were relaxed.[21] The liturgical calendar was also revised, resulting in the elimination of feast days for some saints of antiquity who were now acknowledged to have never existed.[22] John XXIII, who died in 1963 before the council ended, often spoke of his wish to open the Church's windows to let in fresh air. He certainly succeeded.

As the council deliberated, *The Nun in the World* (1963), a book by Belgian Cardinal Léon-Joseph Suenens, signalled a possible future direction for convent life. Suenens argued that monastic traditions had isolated nuns and limited their potential contribution to society. He wanted the sisters to take a new leadership role in the Church and engage actively with the world. The cardinal's ideas resonated with the Sister Formation Conference and sparked discussions about rules and customs before the council endorsed such a move.[23]

Although a small number were allowed to attend the final two sessions of the Vatican Council, nuns played no role in drawing up the key documents that emerged from its deliberations.[24] The document that affected them most profoundly was *Perfectae Caritatis*, or *Adaptation and Renewal of Religious Life*, released on 28 October 1965. Emphasizing the enduring importance of the vows or evangelical counsels, *Perfectae Caritatis* was lavish in its praise of those who bound "themselves to the Lord in a special way." Even so, it suggested that communities adapt their manner of living, praying, and working to "the changed conditions of the time." It proposed, for example, that the religious habit "meet the requirements of health," and be suited to the needs of particular ministries, while remaining "simple and modest." And it urged nuns to acquire "an adequate knowledge of the social conditions of the times they live in." In bringing about renewal, communities were to involve all their members in special gatherings known as "general chapters." All changes would require the approval of the Holy See or the local bishop.[25]

Further changes to convent life were implicit in the concluding document of the council, *Gaudium et Spes*, or the *Pastoral Constitution of the Church in the Modern World* (7 December 1965). This lengthy piece rejected any separation between religion and "earthly affairs," pronounced on matters as diverse as science, culture, atheism, and free love, and asserted the Church's leadership in combatting war and injustice in the world.[26] Active engagement with the modern world and its concerns cast doubts on the value of the social isolation that had long been part of monastic tradition.[27]

The American nuns who attended Vatican II as observers returned home excited about the possibilities of adapting to modern times. *Perfectae Caritatis* gave them the green light to proceed with changes that they and many of their colleagues felt were long overdue. The "general chapters" that were assembled to determine the details of renewal for each congregation were fully participatory, and led inevitably to disputes and polarization. Some nuns were comfortable with the old ways of doing things, and resisted change. Others rejoiced at new possibilities. Where once conformity and harmony reigned – at least on the surface – there was now open disagreement.[28]

In keeping with the Church's commitment to engage with the world and with the idea that nuns should become aware of the society in which they were living, restrictions on access to radio, television, and newspapers were relaxed. It was the same for restrictions on personal movement: nuns were now able to leave their convents without permission, to visit families, go shopping, drive cars, eat in restaurants, and even interact with men. Many congregations voted to allow their members to use their original family names once more. And inflexible rules respecting compulsory bedtimes, silence, and prayer schedules became things of the past.[29]

To outsiders, the modernization of the habit was the most obvious manifestation of change. After much internal debate, some congregations began to experiment with habits consisting of below-the-knee-length pinafore dresses in subdued colours and a small cap with attached veil, not unlike that worn by postulants. It also became possible to add a wristwatch as an accessory. The new attire quickly grew in popularity because of its practicality and the idea that traditional habits created distance between nuns and laity. By the 1970s more and more congregations were turning to clothing that made them indistinguishable from seculars, save for a small silver cross and old-fashioned shoes. Abandoning the habit was controversial, and was distressing to nuns of a conservative outlook. Some felt that the habit accorded them instant respect as persons of holiness whose personal sacrifices served to remind an indifferent world of the kingdom of heaven. There was also a sense that the loss of habit demystified religious life and the status of nuns as consecrated persons.[30]

Modifying or abandoning the habit eased the transition to the outside world for nuns who decided to leave. It often involved taking an interest in one's appearance and in some cases, even losing weight. When nuns were dressed in modern attire, men began to notice them in a different way, and they enjoyed the attention. One of sociologist Lucinda SanGiovanni's informants remembered it this way: "Getting out of the habit really did start things off. On a teasing basis men would begin to respond to you as a woman."[31]

The Vatican Council put an end to an age-old source of discord when it advised: "Unless the state of affairs suggests otherwise, care must be taken to produce in women's communities a single category of sister." This was the signal to end the class system that still prevailed in many congregations. On 2 July 1966, the Sisters of Charity of Providence (Seattle) formally admitted the remaining twenty-three lay sisters to all the privileges of choir sisters.[32] Vilma Seelaus had entered the Carmelites of Newport, Rhode Island, in 1946 as a lay sister. In 1968, when the first general chapter was held following the abolition of the lay-choir distinction, she was elected prioress – something that could never have happened even three years previously.[33]

The vows of poverty, chastity, and obedience needed redefinition with all these changes taking place, and none more so than obedience. The inclusion of everyone in the deliberations over renewal was the first breakthrough for collegial decision-making in the convent. This was in keeping with the Church's new definition of itself as "the people of God," an expression with an egalitarian ring to it. In 1966 around 28 per cent of convents had put some democratic structure in place; by 1982 that was 84 per cent.[34] Consultations and committees shattered the autocratic power of mothers superior. One practical outcome was that nuns achieved a voice in the work assignment of their apostolate. Given a choice in the matter, many abandoned teaching school to seek personal satisfaction in law, social work, prison literacy programs, and the like.[35]

Pursuing individual professions rather than working in a congregation-owned institution meant that nuns found themselves increasingly living away from the convent in apartments or houses, alone or in small groups. These arrangements required either personal allowances or the retention of some of their salaries. The conception of shared poverty, in which nuns never handled money but took what they needed from a communal closet – with permission – no longer worked under these circumstances. Poverty came to mean just living frugally.[36]

The chastity aspect of religious life did not change with Vatican II. The protective structures that had traditionally sustained it did, however, wither away. Nuns frequently found themselves living and working with men and women who had no commitment to sexual restraint and probably little appreciation for it. The vow was still intact, but just more difficult to keep.[37]

These changes did not take place in the isolation of individual communities. Ever since the Sister Formation Conference brought nuns together to seek paths to better education, communities were no longer cut off from one another. The Conference of Major Superiors of Women also played a role here. In place since the mid-1950s, it served as a national coordinating body. It should be noted that, in 1967, the apostolic delegate, Cardinal Egidio Vagnozzi, forbade contemplative nuns from participating in the CMSW. And in 1969 the apostolic letter *Venite Seorsum* stressed the continuing importance of cloister for contemplatives. These nuns did experience some modernization as a consequence of the Vatican Council, but in a very constrained and conservative manner. They organized themselves into their own national body, the Association of Contemplative Sisters, in 1969.[38]

In 1971 the CMSW changed its name to the Leadership Conference of Women Religious (LCWR) and became known for its commitment to modernizing religious life. The Vatican, already uncomfortable with the word "leadership" in the title, began to wonder if nuns were becoming a bit too independent.[39] Conservative American bishops shared this concern, and were none too pleased to see nuns joining in civil-rights and anti-war protests and being arrested on occasion because of it.[40]

In a celebrated case highlighting these tensions, Archbishop James McIntyre of Los Angeles refused to approve the new rules adopted by the Sisters of the Immaculate Heart of Mary (Hollywood) in 1967. When the nuns proceeded with the changes anyway, McIntyre dispensed most of them from their vows and fired them from archdiocesan schools.[41] Cardinal Ildebrando Antoniutti, head of the Congregation of Religious, in commenting on disputes such as this, lamented the tendency of nuns to embrace "erroneous ideas about the promotion of women" that "smothered their natural instinct towards humble and retiring self-giving."[42]

As the 1970s unfolded, the LCWR found itself increasingly at odds with the Congregation for Religious and with conservative American bishops about the direction of renewal. The difficulties became more pronounced with the election of Karol Wojtyla to the Throne of Peter in 1978. Pope John Paul II, as he became known, had little sympathy for the modernizations initiated by Vatican II. His efforts to return religious life to what it had been before the council meant continuous strife between American nuns and the male Church hierarchy.[43] The hierarchy wanted "faithful companions," "little daughters," "mission helpers," "poor handmaids," and "sister servants," but modern nuns were having none of it.[44]

It is worth observing that not all nuns shared in the LCWR agenda, which the hierarchy viewed as tainted with feminism. Shortly after the Leadership Conference adopted its new name, about 10 per cent of the membership broke away to form Consortium Perfectae Caritatis (CPC), an organization comprising conservative communities that were willing to defer to Rome and the bishops.[45] The CPC was later known as the Council of Major Superiors of Women Religious (CMSWR). Conflict existed, then, at several levels: between conservative and progressive members of the same community; between the LCWR and the CPC/CMSWR; and between the LCWR and the hierarchy. The details of these conflicts are not central to our

TABLE 8.2 · NUMBER OF NUNS LEAVING RELIGIOUS LIFE
(1950 TO 1980)

1950	381
1955	590
1960	762
1965	1,562
1970	4,337
1975	1,191
1980	751

TABLE 8.3 · NUNS LEAVING BEFORE AND AFTER FINAL VOWS
(1970 TO 1980)

Year	Nuns Leaving	Before Final Vows		After Final Vows	
1970	4,337	1,723	(44%)	2,416	(56%)
1975	1,191	294	(25%)	897	(75%)
1980	751	147	(20%)	604	(80%)

inquiry, but their existence forms an important background to the exodus from convents.

Table 8.2 shows the pattern of the exodus between 1950 and 1980.[46] It has already been noted that 1965 was a critical year, in that the total number of nuns in the country peaked at around 180,000. Moreover, the numbers leaving suddenly became more pronounced. The greatest exodus occurred in 1970 – 4,337 – and the hemorrhaging continued for much of the succeeding decade. Between 1966 and 1981 convents lost 31,763 nuns through indults of secularization. For most congregations this meant a decline of 20 to 30 per cent in their membership, while deaths added further losses.[47]

Departures before 1965 were different from those after that date in one significant respect. Prior to 1965, the majority of those who left were junior professed nuns – which is to say, they were in the first five years of religious life and had yet to take their final vows. They were young women who realized that the convent was not for

186 · *Into Silence and Servitude*

them and left before making a lifelong commitment. After 1965 this pattern reversed itself: the majority of those leaving had already taken their final vows. Table 8.3 shows these numbers.[48]

When asked why this was happening, mothers superior tended to point to moral failure: "When nuns in perpetual vows forsake their vocation they are yielding to pride or an evil desire of the world," and "I rate as causes mental instability and inconstancy, faults of character ... infidelity to prayer."[49] But when those who left were asked their reasons, their answers were quite different. Many identified the cause as their realization that they had never had a vocation. There were also at times a bitterness at the wasted years and an anger at the high-pressure recruitment that had put them in the convent in the first place. Here are two examples: "I should never have entered. It took me twenty years to realize that. But I went right through parochial school so entering religious life was no big decision. Once you entered you simply couldn't leave";[50] "Nine years after entering, I left. I came to realize that I hadn't been mature enough at seventeen to make the decision I did, to renounce a life I had never experienced."[51]

A survey conducted in 1966 identified a general dissatisfaction with religious life as a major cause of defections. For some, the discontent arose from internal squabbles over the direction of renewal; for others, it was impatience with the slow pace of change.[52] Responding to a questionnaire around 1970 on why she had left, one former nun said: "I did not really want to leave the community but I couldn't accept the rigid form of government that existed and was refusing to change, even with renewal in the Church."[53] Another left for the opposite reason: "The liberals went too far to the left with the freedom thing. It turned me off and may have been the deciding factor in my leaving because I felt that there was no element of community."[54] As the years passed, conflict with bishops and the Vatican over renewal fostered further disillusionment.

Renewal itself brought its own challenges. As nuns shed their habits, began to live away from convents, to work in roles unconnected with Church ministries, and to forsake the staffing of institutions associated with their communities, the meaning and purpose of religious life was no longer as clear as it once had been. There seemed to be little difference between how nuns and lay people lived and worked. In the words of one former nun: "With all these changes in the convent, I didn't see religious living a life any different from the families and people with whom you worked every day. The sense of community was gone."[55] The dissolving of community life was also decisive in the departures of Priscilla and Janet in 1972. Janet felt that the relaxed rules made her feel adrift in the world and that she could better serve the Church in civilian life rather than in what she described as "the decaying shell of what had been a great religious order."[56]

The case of Saundra Willingham, an African-American, illustrates two dimensions of the convent exodus: the role of higher education in cultivating independent thinking and the failure of congregations to remain relevant. Willingham was educated in Catholic schools in Cincinnati, Ohio, and entered the Sisters of Notre Dame upon graduating in 1960. After first vows, she was sent to teach in an inner-city school. As the only African-American in the convent, she felt that she was being put on display as an example of racial integration and evidence of the congregation's progressiveness. But the subtle racist remarks of her fellow nuns and their indifference to the civil-rights movement told her otherwise. As she began to take university courses in the middle of the decade, her political consciousness was raised and she cast a critical eye on the "all-pervasive whiteness of the convent culture." In 1968 she was eligible for her final vows, but walked away instead.[57]

A combination of overwork and the constraints of convent life led sometimes to a physical and emotional exhaustion that prompted departure. This was the case with Midge Turk, who left the "Hollywood nuns" in 1966.[58] Three of Gass's informants – Elizabeth, Beverly, and Jan-2 – had similar stories to tell.[59] One ex-nun explained her disillusionment to Gerelyn Hollingsworth this way: "I left the convent because I couldn't stand it any longer. I was nervous and often ill ... All I had to look forward to was teaching little kids the rest of my life." And it didn't help that she found no enjoyment in teaching.[60] One of those who spoke to SanGiovanni recalled "just wanting to live a normal life," while another saw herself "hanging loose and enjoying myself." They told of the great pleasure of sleeping in and doing things without permission once out in the world.[61] For Shirley Dyckes, the problem was less about obedience and more about poverty and chastity: "I started to think about the fun of making money and spending it. I wanted an apartment of my own, with rooms I could decorate, a job I could work, and men I could date."[62]

Chastity was the requirement that still divided the religious from the secular life, and it was hardly surprising that nuns began to ask if it was worth it when their sense of identity and distinctiveness was being rapidly eroded.[63] Even before the relaxing of rules of enclosure in the 1960s, chastity had been a challenge for the convent system. Prayers, confession, exhausting work schedules, and flagellation had never quite succeeded in obliterating sexual feelings and desires. Turk admitted that it had been the most troubling vow for her. Her confessor had advised her to combat impure thoughts by keeping busy.[64]

The evidence does suggest that most nuns succeeded in keeping this vow, and for those who failed to do so, lesbian relationships and/or masturbation were the outlets of choice. Halstead and Halstead's survey of former nuns in the mid-1970s concluded that 21 per cent of them had had homosexual encounters while in the convent and that 17 per cent had masturbated.[65] Statistics on intimate matters are always problematic, and surveying former nuns rather than nuns would bring different results. It is probably best to go with Turk's imprecise description of the matter during her eighteen years with the Sisters of the Immaculate Heart of Mary: "There were a few relationships between nuns and there was a problem with masturbation."[66]

And then there were men. Traditional convent life provided few opportunities for nuns to meet them. In fact, the segregation of the sexes was the whole point of cloister. And even when social contact with males was unavoidable, it was always governed by strict protocols enshrined in congregation rules, in order to prevent familiarity.

The looser rules respecting dress, mobility, and living/working arrangements in effect after Vatican II meant more mixed company and the possibility of relationships. The looser rules also applied to the manner in which nuns could interact with priests, a double jeopardy for the Church respecting its celibate ranks. After fifteen years with the Poor Clares, Beryl Bissell left in October 1972 when she fell in love with an Italian priest, Padre Vittorio, who was quite a bit older than she was.[67] Mary Gilligan's journey to the outside began in 1967 when she found herself attracted to a Jesuit named Tim who gave retreats for sisters.[68] Shirley Dyckes began to question her vocation with the Holy Cross Sisters when teaching high school in Pericles, New York, in the 1960s. Here she was smitten with blond, square-jawed Father Xavier (a pseudonym) and realized that her platonic friendships with men, who were mainly priests, were not enough. She left in 1969 and later married Clarence Kelley, director of the FBI.[69]

In SanGiovanni's survey of twenty former nuns who had left a teaching congregation, twelve admitted to romantic encounters with priests prior to leaving religious life, and in about half of these cases the relationships had been sexual.[70] In a celebrated case in 1969, Father Philip Berrigan, radical anti-war activist, fell in love with Elizabeth McAlister, a Sister of the Sacred Heart, while he was serving time in prison for destroying military draft files. The couple married in 1973 following his release.[71] Theresa Padovano entered the Sisters of Charity of Leavenworth, Kansas, in 1958 when she was sixteen. She taught in her congregation's schools for much of the 1960s, and then applied for a leave to complete a master's degree at St Mary's Seminary in Houston, Texas. Here she fell for Tony, a priest who was one of her instructors. They decided to forsake their vows and marry. Later they had four children, whom they sent to public schools.[72]

The survey of 1966, referred to earlier in this chapter, identified the desire to marry as a major motivation for leaving religious life. No less than 33 per cent of junior professed nuns gave this as their principal reason; the figure was 20 per cent for nuns in perpetual vows, whom we can assume were a bit older.[73] The surveys of ex-nuns by Gass and Hollingsworth came up with similar ratios respecting the reasons for leaving. K.T. left in 1969 after a series of emotional attachments to men. By the time her dispensation arrived, she was already dating the man who would become her husband. Julia was influenced to forsake her vows in 1973 by the unpleasant politics of the convent and by a fear of becoming like the other sisters – "these embittered old prunes." But her real issue was men: "I found them quite attractive and that was incompatible with the vow of chastity."[74] One of Hollingsworth's informants put her reasons bluntly:

"I left the convent because I could no longer live the vows. I wanted money, a love life, and initiative in my own life."[75]

By 1966 Rachel Ethier was growing increasingly disillusioned with religious life. She had been with the Daughters of Wisdom since 1957 and was impatient with her congregation's slow pace of modernization. The vow of obedience was still inflexibly interpreted, and her university studies encouraged a spirit of independence that annoyed her superiors. Some men whom she met at university showed an interest in her, and she began to fear becoming like some of the older nuns she knew, "twisted, hard, and I might even say cruel." In October 1967, in a letter requesting an indult of exclaustration, she remarked: "I entered the community at seventeen after six years of boarding school. I realize now that a real choice for religious life was never really made before, though I thought I had made it many times. I had never really considered marriage as a possibility."[76]

In the four-year period from 1966 to 1969, the Poor Handmaids of Jesus Christ lost fifty-five professed nuns. The realization that they had never had religious vocations was the principal reason given for these defections. Dissatisfaction with convent life, which some found a source of mental strain, was another major reason. Obedience had been a problem for some of those who left, and, in ten cases, a desire to marry or be in a relationship with a man or woman was the motivation. Juliana L., for example, had repeatedly "sought the attention of a man." Loretta T. had been "interested in the opposite sex and asked for a dispensation." Kathryn S. had "desired to be a wife and mother." Irene U. had "found it difficult to keep the vow of chastity" and needed "human love." Joan W. had experienced "strong temptations against the vow of chastity" as well as "strong attachments to the other sisters."[77]

Were some nuns "longing for the fleshpots of Egypt"? It appears that they were. Stories of nuns leaving to marry priests and other men caused much prurient speculation and was damaging to the Church, and to the convent system in particular. Nothing could compare, however, to the impact of a story that appeared in the media in April 1976: "Nun kills her baby." Carol Murphy, thirty-seven years old, was the subject of the story. Known in religion as Sister Maureen, she was director of Trinity Montessori School in Pittsford, a suburb of Rochester, New York, and a member of the Sisters of St Joseph. On the morning of 27 April, she stayed home from work, explaining that she was not feeling well. Later that afternoon, when the other nuns returned to the convent at the end of the teaching day, they found her lying in a pool of blood on her bedroom floor. Sister Maureen was rushed to hospital, where it was discovered that she had given birth to a baby. She denied that this could have happened and claimed to remember nothing. Later, when it was explained to her that a dead baby boy had been found in a wastebasket hidden behind furniture in her bedroom, she maintained her denials.

Congregations had expelled members for much less, but the Sisters of St Joseph decided to support Sister Maureen and kept her hidden away from the media glare while she was on bail awaiting trial. In February 1977, the trial took place at Monroe District Court in Rochester. Sister Maureen was charged with the manslaughter rather than the murder of "Baby Boy Murphy," on the grounds that she had been "acting under the influence of extreme emotional disturbance." She denied the charge and her defence attorney argued successfully that the trauma of the birth absolved her of any responsibility for the death of the boy. After her acquittal, Sister Maureen disappeared, and it is not known what became of her. The identity of the baby's father was never revealed.

The publicity surrounding the case did not serve the Church well. There was much criticism of its opposition to sex education, birth control, and abortion, which were linked to the story. Feminists were angered that a woman could find herself with an unwanted pregnancy, unaware of the choices open to her, and unwilling or unable to seek medical assistance. Some of the anger was directed at the Convent of Our Lady of Lourdes, the community to which Sister Maureen belonged. How could the nuns with whom she lived be so ignorant of her condition, it was asked.[78]

The breakdown of barriers between the cloister and the world after the Vatican Council made it easier for nuns to leave in several respects. The secular world was not the domain of wickedness that it was once portrayed as being, and it became possible to join it "with less opposition or shame."[79] In a growing number of congregations the departing were no longer spirited away in the middle of the night. They were allowed to announce their intentions to colleagues and to bid them farewell.[80] The stigma of failure and disgrace was fading and, as more nuns left, the exodus acquired a "psychological momentum." The sight of nuns packing their bags inspired others to follow, when they realized that leaving was a realistic choice.[81]

And yet some hesitated, fearing they might not make it in the world. What would it be like to support yourself, to secure accommodation, to choose the right clothes, to make friends, to learn to drive a car. But as word filtered back that those who had left were adjusting well, the exodus accelerated. Two of SanGiovanni's informants were strongly influenced in their decision to leave by news of former companions doing well on the outside.[82]

The vows were a further source of hesitation. As we have seen, most of those who left the convent between 1970 and 1980 had taken final vows, and these commitments formed a psychological stumbling block that barred their exit. Before leaving, they had to convince themselves that the vows had really been temporary, rather than permanent, in nature. There was much soul-searching here, and it was not unusual for nuns to remain in religious life many years after the initial disillusionment that ultimately prompted their departure.[83]

The probability of success on the outside had much to do with the career opportunities available in the world for qualified professionals, and many nuns, as a consequence of Sister Formation, had marketable credentials in hand. In one of her studies, Helen Ebaugh found that those who left religious life were likely to be more educated than those who stayed behind.[84] The Hollywood nuns who were expelled by Archbishop McIntyre serve as an example here. In 1970 it was discovered that around thirty of them were teaching in the public schools of Los Angeles.[85] The memoirs of several former nuns show a similar pattern.[86]

Departures depleted the numerical strength of congregations, but also undermined the morale of those who remained. It was none too encouraging to see the most educated making for the exits, and with them the next generation of leadership.[87] There was some resentment at those who left and the effect of their leaving on the community – and moral judgments too:

TABLE 8.4 · NUMBER OF NOVICE NUNS NATIONALLY (1958 TO 1980)

1958–62	32,423
1966–70	8,699
1976–80	2,767

One third of our community left. A deep sadness gripped our hearts to see them leave the life of dedication they had vowed to God. Their departure created a fissure in the integrity of the community. Their work had to be assumed by others. Most of those who left were good sisters until a short time before they left. Some fell into some vice such as falling in love with a man or building up a craving to have a family of their own.[88]

Others who stayed the course were disappointed rather than bitter at the departures. Happy with their own lives in religion, they were determined to reshape their communities and retain relevance. Sister Georgine Loacker, who entered the School Sisters of Notre Dame in 1942, remained convinced throughout the turmoil of the 1960s and beyond that the religious life was the best life possible, because of its meaningful challenges.[89] Sister Rosemary Dillman, after a long career with the Sisters of Charity of Providence (Seattle), had no regrets and had thoroughly enjoyed her many years in the classroom. She was a little saddened that so few women since the 1960s had chosen to take up the work of her congregation.[90] Sister Mariane Mader had never considered an alternative to her life with the Sisters of Providence (St Mary-of-the-Woods) and loved being part of a supportive community of like-minded women. But she and her companions were concerned for the future. Most members of the congregation were no longer young, and the congregation had only one novice in 2013.[91]

Sisters Rosemary and Mariane were pointing to another problem that threatened the future of congregations: the virtual disappearance of new recruits. It was a phenomenon that coincided with the great exodus. Table 8.4 shows the total number of young women

FIGURE 8.1 · POOR HANDMAIDS OF JESUS CHRIST

Number of postulants admitted and the corresponding number of them who became novices

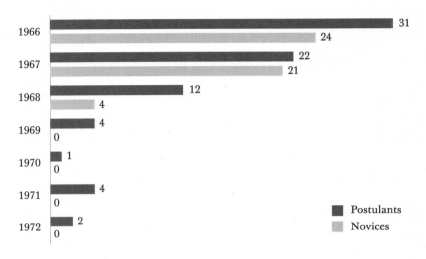

in convent novitiates during three staggered five-year periods.[92] A survey conducted around 1970 presented this trend another way. The median number of novices entering the 287 congregations providing information had been thirteen in 1960, but that number had fallen to three in 1970. Moreover, 27 per cent of these congregations had nobody entering their novitiates at the latter date.[93] We can see the plummeting numbers more clearly in the case of one congregation represented in Figure 8.1.

The number of novices with the Poor Handmaids went from an historic high of twenty-four in 1966 to zero just three years later. And while the congregation was still receiving a small trickle of postulants, none of them were going on to the novitiate. A similar pattern is discernable in a much larger congregation, the Maryknoll Sisters. In 1963 the Maryknollers had 128 postulants (an historic high), ninety-seven of whom went on to become novices. By 1970 the postulants numbered only two, although both of them did enter as novices.[94]

The turmoil associated with renewal that afflicted congregations during the 1960s and 1970s enables us partly to understand the collapse of recruitment. As constitutions and apostolates underwent radical revision, congregations lost the clear purposes that had once bound them together. With uncertainty over future directions, communities found it difficult to recruit aggressively, as in the past. How could you ask someone to commit to religious vows when the very nature of that commitment was the subject of internal controversy?[95] Nor could nuns who were questioning their own commitment be expected to seek out new members with any conviction. As one potential candidate said to Mary Ann Donovan, "If the members do not look convincing and convinced, forget it."[96] And the actual abandonment of their vows by so many nuns – widely publicized in the media – acted as a significant deterrent to potential recruits.[97] Who would want to join what appeared to be a sinking ship?[98]

The exodus from religious life and the introduction of individual career choice for those who remained in the system radically reduced the number of sisters directing classrooms in Catholic schools. As we saw in Chapter 2, the ability of teaching sisters to influence and inspire girls to emulate them was perhaps the most significant factor in convent recruitment. The virtual disappearance of this influence accelerated the decline in the number of new recruits.[99]

In Chapter 4 we observed that parental objections to their children's religious vocations were considered a major obstacle to recruitment – even in the days when novitiates were full. The Church accused parents in the 1940s and 1950s of excessive concern for the material success and happiness of their children. The parents of the 1960s and 1970s were of a similar disposition, and even more so.[100] Father James Hennesey noted that the Church had lost much of its influence on Catholic families as they achieved upward mobility and moved to the suburbs from ethnic enclaves. He believed that "vocational decisions" had been adversely affected by these trends.[101] When *Humanae Vitae* was released in July 1968, the encyclical's condemnation of artificial birth control as "intrinsically evil" was rejected by most lay Catholics. Father Carroll Stuhlmueller sensed a growing alienation. Noting widespread disagreement among the laity with the Church's teachings on sexuality – and especially its views on contraception and masturbation – he saw little likelihood of parents encouraging lives of celibacy for their children.[102]

Nor did their children find the idea of celibacy appealing. The baby-boom generation that came of age in the 1960s had been, in historian Doug Owram's words, "born at the right time." These were young people who had avoided the Depression and the Second World War and had grown up in an era of prosperity and rising expectations. Self-fulfillment was part of their mantra, and during the Age of Aquarius this included sexual fulfillment. The increasing availability of birth control, the decline of censorship, and the celebration of sexuality in popular culture undermined the age-old double standard and fundamentally changed the ways in which teenage dating and relationships were conducted.[103] Helen Gurley Brown's *Sex and the Single Girl* (1962) advocated education and independent careers for women, as well as the enjoyment of sex and the company of a variety of men. And when Gurley Brown became editor of *Cosmopolitan* magazine shortly afterwards, she used it as a vehicle to promote the same philosophy.[104]

It became impossible under the circumstances to keep the young in the dark about human reproduction or to fill them with shame and guilt respecting sexual desire. Sister Sarah Marie Sherman, in writing about celibacy's lack of appeal, expressed the Church's frustration at this turn of events: "One apparent reason is the supersaturation of our culture with sexual values and fulfillment 'overkill.' Subtly, the present generation (and those to come?) are being led to believe that life without sex is a life without anything."[105]

The young people of the 1960s were far more likely to finish high school and go on to college than were their parents, and this was as true for females as it was for males. More education meant more career opportunities. Catholic girls were no longer faced with two stark choices in life: become a wife or a nun. Moreover, the feminist movement encouraged girls to pursue non-traditional careers as paths to independence. And even when girls chose teaching or nursing, which they often did, they were much more inclined to practise these professions in public institutions for decent pay, and without the constraints of religious life. Entering a convent for career purposes had lost its appeal.[106] With the establishment of the

Peace Corps in 1961, those inspired to work for social justice had an outlet to do so without becoming missionaries or taking religious vows.[107] Besides, nuns were increasingly viewed by the public as a bit silly, childish, and out of touch. They had an image problem; they were just not cool.[108]

A survey conducted in Westchester County, New York, in the mid-1960s sought to discern the attitude to religious vocations of Catholic high-school girls and college women. The respondents, who had all been educated by nuns, were strongly negative in their views. They cited "restraint on freedom" as the major difficulty with religious life. It was most objectionable, they said, that others would decide for them "where they would live, what type of work they would spend the rest of their lives doing, what they would wear, and what they would eat." A few of those surveyed, while confirming that they were good Catholics, expressed disagreement with the Church's position on racial segregation, the treatment of minorities, and birth control.[109]

Diminishing numbers because of defection, death, and lack of new recruits, combined with aging memberships, sapped the vitality of congregations. By the latter half of the 1980s, reports began to appear of communities amalgamating to pool resources and to avoid extinction.[110] Among the Sisters of Divine Providence (San Antonio) morale sank as their organization ebbed away. There was also some resentment among younger members because of the growing commitment to caring for the elderly – something they had not really signed on for.[111] The general aging of congregations has had an accelerating negative effect on recruitment. When most members are in their sixties or over, it is increasingly difficult to make a community attractive to what are called "millennials" – those born after 1982.[112]

The future of female monasticism in America is further clouded by recent studies showing a younger generation of Catholics largely skeptical of doctrinal orthodoxy. Less than a quarter of those in their twenties and thirties accept Church teaching on abortion, contraception, divorces, homosexuality, and premarital sex. This is a significant rejection of authority, and the rejection is even greater among women than among men – an hardly encouraging sign for recruitment to religious sisterhoods. And while it is true that some

TABLE 8.5 · NUMBER OF STUDENTS IN THE CATHOLIC
ELEMENTARY SCHOOLS (1975 TO 2015)

1975	2,557,000
1985	2,005,000
1995	1,815,000
2005	1,559,000
2015	1,358,000

congregations are showing signs of growth, the numbers are so insignificant that they do not affect the overall downward trend.[113]

The effects of all of this on Catholic schools are not difficult to imagine. In 1965 there were 114,000 nuns working in education, historically their most significant apostolate; today's number is less than 7,000, a decline of 94 per cent.[114] We can look at these numbers from another angle: only 2.2 per cent of teachers in contemporary Catholic schools are nuns/sisters. Another 1 per cent are priests and brothers. It means that the teaching force is now overwhelmingly lay – 96.8 per cent to be exact – and preponderantly female (75.1 per cent) at that.[115]

Catholic schools survived, then, by employing lay teachers to replace the vanishing nuns. But lay teachers required salaries, driving costs and fees higher. Today the average fee for elementary schools is $3,673, and $9,622 for secondary schools.[116] Some parents can no longer afford it, while others question whether it is worth the additional expense. After Vatican II, the Church was not as adamant in insisting on Catholic education for all children of the faith and on the grave dangers posed by state institutions. This more tolerant attitude allowed public schools to be viewed as an acceptable alternative – and a free one at that.[117]

Unsurprisingly, the number of Catholic children attending the Church's schools has been declining steadily in recent decades, as Table 8.5 shows.[118]

While costs are certainly a factor, they are tied in with the changing demographics and ethnic composition of the faithful. Catholics of European origin generally ignore the Church's teaching on birth control and have fewer children. Hispanics, on the other hand, have

been for some time the fastest-growing and youngest Catholic minority, making up almost 40 per cent of the total membership today.
But only 3 per cent of Hispanic schoolchildren receive a Catholic
education. Relative poverty and a sense that Catholic schools are
elitist and unwelcoming are the main reasons that they stay away.[119]

Among the Catholic population in general, there is a general decline in parish participation and in church attendance, all of which
adversely affects support for parochial schools. Weekly Mass attendance fell from 47 per cent of Church members in 1974 to 24 per
cent in 2012. Empty pews mean less in collection plates and fewer
financial resources to subsidize schools. While the participation decline has multiple explanations, the priest sex-abuse scandal that
hit the Church badly, beginning in the 1980s, has been particularly
significant. It has meant a loss of confidence in the hierarchy and
some skepticism at its admonitions in support of Catholic schools.
Besides, the scandal cost the Church over three billion in compensation settlements and at least eleven dioceses have had to seek
bankruptcy protection. It is hardly surprising that school subsidies
are harder to come by.[120]

Nor is it helpful that allegations of abuse against nuns have
come to light. By 2006 an estimated four hundred men and women
had complained of having been sexually molested by nuns during
their youth. In the state of Minnesota alone, credible charges were
brought against the School Sisters of Notre Dame in Mankato,
the Sisters of St Francis in Rochester, and the Ursulines in Old
Frontenac.[121]

The Ursulines in the Oregon Province were also in trouble.
Eleven nuns of this congregation were charged with sexually abus-
ing children at the Ursuline Academy, a school in St Ignatius on
the Flathead Indian Reservation in Montana. The lawsuit named
Mother Loyola, the superior, as one of the principal abusers. Now
deceased, Mother Loyola was described as a large German woman
and strict disciplinarian. Some of those abused by her were convinced that she was a Nazi war criminal hiding out in the West;
others suspected that she was really a man in drag – at least until
confronted with indisputable evidence to the contrary. The case was
settled out of court in December 2014, with the congregation agreeing to pay the victims $4.45 million in compensation.[122] This was

the Church's preferred method of settling cases such as this, since it minimized embarrassing publicity and scrutiny.[123]

The full extent of abuse by women religious is unknown. In trying to get to the bottom of it, the Survivors' Network of those Abused by Priests (SNAP) has encountered nothing but obstructions. For more than a decade, SNAP has lobbied the Leadership Conference of Women Religious, asking to speak at its annual meeting and urging measures to protect the vulnerable and heal the victims. The LCWR has refused to cooperate, insisting the problem is insignificant and outside of its jurisdiction.[124]

The nuns are not coming back, and Catholic schools continue their enrolment decline. In states such as Indiana, where "educational vouchers" are allowed, some schools are actually growing. But vouchers – in effect, direct public subsidies to parents of school-age children that can be applied to any school – are controversial and are opposed by teachers' unions and champions of public schooling. The overall effect has simply been to slow the rate of decline.[125]

Subtle changes in the Catholic identity of the schools accompany the decline. The latest figures show that non-Catholics constitute 16.4 per cent of total enrolment. These are the children of parents who have lost confidence in public education and see any private school as a better choice. And with tuition-paying parents steering school priorities, there is often greater attention to academics and athletics at the expense of religion.[126] In 1994, a survey of parents with children in the Catholic schools of Orlando, Florida, found that they had chosen such an education because of academics, safety, and discipline. Religious instruction was not even among their top ten motivations.[127] A 1997 report by Archbishop Daniel Buechlein of Indianapolis deplored deficiencies in the teaching of religion in Catholic schools. The report noted that there was "insufficient attention to the Trinity," "insufficient emphasis on the divinity of Christ," "insufficient recognition of the transforming effects of grace," and "a pattern of deficiency in the teaching on original sin and sin in general."[128] The traditional Catholic school, where nuns ruled with rulers and where sin in all its varieties received the attention it was due, is a thing of the past.

CONCLUSION

Does secularization theory provide an explanation for the transformation of American Catholicism since the 1960s, and, in particular, the collapse of the convent system? This theory is usually traced
to classical sociologists Auguste Comte, Emile Durkheim, and Max
Weber, who employed it to account for the waning of religion's
social and political influence in Western Europe. Secularization
was said to have its origins in the emergence of religiously plural societies following the Reformation. The fragmentation of Christianity into many churches inevitably diminished the authority of each
one, toleration became the price of social peace, and parochialism
and isolation were replaced by integration across communities of
faith. The separation of the political from the sacred meant a loss
for the latter, and the practice of religion became a private rather
than a public affair.

Modernization accelerated the process. The growth of specialized
institutions with secular aims in law, politics, education, science,
and media reduced the status of religion to just another organization among many. Materialist values connected with the social and
economic ambitions of the bourgeoisie replaced those of a purely
spiritual nature. In modern secular societies, religious practice and
belief became matters of individual choice and were not imposed
either by law or institutional domination. With religion relegated to
the private sphere, commitment weakened, dogma was questioned,
and clerical authority was challenged.[129]

In the United States, secularization is a highly contested notion,
with some scholars arguing that, while it might have applicability
in Europe, it lacks explanatory power on this side of the Atlantic.
Rodney Stark, for instance, would like to bury secularization for
good.[130] There is also an entertaining but rather pointless debate respecting the founding fathers and whether they intended to create a
secular or Christian nation.[131]

These disputes need not detain us here, but it does seem that
secularization may provide a useful prism through which to view
the events described in this chapter. Did the American Catholic
community become secularized in the postwar period? Or, put

another way, did secularization undermine the cohesiveness and identity of that community?

The exclusive nature of the pre-war Catholic ghettoes with their vibrant parish institutions has probably been exaggerated. A majority of Catholic parents always sent their children to public schools – and especially so for second-level studies – removing them from clerical influence and fostering integration across denominations. In addition, public schools provided outlets for countless Catholic girls and young women who wished to become teachers without becoming nuns. The tendency to embrace public education became more pronounced after the war as Catholics moved to the suburbs, and more pronounced still when parish and diocesan schools went into decline after 1965. Public education is one of the more striking achievements of the modern state, and its secular aims appealed to upwardly mobile Catholic families. Father Martin Stevens was not wrong in describing secularism as a "creeping rot" (Chapter 4) that encouraged parents to oppose their daughters' religious vocations. That opposition triumphed completely with the generation that finished school in the mid-1960s. The girls and young women who came of age at this time totally rejected the religious life and sought instead to embrace the world and all it had to offer.

Nuns, too, were not immune to secularizing influences. As they acquired more education – and with it, more contact with the outside world – they began to challenge the restrictions and constraints of the cloister. Contact with the world, despite its nagging imperfections, meant exposure to modern secular values that had compelling appeal: equality of opportunity, participatory democracy, freedom of expression, and the individual pursuit of happiness and material success. The dissonance between these values and those of the convent was not lost on educated nuns, and a critical, questioning attitude made its appearance. The nun as poor little helper was replaced by the nun as independent, educated woman. But the latter definition was an uneasy fit and difficult to reconcile with any workable conception of monastic life. Why be a nun at all? This was the question that inevitably came to mind and that prompted many to forsake their vows, which, in any case, no longer seemed so important.

Vatican II helped break down the walls that protected convent culture from the worldly forces that surrounded it. The intention was not to destroy the convent, but to adapt it to modernity. The nature of that adaptation was never fully formulated, however. Nor is it clear how it might have been done. In the upheavals that followed, the very necessity of a convent system, whether in the older or a newer version, came to be questioned.

We can also discern the effects of secularization on the larger Catholic community. The decline in church attendance and parish participation signalled a weakening in religious commitment. Alienation from the hierarchy – prompted inter alia by *Humanae Vitae* and sex-abuse scandals – weakened further this commitment. Surveys of the laity, and especially the young, have shown much disagreement with the Church's teaching on sexual and reproductive matters. The faithful today are sometimes described as "cafeteria Catholics," who make individual choices respecting the teachings they wish to accept or reject. The conditions described here are fully consistent with the way religion functions in modern secular societies.

The Second Vatican Council sought to open the Church to the world – that it might change it. Quite the opposite may have happened. It seems more plausible to argue that the secular spirit invaded the Church and undermined one of its more enduring institutions, female monasticism.

Conclusion

. . . .

As the Catholic Church developed its network of institutions in America in conjunction with immigration and population growth, the teaching sister became its most visible figure. When parents sent their children to the Church's schools, they expected them to be taught by nuns, and this was usually so. The nun as the ideal teacher for girls – and for young boys too – became an axiom of Catholic education. Since nuns were called by God to an exalted way of life, the moral formation of youth was presumed to be safe in their hands. Nor was their dedication in doubt; unhampered by the demands of family life, nuns would devote their energies exclusively to their students.

The key role played by nuns in staffing parochial schools and diocesan high schools can only partly be attributed to their image as moral exemplars, however. An economic imperative was also at play. Catholic schools, as private institutions without public funding, were reliant on fees and donations to meet operating costs, and especially teachers' salaries. Since nuns worked for stipends amounting to but a fraction of what public-school teachers earned, their deployment in the classroom allowed for limited expenditure and modest fees. In this way, Catholic schooling was made affordable to a wider spectrum of families.

Nuns, therefore, were in great demand. Where did they come from and was it possible to increase their numbers? Girls and young women who were attracted to the religious life had always been around. Convinced they had a vocation or a special calling from God, they willingly entered the cloister. In pursuing this calling, they hoped to achieve personal sanctification and eternal salvation. Secondary motivations may also have been present: a desire to serve the poor, to convert pagans in faraway lands, to pursue a career, or to avoid the complications of marriage and child-rearing. Those who volunteered in this manner were often sufficiently numerous to keep congregations functioning or even to expand their operations, depending on social and economic circumstances.

But when the number of volunteers was insufficient, some form of intervention was in order. Elements of intervention were seen as early as the nineteenth century, when congregations sent emissaries to Ireland on recruiting drives. Nuns at home, especially after the Baltimore Council in 1884, were encouraged to seek suitable candidates among their students as the staffing needs of the Catholic school system expanded. Insufficiencies in the number of nuns continued into the twentieth century and threatened to reach crisis proportions following the Second World War with the appearance of the baby-boom children. Accommodating the children of that generation who sought Catholic schooling would not have been possible without a substantial increase in the number of teaching sisters. The solution was active recruitment – the systematic identification of students who appeared to be suitable to the religious life, followed by measures of persuasion.

Every teaching sister now became a recruiter in her own classroom, but even this arrangement appeared inadequate to the task. Congregations committed to expansion began to appoint recruitment professionals or vocations directors assigned to work full time in securing new recruits. It was an American solution to an American problem. Drawing on insights from sociology, psychology, and marketing, the professionals constructed a set of field-tested recruitment strategies that they shared among themselves. These strategies in turn formed the basis of a nationwide campaign that reached into Catholic schools and that also – insofar as this was possible – targeted Catholic students attending public schools.

Active recruitment required that the understanding of a vocation be presented to the young as simply a willingness to serve. The religious life was portrayed as most pleasing to God, who promised a hundredfold reward to those who pursued it. Yet many of the details of what the life actually entailed were not readily disclosed to those encouraged to enter. They were also urged to enter as soon as they felt attracted to the idea, even if they were young at the time. A vocation was said to be a fragile entity, easily lost through hesitation.

Recruitment in this manner drew the ire of many parents, who sensed that their children were being pressured into career decisions without the maturity and experience to comprehend the magnitude of the commitment. Parental objections blunted the recruitment campaign in some measure, but the numbers entering religious sisterhoods continued to rise.

The recruitment professionals were aware that conviction and commitment among those persuaded to enter, as distinct from those who readily volunteered, might waver, but reasoned that the rigourous training to which postulants and novices were subjected would winnow out the unsuitable. The training was certainly strict – sometimes to the point of severity – and it did result in withdrawals and expulsions along the way. But persuasion continued in play during training: if postulants or novices who were considered "convent material" by the sponsoring congregation wished to withdraw from the program, they were usually actively encouraged to stay until completion.

By the 1950s and early 1960s, American convents housed substantial numbers of nuns who had entered religious life at a young age as a consequence of active recruitment. Many harboured doubts about the authenticity of their vocations. The constraints of the life and exhausting work details accentuated these doubts. University courses, taken to improve their professional credentials, opened windows on a world of possibilities outside of the convent and added to the doubts. It became possible to question things that until then had been unquestioned, even the very raison d'être of religious life and why they were part of it.

By the mid-1960s, the convent system was in a fragile state. When the Second Vatican Council proposed adapting religious life to modern conditions, it launched a process that sent the system into a downward spiral. Ancient rules and protocols were now modified or even cast aside, undermining the very structures upon which monasticism was founded: cloistered isolation from the world and its concerns, strict adherence to the vows, inflexible daily routines, clearly defined community purposes, and distinctive attire. In truth, convents were medieval institutions that defied modernization.

Change quickly turned to disintegration, and this took place on two fronts: unprecedented desertions from religious life and the virtual disappearance of new recruits.

The desertions are a complex phenomenon, but surveys of those who left indicate two dominant reasons that are worthy of some thought: an awareness of never having had a religious vocation in the first place; and a desire to have children and/or be in an intimate human relationship. That so many could be in religious life with serious doubts about their vocation redirects us to the circumstances in which they entered. The memoirs and recollections of those who left the convent suggest that the vocation was not always their own idea, but rather was suggested to them by persuasive recruiters. That so many sought a human relationship is also noteworthy. Were they completely cognizant of what they were forsaking when they entered? Again, the testimony of those who left provides strong evidence that they were not. The absence of true vocations and the desire for human intimacy are only part of the desertion picture, but they may be a clue in explaining the astonishing rapidity of the exodus from religious life.

Multiple factors were also at play in the disappearance of new recruits. The growing secularization of the Catholic community, as manifested in its social and economic ambitions and integration into the larger society, left little room for the convent as a desirable destination for its children. And the baby-boom generation, with its high expectations for personal fulfillment, could see no merit in a life lived under vigilance and constraint.

Two aspects of active recruitment that had been critical in expanding the convent system now disappeared, also affecting the supply of postulants and novices. The first of these was the swift decline in the number of teaching sisters in Catholic schools. The decline had to do with desertions from religious life, as well as the abandonment of teaching by sisters who stayed in the system after Vatican II. The sister who could inspire her students and encourage the suitable among them to follow in her path played a critical role in recruitment. Her departure from the classroom was an incalculable loss.

The second recruitment mechanism to fade away was the aspirancy high school. In some ways, aspirancies were the highest expression of active recruitment and had the numbers to prove it. Aspirants were girls who discerned the elements of a vocation around the ages thirteen to fourteen. Early identification was followed by an education program infused with convent culture and conducted in isolation from the social activities of contemporary adolescence. Those completing the program were ushered into the postulancy with minimal exposure to the outside world and its concerns.

The shutting down of the aspirancies symbolized the end of active recruitment as it had been practised before the Second Vatican Council. Recruits did not disappear completely, but from then on, they were greatly diminished in number. The new postulants and novices were young women who entered religious life from sincere personal conviction rather than in response to persuasion.

In their heyday, the structures of active recruitment were primarily concerned with boosting the number of nuns employed in the Church's institutions, and in its schools in particular. In a private-school system requiring stringent cost controls, the teaching sister was the ideal worker. The sister's vow of poverty required her to work for little more than room and board – and a frugal one at that. Her vow of obedience obliged her to accept any assignment, no matter how onerous or disagreeable, and restrained any troublesome tendencies towards personal autonomy. And her vow of chastity eliminated complications to do with maternity leave, daycare, and the like.

Women's work has always been undervalued, and usually underpaid or unpaid. The operations of the convent system illustrate another dimension of female labour exploitation. Small wonder that it did not endure. It may well be that the Church was only comfortable with educated professional females as long as they were poor, chaste, and obedient. Operating under the constraints of monasticism, they represented no threat to patriarchy.

A Note on Sources

. . . .

Otto von Bismarck once observed that those fond of sausages and legislation should avoid watching them being made. I think the same could be said about books and those who enjoy reading them. Most readers want to engage with a topic without first enduring the tedium of the author's challenges in writing about it. That being said, there will be those who question how I went about my research, wonder at the scope and representativeness of my sources, and attempt to categorize this book within the several paradigms of writing on women religious. This Note is presented as an antidote to their concerns.

Let's deal with archives first. It is well to remember that convent archives are private institutions and are under no obligation to admit researchers. My initial plan was to examine the archival collections of eight communities that appeared to welcome the public and that were reasonably representative. I wanted communities that were preponderantly engaged in teaching, because of the connection between Catholic schools and recruitment. And I wanted some that conducted aspirancies and some that did not. It did not quite work out as intended.

The archives of two communities that conducted aspirancies welcomed me: those of the Sisters of Providence, St Mary-of-the-Woods, Indiana, and those of the Poor Handmaids of Jesus Christ – the latter actually housed in Notre Dame University, Indiana. A third community in the same category in a neighbouring state initially agreed to admit me, but when I turned up to do the work on the week agreed to beforehand, I was told there was no one to help me and I could not be accommodated.

The archives of two communities without aspirancies opened their doors to me: those of the Sisters of Charity of Providence in Seattle, Washington, and those of the Maryknoll Sisters in Ossining, New York. There were three others in this category that initially seemed receptive to my inquiries but balked at the fact that I was teaching at a secular rather than at a Catholic university. It did me no good to explain that virtually all Canadian universities are public institutions and, while some have small Catholic colleges attached, we have no equivalents to Notre Dame, the Catholic University of America (CUA), Fordham, and the like. Affiliation with a Catholic university was the price of admission, and I did not have it. I approached one more community archives that appeared to be well organized, but was presented with terms and conditions for access that I found unacceptable. What I describe here will come as no great surprise to secular historians who have written about Catholic institutions or have attempted to do so. Catholic and secular historians often operate in very different worlds – and, regrettably, in different academic associations.

And so I ended up with four convent archives rather than the eight that I had originally envisaged. It is hard to say with any certainty if they were representative, but they were fairly typical. The quality and consistency of the records maintained was often uneven. Material on postulants was noticeably scarce, for example. The archival part of my research was useful for insight into programs of study and statistics on admissions and perseverance, but left much that was untold. There was little sense of what it was like to be there – to be recruited, to deal with dubious parents, and to negotiate the aspiracy, postulancy, and novitiate. For an understanding of the significant markers on the road to religious vows, I turned to oral history and to the memoirs of nuns and former nuns. When these sources were combined with archival records, I had evidence from at least twenty different congregations – some of them contemplative – and much greater confidence in making generalizations.

Memoirs, of course, can easily deceive. Memory is filtered through subsequent experience, making the recollections of a nun, for example, potentially very different from those of an ex-nun. Nor is such a simple categorization easily imposed. Madeline DeFrees published her memoir, *The Springs of Silence*, in 1954 when she was with the Sisters of the Holy Names, only to leave the congregation two decades later. Do we classify her as a nun or an ex-nun? The burgeoning body of autobiographical writing by former nuns has almost established itself as a distinct literary genre. And yet quality and reliability vary greatly. Some books in the genre are of little use to historians. Poorly written and published by dubious vanity presses, they often fail to identify the author's congregation or the years during which she was a member of it. Some are barely disguised revivals of the nineteenth-century "escaped nun" narrative. But there is much of value here too – thoughtful and detailed accounts of personal experience that allow history to come alive.

Books of advice by priests for nuns constitute another category of sources. Sometimes the work of experienced retreat masters, sometimes not, these books take on relevance when addressing questions of recruitment and training. The works of Father Godfrey Poage – a major champion of active recruitment – belong here. Books of advice require a word of caution too, since it is hard to say how many people actually read them or took their advice to heart. They do, however, reveal the thinking of influential priests on religious life, and priests played a critical role in convents, as chaplains, confessors, retreat masters, and novitiate instructors.

A number of Catholic journals and periodicals, many of them no longer being published, give occasional insight into questions of recruitment and religious formation: for example, the *Catholic Educational Review*, the *Ecclesiastical Review*, and *Sponsa Regis*. One source that can be classified here stands out for its consistency in addressing these issues: the *National Catholic Educational Association Bulletin*, and in particular the sections recording the deliberations of the association's Vocations Committee. The publications arising from the Vocational Institutes held at Notre Dame University beginning in the late 1940s and continuing through the subsequent decade are also of direct relevance.

In the introductory and concluding chapters, I relied principally on secondary sources, although primary materials and memoirs did come into play. Of course, I did not read everything written on the subject; that would be impossible in a lifetime, let alone in an academic career, and this is especially so in the case of congregational histories. This is not to admit to a want of diligence on my part and, if you suspect otherwise, try reading all 729 pages of Sister Sheila Hackett's *Dominican Women in Texas* (1986). And be sure not to drop it on your foot if you doze off in the middle of it.

1 Quoted in Wulstan, "Overcoming the Prejudice to Vocation Clubs," 171.

2 Wakin and Scheuer, "The American Nun: Poor, Chaste, and Restive," 40.

3 "'God's Geese' Watched Over Flocks of Girls," *Los Angeles Times*, 29 June 1997.

4 Mary of St Teresita, *The Social Work of the Sisters of the Good Shepherd*, 78.

5 Kuhns, *The Habit*, 68, 69.

6 While rules and constitutions are usually employed as interchangeable terms, the rule, strictly speaking, refers to the basic principles prescribed by a saint many centuries ago. Constitutions are more elaborate documents providing the details of governance that are founded on the rule.

7 This idea has no foundation in the official books of the Bible and is usually traced to the *Infancy Gospel of James*, or the *Protevangelium Jacobi*, which was written around 150 CE. Ehrman, *Forgery and Counterforgery*, 485–93.

8 Freeman, *The Closing of the Western Mind*, 246–8.

9 Saints Agnes, Lucy, Margaret of Antioch, and Catherine of Alexandria fall into this fictional category, and they were eliminated from the liturgical calendar in 1969. See Jansen, *Making the Magdalen*, 335, 336.

10 MacCulloch, *Christianity*, 200–1.

11 McNamara, *Sisters in Arms*, 62–4.

12 MacCulloch, *Christianity*, 203–5, Reynes, *Couvents de femmes*, 8, 9.

13 Freeman, *The Closing of the Western Mind*, 251–2; MacCulloch, *Christianity*, 317–18; McNamara, *Sisters in Arms*, 33, 34.

14 Grout and Palisca, *A History of Western Music*, 17–48; Diekmann, "Living with the Church in Prayer and Reading," 209–26.

15 Quoted in Reynes, *Couvents de femmes*, 122, 123.

16 Rapley, *The Lord as Their Portion*, 39.

17 Kuhns, *The Habit*, 53–5, 65–7.

18 McNamara, *Sisters in Arms*, 95–102.

19 Ibid., 193–4; Rapley, *The Lord as Their Portion*, 39.

20 Evangelisti, *Nuns*, 31, 32; McNamara, *Sisters in Arms*, 79, 80.

21 Evangelisti, *Nuns*, 4, 5, 21, 22; Rapley, *The Lord as Their Portion*, 214; Shahar, *The Fourth Estate*, 39, 40.

22 Evangelisti, *Nuns*, 21. Diderot's novel, *La religieuse* (*The Nun*) tells the story of a young woman sent to a convent against her will. The most recent movie version of the novel is directed by Guillaume Nicloux (2013).

23 Reynes, *Couvents de femmes*, 19–36.

24 McNamara, *Sisters in Arms*, 159, 185.

25 Cohen, *The Evolution of Women's Asylums Since 1500*, 14–17; McCarthy, *Origins of the Magdalene Laundries*, 72–89.

26 Evangelisti, *Nuns*, 6; Laven, *Virgins of Venice*, 147–66; Levack, *The Devil Within*, 175–9; McNamara, *Sisters in Arms*, 358–68.

27 Evangelisti, *Nuns*, 202; Rapley, *The Lord as Their Portion*, 83.

28 MacCulloch, *Christianity*, 421.

29 Evangelisti, *Nuns*, 33–9.

30 Rapley, *The Lord as Their Portion*, 124, 141.

31 Evangelisti, *Nuns*, 176–81.

32 Ibid., 204–11; Rapley, *The Dévotes*, 48–60.

33 "Little Office of Our Lady," *New Advent Catholic Encyclopedia*. http://www.newadvent.org/cathen/09294a.htm (accessed 17 June 2015). For a fuller discussion of the difference between the two Offices, see Diekmann, "Living with the Church in Prayer and Reading," 209–26.

34 For further insight into the new forms of active monastic life that emerged at this time, see Bireley, *The Refashioning of Catholicism, 1450–1700*. Bireley, himself a Jesuit priest, argues that the Counter Reformation was not just a reaction to the challenge of Protestantism, but a more profound response to the political, social, and economic changes that were transforming European society at the time.

35 Rapley, *The Lord as Their Portion*, 172–7.

36 Bernoville, *Saint Mary Euphrasia Pelletier*, 36–40; Coburn and Smith, *Spirited Lives*, 20–35; Rapley, *The Dévotes*, 34–41, 79–94.

37 Hennesey, *American Catholics*, 11–14.

38 Evangelisti, *Nuns*, 192–7.

39 Butler, *Across God's Frontiers*, 17.

40 Chabot, "Guyart, Marie, *dite* Marie de l'Incarnation."

41 McGuinness, *Called to Serve*, 19, 20.

42 Butler, *Across God's Frontiers*, 17.

43 Hennesey, *American Catholics*, 86, 87; McGuinness, *Called to Serve*, 22–6.

44 Hennesey, *American Catholics*, 87; Rapley, *The Lord as Their Portion*, 297.

45 McGuinness, *Called to Serve*, 28–31; Rapley, *The Lord as Their Portion*, 298–9.

46 Walch, *Parish School*, 23, 24.

47 McGuinness, *Called to Serve*, 47.

48 Coburn and Smith, *Spirited Lives*, 43–65.

49 Mitchell, *Mother Théodore Guérin*, 27–86.

50 Mary of St Teresita, *The Social Work of the Sisters of the Good Shepherd*, 42–50.

51 Butler, *Across God's Frontiers*, 19, 20; Sister Mary James, *Providence*, 28–51; Nelson, "'The Harvest That Lies Before Us,'" 151–71.

52 McGuinness, *Called to Serve*, 32–5, 62, 63, 80.

53 Hennesey, *American Catholics*, 143, 144; McGuinness, *Called to Serve*, 20, 61, 62.

54 Ellis, *American Catholicism*, 90, 91; Hennesey, *American Catholics*, 153.

55 McGuinness, *Called to Serve*, 61.

56 Schultz, *Veil of Fear*. This volume reproduces two books in the escaped-nun genre: Rebecca Reed's *Six Months in a Convent* and Maria Monk's *Awful Disclosures of the Hôtel Dieu Nunnery*. See also, Sullivan, "Blasphemes of Modernity." There is a lengthy discussion of this topic in Ewens, *The Role of the Nun in Nineteenth-Century America*, 115–57.

57 Ewens, *The Role of the Nun in Nineteenth-Century America*, 173–95.

58 McGuinness, *Called to Serve*, 90–105; Rapley, *The Lord as Their Portion*, 303–5.

59 Dolan, *The Immigrant Church*, 47–62.

60 Lazerson, "Understanding American Catholic Educational History," 300, 301.

61 Walch, *Parish School*, 26–43.

62 McGuinness, *Called to Serve*, 74, 75; Walch, *Parish School*, 60–2.

63 Sprows Cummings, "The Wageless Work of Paradise," 117–20.

64 Caspary, *Witness to Integrity*, 12, 13, 26–8.

65 Hoy, "The Journey Out," 73–88.

66 Coburn and Smith, *Spirited Lives*, 87–9.

67 Butler, *Across God's Frontiers*, 24, 252–5.

68 Hoy, "The Journey Out," 86. Mary Peckham Magray argues that poor Irish girls preferred to pursue religious life abroad, where they had a better chance of becoming choir sisters, rather than at home. In Ireland they would have been assigned to manual labour as lay sisters. She is probably correct, but clearly it didn't always work out that way. Peckham Magray, *The Transforming Power of Nuns*, 105.

69 SPSMWA, unclassified file containing the necrologies of several co-adjutrix sisters shown to me by Sister Donna Butler, 22 May 2013, St Mary-of-the-Woods.

70 Conversation with Sister Donna Butler, 22 May 2013, St Mary-of-the-Woods. Anne Butler points out that tension over this distinction existed in other congregations too, and that one group of Benedictines abolished the distinction after much agitation as early as 1894. Butler, *Across God's Frontiers*, 292, 293.

71 Coburn and Smith, *Spirited Lives*, 129, 130, 144.

72 McGuinness, *Called to Serve*, 157–8.

73 Butler, *Across God's Frontiers*, 142–4; Coburn and Smith, *Spirited Lives*, 147, 164–7, 172; McGuinness, *Called to Serve*, 70–2; Oates, "Catholic Female Academies on the Frontier," 125–7.

74 Brewer, *Nuns and the Education of American Catholic Women*, 116.

75 Hennesey, *American Catholics*, 173, 174; McCarthy, *Guide to the Catholic Sisterhoods in the United States*, 204, 270.

76 Praszalowicz, "Polish American Sisterhoods," 47, 48.

77 McCarthy, *Guide to the Catholic Sisterhoods in the United States*, 26, 49.

78 Roby, "Les Canadiens français des États-Unis," 3, 4, 11, 18–20.

79 Butler, *Across God's Frontiers*, 17; Stewart, *Marvels of Charity*, 308, 309. Later upheavals, such as the establishment of the Spanish Republic in 1931 and the Cuban Revolution in 1959, brought more refugee nuns to America and for the same reasons.

80 Dolan, *The American Catholic Experience*, 276–82; LeMay, *From Open Door to Dutch Door*, 73–102; Walch, *Parish School*, 76–83.

81 UNDA/CHJC, 113/03, Entrance Book/Postulants' Book.

82 SCPA, File: Correspondence Re: Profession, Holy Habit, 1923–1979. The annual correspondence with Providence Maison Mère, Montréal, about the "novices vocales" to be admitted to vows was in French until 1954. Conversation with Sister Rosemary Dillman, Seattle, 3 December 2013. Sister Rosemary admitted that the choir sisters tended to look down on the lay or coadjutrix sisters, who often spoke very little English.

83 Davidson, "The Catholic Church in the United States," 187, 188; Gillis, *Roman Catholicism in America*, 65, 66; Tentler, ed., *The Church Confronts Modernity*, 12, 13.

84 Woods, *The Church Confronts Modernity*, 27–30, 88–97.

85 Ibid., 49, 50.

86 Pius XI, *Divini Illius Magistri*, Sections 59, 60.

87 "Rev. George B. Ford, a Crusader for Civil Rights and Ecumenism," *New York Times*, 3 August 1978; Arthur E. Bestor, *Educational Wastelands: The Retreat from Learning in Our Public Schools* (1953). Bestor was a professor of history at the University of Illinois and a specialist in the history of early American utopian communities.

88 Spring, *The American School*, 221–3.

89 Dwyer-McNulty, *Common Threads*, 106–8, 130.

90 Meyers, *The Education of Sisters*, 43, 70–3.
91 Orsi, *Thank You, St Jude*, 30, 45.
92 SCPA, Box 19, Surveys, Reports, File: Providence Vocation Survey, Thomas J. Harte, "Research on Religious Vocations in the United States."
93 Walch, *Parish School*, 170–6.
94 Deady, "The Role of the Religious Teacher in America," 130; Sister Mary Patrick, "Share the Sisters," and subsequent discussion, 134–47.
95 Sullivan, *Visual Habits*, 128, 129.
96 Cicognani, "The Religious in the U.S.," 11–16.
97 Mother Marie Helene, "The Spiritual Possibilities of Teaching as a Vocation," 119.
98 Briggs, *Double-Crossed*, 48.
99 Wakin and Scheuer, "The American Nun: Poor, Chaste, and Restive," 36.
100 Sister M. Madeleva, "The Education of Our Young Religious Teachers," 253–6.
101 Quinonez and Turner, *The Transformation of American Catholic Sisters*, 12–13; Wittberg, *The Rise and Fall of Catholic Religious Orders*, 210–11.
102 Sister Mary Emil, "The Survey Report on Teacher Preparation," 224–9; Quinonez and Turner, *The Transformation of American Catholic Sisters*, 6–8.
103 Briggs, *Double-Crossed*, 42.
104 Beane, *From Framework to Freedom*, 5–11.
105 Ibid., 82, 83.
106 Schneider, "American Sisters and the Roots of Change," 66.
107 O'Donnell, "The Lay Teacher in Catholic Education," 94.
108 Wakin and Scheuer, "The American Nun: Poor, Chaste, and Restive," 38.
109 Sister M. Annette, "An Environment Conducive to Mental and Physical Health," 114.
110 Vaughan, "The Psychological Screening of Candidates," 212.

CHAPTER 2

1 Pius XII, "Women's Duties in Social and Political Life," 324.
2 Sister Jean Clare, "The Primary Objective of Christian Education – Developing a Sense of Vocation," 446, 447.
3 Del SS.mo Rosario, "The Theology of Religious Vocations," 147.
4 Bernstein, *Nuns*, 46.
5 Pius XII, *Sacra Virginitas*, 6.
6 Ibid., 9, 10.
7 McGoldrick, *The Martyrdom of Change*, 31, 32.

8 Harris, "Virginity," 347, 348; Pius XII, *Sacra Virginitas*, 3.

9 Goyenche, "The States of Perfection in the Church Today," 143.

10 Hagan, "Some Factors in the Development of the Religious Vocations of Women," Part I, 621.

11 Bonduelle, "The Recognition of a Vocation," 41.

12 Bowdern, "A Study of Vocations," 601–3.

13 Bonduelle, "The Recognition of a Vocation," 42.

14 Frison, *Selection and Incorporation of Candidates for the Religious Life*, 7–9; A Vincentian Father, *Vocations Explained*, Chapter 8.

15 Kane, *Why I Entered the Convent*, xvi.

16 Del SS.mo Rosario, "The Theology of Religious Vocations," 149; Frison, *Selection and Incorporation of Candidates for the Religious Life*, 5–6.

17 Peters, *The 1917 Pio-Benedictine Code of Canon Law*, 209–12.

18 Titley, "Heil Mary," 5, 6. See also Kirsch, *The Spiritual Direction of Sisters*, 408. Kirsch, a Capuchin priest, warned confessors to be cautious in recommending doubtful cases. "The convent," he said, "should never be considered merely a refuge of sinners."

19 Best-Colgan, *Two Girls from the Bay*, 123, 124.

20 Bergh, "Canonical Impediments," 87.

21 For example, the Mexican Josephite Sisters, the Sisters of Providence of St-Mary-of-the-Woods, and the Sacramentine Nuns. McCarthy, *Guide to the Catholic Sisterhoods*, 241, 248, 318.

22 For example, the Daughters of Charity of the Most Precious Blood, the Dominican Sisters of Saint Catherine of Siena, and the Sisters of the Poor of St Francis. McCarthy, *Guide to the Catholic Sisterhoods*, 237, 278, 287.

23 Omez, "Negative Criteria of Vocation," 100.

24 D'Arienzo, "My Pact with Camillus," 27.

25 McGuinness, *Called to Serve*, 130–1; Rogers, *Habits of Change*, 188–9.

26 A Vincentian Father, *Vocations Explained*, Chapter 8. See also Bowdern, "A Study of Vocations," 401, and Cahill, "Factors in Religious Vocations of a Dominican Community," 42, for surveys that showed the dominance of these motivations among novices and nuns.

27 Hagan, "Some Factors in the Development of Religious Vocations of Women," 621; McCarthy, *Guide to the Catholic Sisterhoods*, 253.

28 Frison, *Selection and Incorporation of Candidates for the Religious Life*, 16–19; McCorry, "Basic Concepts of Vocation," 357; Motte, "The Obligation to Follow a Vocation," 22.

29 Motte, "The Obligation to Follow a Vocation," 33–5.

30 A Redemptorist Father, *A Treatise on Religious Vocation*, 38–9.

31 A Vincentian Father, *Vocations Explained*, Chapter 2.

32 Barrett, "A Study of the Influences of Catholic High School Experiences," 76–9.
33 SCPA, Formation, Box 19, File: Vocation Questionnaire. There is no date on the survey, but it can be narrowed down to between 1955 and 1965.
34 Poage, *For More Vocations*, viii.
35 Ferrer, "The Church's Need of Vocations," 295.
36 Bowdern, "A Study of Vocations," 21.
37 Pius XII, *Sacra Virginitas*, 14.
38 Woods, *The Church Confronts Modernity*, 52–62.
39 Pius XI, *Divini Illius Magistri*, Section 64.
40 Frison, *Selection and Incorporation of Candidates for Religious Life*, 56.
41 Houtart, "The Sociology of Vocations," 22–35. Houtart, born 1925, was a prominent Belgian sociologist of religion in the 1950s and 1960s. Later, he championed the cause of Palestinian statehood and became a well-known critic of globalization. Nominated for the 2011 Nobel Peace Prize, he asked that his name be withdrawn late in 2010 when he admitted to the sexual molestation of a youth many years earlier. "François Houtart, Belgian Activist Priest, Admits Sexual Abuse," *Huffington Post*, 29 December 2010.
42 Steinmetz, "American Sociology Before and After World War II," 343–62.
43 Desmond, "A Study of the Social Background Factors in Vocations," 11–14.
44 Willenbring, "The Origin and Development of Vocations to the Sisterhoods in North Dakota," 1–2.
45 Swatos, ed., *The Encyclopedia of Religion and Society*, 222. Thomas J. Harte (1914–1974) was born in Ireland and emigrated to the United States at the age of fourteen. He was a member of the Redemptorist Order and professor of sociology at the Catholic University of America. He was president of the American Catholic Sociological Society in 1951 and made no secret of his low regard for scholarship in the field.
46 This fact was acknowledged by one of the most respected Catholic sociologists, Father Joseph H. Fichter. Fichter, *Religion as an Occupation*, 23.
47 SCPA, Formation, Box 19, File: Providence Vocation Survey, background materials. Typescript paper by Thomas J. Harte, "Research on Religious Vocations in the United States," 3–5.
48 Poage, *Recruiting for Christ*, 96–8. Joseph Fichter affirmed Poage's view on the importance of piety as an indicator of "convent material." He said that a girl needed to be more than just "good" in the sense that

that word was normally understood. On the other hand, she did not have to be a saint, but should have a desire to become holy. Fichter, *Religion as an Occupation*, 47.

49 For example, Pius XI, *Divini Illius Magistri*, Section 90. See also Gillis, *Roman Catholicism in America*, 223–9.

50 Cahill, "Factors in Religious Vocations of a Dominican Community," 38–9.

51 Fichter, *Parochial School*, 101.

52 M. Christina, "Study of the Catholic Family Through Three Generations," 145.

53 "Catholic University Research Abstracts," 267; Desmond, "A Study of the Social Background Factors in Vocations," 33, 48–50; Hagan, "Some Factors in the Development of Religious Vocations in Women," 627.

54 M. Christina, "Study of the Catholic Family Through Three Generations," 149.

55 Cahill, "Factors in Religious Vocations of a Dominican Community," 35–6; Desmond, "A Study of the Social Background Factors in Vocations," 17; Hagan, "Some Factors in the Development of Religious Vocations in Women," 624–5.

56 Fichter, *Religion as an Occupation*, 35, 36.

57 Hoedl, "A Study of the Relationship of Several Types of Secondary Schools," 76, 137–8.

58 Hagan, "Some Factors in the Development of Religious Vocations of Women," 712–13.

59 Hoedl, "A Study of the Relationship of Several Types of Secondary Schools," 24–6, 80–3.

60 Barrett, "A Study of the Influences of Catholic High School Experiences," 49–50; Desmond, "A Study of the Social Background Factors in Vocations," 95–100; Hagan, "Some Factors in the Development of Religious Vocations of Women," 796–7.

61 Barrett, "A Study of the Influences of Catholic High School Experiences," 60–2.

62 Garesché, "The Influence of Schools on Religious Vocations," 194–5.

63 Barrett, "A Study of the Influences of Catholic High-School Experiences," 63–5; Cahill, "Factors in Religious Vocations of a Dominican Community," 43; Willenbring, "The Origin and Development of Vocations to the Sisterhoods," 44–5.

64 Willenbring, "The Origin and Development of Vocations to the Sisterhoods," 44–5.

65 Sister Mary George, "Proper Relationship Between Teacher and Prospective Vocation," 385.

66 Hoedl, "A Study of the Relationship of Several Types of Secondary Schools," 111.

67 One study suggested that about 25 per cent of sisters joined congregations different from the one from which they had received their education. They may have been motivated in doing so by a desire to pursue a career not available in exclusively teaching congregations. Desmond, "A Study of the Social Background Factors in Vocations," 69.

68 Conversation with Sister Rosemary Dillmann, Seattle, 3 December 2013.

69 Barrett, "A Study of the Influences of Catholic High-School Experiences," 67–8.

70 Hagan, "Some Factors in the Development of Religious Vocations in Women," 799.

71 Sister Marian Elizabeth, "Methods of Recruiting Vocations among High School Students," 309–10.

72 Hoedl, "A Study of the Relationship of Several Types of Secondary Schools," 74, 89–90.

73 Ibid., 74–6, 90.

74 Barrett, "A Study of the Influences of Catholic High-School Experiences," 50–1, 65–7.

75 Fichter, *Religion as an Occupation*, 43, 44.

76 Frison, *Selection and Incorporation of Candidates for the Religious Life*, 41.

77 Hagan, "Some Factors in the Development of Religious Vocations in Women," 715–16.

78 Barrett, "A Study of the Influences of Catholic High School Experiences," 26.

79 Ibid., 26–7.

80 Hagan, "Some Factors in the Development of Religious Vocations in Women," 716.

81 Garesché, "The Influence of Schools on Religious Vocations," 198.

82 A Vincentian Father, *Vocations Explained*, Chapter 11.

83 "Catholic University Research Abstracts," 267.

84 Hoedl, "A Study of the Relationship of Several Types of Secondary Schools," 14–15. In fact, Catholic women had engaged in public-school teaching ever since it had become a respectable profession in the nineteenth century. Teaching allowed them to live independently, if frugally. After the Second World War, with the emergence of effective unions, teaching allowed for much greater economic independence. Clifford, *Those Good Gertrudes*, 92, 110, 111, 169; Dwyer-McNulty, *Common Threads*, 94–9; Spring, *The American School*, 125.

85 Barrett, "A Study of the Influences of Catholic High-School Experiences," 65.

86 Hoedl, "A Study of the Relationship of Several Types of Secondary Schools," 14–15.

87 Greeley, *The American Catholic*, 50–68.
88 Davidson, "The Catholic Church in the United States," 193, 194; Tentler, ed., "Introduction," *The Church Confronts Modernity*, 13, 14.
89 Hagan, "Some Factors in the Development of Religious Vocations in Women," 624–7.
90 Cahill, "Factors in Religious Vocations of a Dominican Community," 44, 52; Desmond, "A Study of the Social Background Factors in Vocations," 106–8; Hoedl, "A Study of the Relationship of Several Types of Secondary Schools," 17.
91 "Catholic University Abstracts," 267; Desmond, "A Study of the Social Background Factors in Vocations," 48–50.
92 Hoedl, "A Study of the Relationship of Several Types of Secondary Schools," 24–6.
93 Garesché, "The Influence of Schools on Religious Vocations," 195, 196; Hoedl, "A Study of the Relationship of Several Types of Secondary Schools," 113–15.
94 "Catholic University Abstracts," 267.

CHAPTER 3

1   Sister M. Claudette, "I Remember My Last Date," 38–9.
2   Cushing, *That They May Know Thee*, 158.
3   Dukehart, "Guidance of Prospective Candidates to the Priesthood and Religious Life," 359.
4   Active recruitment was nothing really new. In her study of convents in nineteenth-century Quebec, Marta Danylewycz devotes a few pages to it. With respect to the Congregation of Notre Dame, she notes that teaching sisters in particular were expected to seek out suitable recruits: "Supplying students and other acquaintances with pious readings, encouraging frequent confessions, and offering to cover the cost of boarding were some of the approaches suggested to coax women with 'the qualities required for our institution' into religious life." Danylewycz, *Taking the Veil*, 118–22.
5   "Godfrey Poage," CatholicAuthors.com web archive; "Godfrey Poage," *Chicago Tribune*, 28 June 2001.
6   Poage, *For More Vocations*, viii, xiv.
7   Senieur, "The Thrill of a Lifetime," in Kane, *Why I Became a Priest*, 55–6.
8   Senieur, *Vocational Replies*, 4, 5, 156.
9   Ibid., 103.
10 Ahern, "The Role of the Elementary School Teacher in Fostering Vocations," 422.

11 Sister Mary Isabel, "A Plan for Fostering Vocations in the Elementary School," 254–60.

12 Poage, *Recruiting for Christ*, 125.

13 Conversation with Claire Perkins, Villefranche-sur-Mer, France, 20 October 2014.

14 Poage, *Recruiting for Christ*, 143.

15 Whitney, *The Calling*, 30–1.

16 Cullinan, "The Quest for Vocations," 270.

17 Masterson, *One Nun's Story*, 44–5.

18 Association of the Monasteries and Nuns of the Order of Preachers, *Vocation in Black and White*, 71–2.

19 Sister Mary Jean, "In Search of God," 57.

20 Thérèse of Lisieux, *The Story of a Soul*, 145.

21 For example: "But I don't want to suffer just one torment. I should have to suffer them all to be satisfied. Like you, my adorable Jesus, I want to be scourged and crucified. I want to be flayed like St. Bartholomew. Like St. John, I want to be flung into boiling oil. Like St. Ignatius of Antioch, I long to be ground by the teeth of wild beasts, ground into a bread worthy of God." Ibid., 160.

22 Whitney, *The Calling*, 32. In 2011 Rebecca Camisa directed a HBO documentary on Hart's life, *God Is the Bigger Elvis*. There is also a 2013 autobiography co-written with Richard DeNeut, *The Ear of the Heart: An Actress' Journey from Hollywood to Holy Vows*.

23 Brother André, "The Development of Religious Vocations," 347.

24 Fichter, *Religion as an Occupation*, 39.

25 McCorry, *Most Worthy of All Praise*, 84–6.

26 Gass, *Unconventional Women*, 23.

27 Ibid., 20.

28 Weakley, *Monastery to Matrimony*, 5–10, 27–34.

29 Kane, *Why I Entered the Convent*, 41–5. Kane's book was published first in 1953, but the essay by Sister M. Maura contains no information on the date she entered the School Sisters of Notre Dame.

30 Grueninger Beasley, *The Tears I Couldn't Cry*, 30–9, 284.

31 Hulme, *The Nun's Story*; Sullivan, *Visual Habits*, 104–17. The Warner Brothers' film, directed by Fred Zinnemann, actually toned down some aspects of convent life as depicted in the book in response to pressure from the Church. For example, Sister Luke's hair was shortened rather than shorn off, and she was shown receiving a flagellation whip, but not using it.

32 Poage, *Secrets of Successful Recruiting*, xv–xix.

33 Ferrer, "The Church's Need for Vocations," 295–6.

34 Poage, *For More Vocations*, 319.

35 Sister Mary Daniel, "Successful Vocation Programs," 216.

36 Poage, *Secrets of Successful Recruiting*, 45–7.

37 ACHRCUA/NCEA, Series 3, Box 20, Folder 5, Vocations, 1948–1956: "An Integrated Plan for Fostering Vocations to the Priesthood and Religious Life."

38 ACHRCUA/NCEA, Series 3, Box 9, Folder 9, Vocations, 1949–1951: John C. Wilson to Frederick Hochwalt, 20 April 1950.

39 Cassilly, *What Shall I Be?* 8–9.

40 Senieur, *Vocational Replies*, 14–15.

41 Hunter, *Marriage, Celibacy, and Heresy in Ancient Christianity*.

42 Poage, *Recruiting for Christ*, 147.

43 Orsi, *Thank You, St. Jude*, 46, 58–62, 73, 79.

44 Poage, *Recruiting for Christ*, 84.

45 Ibid., 85–6.

46 Ibid., 147.

47 Ibid., 1.

48 Poage, *For More Vocations*, 26.

49 Helen Horton was a native of Manhattan. Upon graduating from Garden City High School in 1941, she embarked on a career as a cabaret singer under the stage name Molly Horton, and performed at the Stork Club and the Café Pierre. In February 1946, she shocked the entertainment world by entering the Sisters of Charity of New York and remained with the congregation until her death on 8 January 2012. http://www.cny.org/stories/Sister-Helen-Horton-SC (accessed 10 April 2017).

50 This second example of a celebrity abandoning the world might not have been as persuasive as the first. While it was true that, in 1946, Los Angeles "was abuzz" when twenty-two-year-old Stella Consigli abandoned the Ice Follies to take her vows as Sister Mary Gertrude at the Monastery of the Angels below the Hollywood sign, she only remained there three or four years before re-entering the world. "Supporters band together to save Hollywood convent famous for pumpkin bread," *Los Angeles Times*, 9 April 2009.

51 Poage, *For More Vocations*, 34–6.

52 Fichter, *Parochial School*, 102, 103.

53 Congregation of the Sisters of St Joseph, Cleveland, Ohio, "Symposium on Religious Life," 256–68.

54 Gilligan Wong, *Nun*, 23–8.

55 Senieur, *Vocational Replies*, 194.

56 Poage, *Secrets of Successful Recruiting*, 6–7.

57 There is an extensive collection of this literature in the Rare Books and Special Collections of the Catholic University of America's

Mullen Library. One interesting piece here is John T. Gillard's *More Colored Nuns* (1938), which encouraged recruitment to the three congregations reserved exclusively for African-American women.

58 SCPA, Box 29, File: Vocation Brochures, 1943–1960s.

59 SPSMWA, Record Group 1300, Recruitment, File 1, Brochures. It should be noted that cover-girl Marilyn Marschall left the congregation in 1969.

60 Masterson, *One Nun's Story*, 52.

61 Poage, *Recruiting for Christ*, 166–9.

62 Palmer, *Parents and Vocations*, 21–2.

63 Fichter, *Religion as an Occupation*, 51.

64 Packard, *The Hidden Persuaders*, 4–9.

65 Poage, *For More Vocations*, 44.

66 Ibid.

67 Reilly, *What Must I Do?* 3–12.

68 Del Rey Danforth, *Bernie Becomes a Nun*, 72–3, 117.

69 Sister M. Catherine Frederic, *And Spare Me Not in the Making* (1953) was rather similar to Sister Reilly's book, but it offered a more realistic view of sister formation, since it was an actual diary kept by the author during her postulancy and novitiate with the Sisters of the Third Order of St Francis. Barbara and Grey Villet's *Those Whom God Chooses* (1966) was modelled on *Bernie Becomes a Nun* in its reliance on photographs to record the experiences of a group of young women as they became Marist Missionary Sisters.

70 Sullivan, *Visual Habits*, 124–56.

71 Spring, *The American School*, 221.

72 Sister Mary Joanne, "Our Lady of Good Counsel Clubs," 172; Poage, *For More Vocations*, 80; Poage, *Vocational Club Handbook*, 5.

73 Senieur, *Vocational Replies*, 26–7.

74 Ibid., 178–9.

75 Sister Mary Joanne, "Our Lady of Good Counsel Clubs," 177.

76 Poage, *Secrets of Successful Recruiting*, 137.

77 Wulston, "Overcoming the Prejudice to Vocation Clubs," 166–7.

78 Poage, *Secrets of Successful Recruiting*, 123–4.

79 Sister Mary Joanne, "Our Lady of Good Counsel Clubs," 174–5.

80 Poage, *Secrets of Successful Recruiting*, 125.

81 Poage, *For More Vocations*, 77–98.

82 Sister Mary Joanne, "Our Lady of Good Counsel Clubs," 176.

83 Sister Mary Blaise, "Fostering Vocations in Grades Six, Seven, and Eight," 106.

84 Sister Mary Corona, "Recruiting for Vocations to the Sisterhood," 328–9.

85 Senieur, *Vocational Replies*, 177.

86 Poage, *Secrets of Successful Recruiting*, 118–19.

87 Ibid., 137.

88 Sister Mary Joanne, "Our Lady of Good Counsel Clubs," 177.

89 Poage, *Recruiting for Christ*, 147–9.

90 Fichter, *Parochial School*, 103.

91 Poage, *The Secrets of Successful Recruiting*, 161–5.

92 Whitney, *The Calling*, 29–30.

93 Orsi, *Between Heaven and Earth*, 85. The photograph of little girls dressed as nuns reproduced on this page is quite remarkable.

94 Cullinan, "The Quest for Vocations," 272.

95 Brewer, *Nuns and the Education of American Catholic Women*, 83–5; Ward, *Christianity Under the Ancien Régime,* 46.

96 MacDonald, "Entering the Convent as Coming of Age in the 1930s," 88–9.

97 Association of the Monasteries of Nuns of the Order of Preachers, *Vocation in Black and White*, 1–2, 55–6, 79–80, 89–91.

98 The Missionary Oblate Sisters, established in Manitoba in 1902, drew their recruits from small French-Canadian communities on both sides of the Canada-US border. Bruno-Jofré, *The Missionary Oblate Sisters*, 86–8.

99 Poage, *For More Vocations*, 10.

100 Masterson, *One Nun's Story*, 47–8.

101 Howe, *A Change of Habit*, 32–6.

102 Griffin, *The Courage to Choose*, 6, 7, 15, 17.

103 Leahy, *The Summer of Yes*, 1–3, 9–11.

104 Poage, *Recruiting for Christ*, 122–4; Senieur, *Vocational Replies*, 122.

105 Poage, *For More Vocations*, 12–13.

106 ACHRCUA/NCEA, Series 3, Box 9, Folder 9, Vocations 1949–1951: Minutes of the Meeting of the Committee on Vocations, 21 April 1949.

107 MSA, Novitiate, Motherhouse, Admissions Procedure, File 5-4, Vocation Director's interview notes, no date. A similar point was made by Brother Adelbert James, FSC, in an address to the NCEA in 1960: Adelbert James, "Interviews and Vocations," 491.

108 Poage, *For More Vocations*, 110–13.

109 Ethier Rosenbaum, *The Unmaking of a Nun*, 8, 9, 12, 24, 249.

110 Poage, *Secrets of Successful Recruiting*, 71–2.

111 Ibid., 72–3.

112 Sister Mary Corona, "Recruiting for Vocations to the Sisterhoods," 331.

113 Senieur, *Vocational Replies*, 66–7.

114 Reilly, *What Must I Do?* 14–15.

115 Poage, *Secrets of Successful Recruiting*, 70–1.

116 MSA, Lists, Series 5: Box 15, Folder 15/18, Reports, Internal, Entrance, Statistics, 1948–1974.
117 MSA, H3.4 Eastern USA Region, File 2-16: A History of Ladycrest; File 2-17: Topsfield Novitiate, Administrative Papers; File 2-19: Newspaper Clippings (1953–1984). In 1968 there were only two novices remaining in Topsfield and the property was sold the following year to the State of Massachusetts, which planned to turn it into a juvenile-detention centre.

CHAPTER 4

1 Reilly, *What Must I Do?* 13.
2 Mother Catherine Thomas, *My Beloved*, 64.
3 Danylewycz, *Taking the Veil*, 112, 130.
4 McGuinness, *Called to Serve*, 155. There is a brief discussion of the problem of parental objections in McLoughlin, *American Culture and Catholic Schools*, 202–8. Emmett McLoughlin, the "People's Padre," was a former priest, and his book is a bitter and poorly researched attack on the Church.
5 Sister Josphine, OSB, "One Reason for the Dearth of Religious Vocations," 70–2.
6 Pius XI, *Ad Catholici Sacerdotii*, 23 (Section 83).
7 Poage, *For More Vocations*, 143.
8 The study is cited in Fichter, *Religion as an Occupation*, 19.
9 Stevens, "Picketing the Vineyard," 74–5.
10 De Hueck, "What Sisters Can Do," 145. De Hueck was an exiled Russian baroness who established shelters for the down-and-out in Canada and the United States. She was an ardent foe of racism and attacked her Church's indifference to it. She is being considered for canonization. See "The Unlikely Story of Catherine de Hueck," *Ottawa Citizen*, 9 July 2007.
11 See, for example, Palmer, "The Natural Law and International Relations," 40.
12 Palmer, *Parents and Vocations*, 10–11.
13 Brother André, "The Development of a Religious Vocation," 343–4.
14 Gass, *Unconventional Women*, 20–31.
15 Drydyk died on 15 September 1995, after an active career championing the rights of farm workers. Bernstein, *Nuns*, 54–5; "Drydyk's Life a Paradigm for Justice," *National Catholic Reporter*, 6 October 1995.
16 Dorcy, "Some Call It Madness, Some Call It Love," 48.
17 Whitney, *The Calling*, 47–8.
18 Bissell, *The Scent of God*, 41–4.
19 Kelley, *Love Is Not for Cowards*, 29, 30.

20 Brother of the Christian Schools, *Instructions on Vocations*, 10.
21 Lexau, *Convent Life*, 42.
22 Stevens, "Picketing the Vineyard," 77–8.
23 Palmer, *Parents and Vocations*, 11–12.
24 Fichter, *Religion as an Occupation*, 113.
25 Brother of the Christian Schools, *Instructions on Vocations*, 10.
26 Ibid., 39.
27 See, for example, Brother of the Christian Schools, *Instructions on Vocations*, 10; Reilly, *What Must I Do?* 12; St Alphonso di Liguori, *The True Spouse of Jesus Christ*, 277–9.
28 Reilly, *What Must I Do?* 11.
29 Ibid., 93–4.
30 SCPA, Formation Series, Box 29, File: Vocation Brochures, 1943–1960s, "Who Are the Sisters of Providence?" The same prayer is reproduced in Poage and Treacy, *Parents' Role in Vocations*, 125.
31 DeFrees, *The Springs of Silence*, 93, 94.
32 St Anthony's Vocational Club in Pittsburgh, for example, was active in publishing vocational pamphlets.
33 SCPA, Formation Series, Box 29, no file, brochure: "Information for Parents," no date.
34 Ralenkotter, "Winning Parents," 193. http://www.catholicnewworld.com/archive/cnw2003/091403/obit.html (accessed 12 June 2015).
35 Senieur, *Vocational Replies*, 139–40.
36 Poage, *Secrets of Successful Recruiting*, 87–8.
37 Ibid., 92–8.
38 Palmer, *Parents and Vocations*, 14–15.
39 Stevens, "Picketing the Vineyard," 76, 79.
40 Reilly, *What Must I Do?* 15–16.
41 Senieur, "Why Do My Parents Object?" 81.
42 Palmer, *Parents and Vocations*, 20–1.
43 Senieur, "Why Do My Parents Object?" 84.
44 Reilly, *What Must I Do?* 15.
45 Senieur, "Why Do My Parents Object?" 82.
46 Palmer, *Parents and Vocations*, 12–13.
47 Pius XI, *Divini Illius Magistri*, 13 (Sections 65 and 67).
48 Camilleri, *The Problem of Teen-Age Purity*, 42–3.
49 Ibid., 71.
50 Senieur, "Why Do My Parents Object?" 82.
51 Poage, *For More Vocations*, 148–50.
52 Senieur, *Vocational Replies*, 136–8; Senieur, "Why Do My Parents Object?" 84–5.
53 Stevens, "Picketing the Vineyard," 78.

54 Palmer, *Parents and Vocations*, 16–17.

55 Poage, *For More Vocations*, 156–8.

56 Palmer, *Parents and Vocations*, 19.

57 Brewer, *Nuns and the Education of American Catholic Women*, 93.

58 Schrembs was born in Germany in 1866 and his family emigrated to the United States in 1877. He was Bishop of Toledo, Ohio, from 1911 until 1921 and Bishop of Cleveland from 1921 until his death in 1945. Poluse, "Archbishop Joseph Schrembs's Battle," 428.

59 Brothers of the Christian Schools, *Instructions on Vocations*, 42–3. Invidious comparisons between the happiness of religious and married people had a long history in the Church. St Alphonso di Ligouri argued that the difficulties facing women in marriage – including the dangers and pains of childbirth – "fill their souls with continual regret for not having been called to a happier and more holy state." Di Ligouri, *The True Spouse of Jesus Christ*, 22–4.

60 Senieur, "Why Do My Parents Object?" 85.

61 Palmer, *Parents and Vocations*, 23–4.

62 The quotation is from *Homo Apostolicus*, Tract 13, No 25, and was cited in Brother of the Christian Schools, *Instructions on Vocations* (42), Lexau, *Convent Life* (41), Senieur, *Vocational Replies* (132), and elsewhere.

63 Poage, *For More Vocations*, 165.

64 Stevens, "Picketing the Vineyard," 79.

65 Lord, *Shall My Daughter Be a Nun?* 11, 31.

66 Brother of the Christian Schools, *Instructions on Vocations*, 42.

67 Frederic, *And Spare Me Not in the Making*, 79–80.

68 Lord, *Shall My Daughter Be a Nun?* 12.

69 Zemba, *A Life Like Nun Other*, 56.

70 Gass, *Unconventional Women*, 26.

71 Herbst, *Girlhood's Highest Ideal*, 67. See also Motte, "The Obligation to Follow a Vocation," 18–19. While there were many individuals named Heliodorus in antiquity, the reference here is to St Heliodorus (died c. 399 CE), Bishop of Altino, who was noted for combatting Arianism.

72 Herbst, "Doubts About Vocation," 125.

73 A Redemptorist Father, *A Treatise on Religious Vocation*, 27, 28.

CHAPTER 5

1 Poage, *Recruiting for Christ*, 172.

2 Sister Mary Alene, "The Adolescent Girl and the Aspirancy," 367–9.

3 Hoy, *Good Hearts*, 24–6.

4 UNDA/CHJC, 157/12, Historical Data, 1921–68, typescript history of Ancilla Domini School.

5 The congregation of the Franciscan Sisters of St Joseph was founded in 1897 in Trenton, New Jersey, by Father Hyacinth Fudzinsky and Sister M. Colette Hilbert. Hilbert had originally been with the Charity Sisters of St Charles Borromeo. McCarthy, *Guide to the Catholic Sisterhoods*, 87.

6 Immaculata continues in existence, but as an exclusive private school for girls. http://www.immaculataacademy.com (accessed 29 March 2012).

7 SPSMWA, Record Group 1360, Juniorate/Aspirancy, File 6, Sister M. Angelica (Marymount College, Salina, Kansas) to Mother Superior, Sisters of Providence, 10 August 1953 and 31 March 1954. Sister Rose Thering's survey for her MEd thesis in 1958 was also distributed to fifty communities. Thering, "The Aspirancy," 37.

8 Fichter, *Religion as an Occupation*, 30, 33.

9 Sister Mary Alene, "The Adolescent Girl and the Aspirancy," 365–6.

10 SPSMWA, Record Group 1360, Juniorate/Aspirancy, Materials re. entrance, miscellaneous brochures.

11 Ibid., File 2 Correspondence, 1930–72, Sister Emmanuel (St Patrick's Convent, Stoneham, Mass.) to Mother Mary Raphael, 23 April 1930; Sister Francis Lucile (St Anselm Convent, Chicago) to Mother Mary Raphael, 13 May 1930.

12 UNDA/CHJC, 157/10, Journal of Recruiting and Enrolment, Ancilla Domini School, 1938–62. The notes in this journal showed the Poor Handmaids identifying potential students for the aspirancy, while Sisters Isabelle and Beatildis were travelling about to recruit them.

13 SPSMWA, Record Group 1360, Juniorate/Aspirancy, File 6, Materials re. entrance, miscellaneous brochures.

14 UNDA/CHJC, 157/10, Journal of Recruiting and Enrolment, Ancilla Domini School, 1938–62.

15 UNDA/CHJC, 94/14, Study of Sisters Entering from Ancilla Domini High School, 1922–49, 37–8.

16 Conversation with Sister Mariane Mader, St Mary-of-the-Woods, Indiana, 23 May 2013. In the documentary *Why Is a Nun?*, aspirants at Mt. Alvernia are shown cleaning and working in the laundry. The narrator describes it as the "cheerful application to the most menial tasks."

17 The Sisters of St Francis trace their origins to a community established in Millvale, Pennsylvania, in 1855 under the leadership of a Redemptorist bishop, the Venerable John Nepomucene Neumann and Mother M. Chrysostom. McCarthy, *Guide to the Catholic Sisterhoods*, 96.

18 Howe, *A Change of Habit*, 21, 26. Howe stayed at Mt Alvernia until June 1952 and completed her secondary education at Sacred Heart

High School, a non-residential institution for Catholic girls. Later she joined the Sisters of St Joseph. Mt Alvernia in time evolved into a regular Catholic girls' school and closed due to falling enrolment in 2011. "Millvale's Mount Alvernia High School to Close," *Pittsburgh Post-Gazette*, 11 December 2010.

19 The congregation of the School Sisters of St Francis was established in Cambellsport, Wisconsin, in 1874 by Mother M. Alexia, who had emigrated from Bismarck's Germany. McCarthy, *Guide to the Catholic Sisterhoods*, 90.

20 Zemba, *A Life Like Nun Other*, 2.

21 Dwyer-McNulty, *Common Threads*, 89, 100.

22 *Why Is a Nun?* shows these uniforms at Mt Alvernia.

23 Gilligan Wong, *Nun*, 22–3, 26–7, 31–2. Gilligan became a professed Sister of Providence in 1961 and kept her vows until 1968. In her memoir, she fictionalizes her congregation as the Sisters of Blessing.

24 The congregation was established in France in 1762 by the Venerable John Martin Moye, with the assistance of Marguerite Le Compte. In 1866 two sisters came to Texas with Bishop Claude Dubuis and made their headquarters in Castroville. Their aspirancy was known as Moye–St Louis High School. The Sisters opened additional aspirancy sites in Oklahoma and Louisiana in 1964, but they were never a success. In 1966 no new aspirants were admitted to Moye–St Louis and it closed in 1968. McCarthy, *Guide to the Catholic Sisterhoods*, 65. Morkovsky, *Living in God's Providence*, 346–7.

25 Ebaugh, *Women in the Vanishing Cloister*, 96–7. In a typical sociological approach, Ebaugh does not name the congregation she studied in this book, giving them the pseudonym "Sisters of Service." The real identity of the congregation was easy to figure out. The Sisters of Service do actually exist. Founded in Toronto, Canada, in 1922, they established a branch in Fargo, North Dakota, in 1939. McCarthy, *Guide to the Catholic Sisterhoods*, 257.

26 Howe, *A Change of Habit*, 25.

27 Poage, *Recruiting for Christ*, 119.

28 Senieur, *Vocational Replies*, 90–1.

29 Sister Mary Alene, "The Adolescent Girl and the Aspirancy," 367.

30 SPSMWA, Record Group 1630, Juniorate/Aspirancy Group 6, Sister M. Angelica to Mother Superior, 31 March 1954.

31 UNDA/CHJC, 157/13, Villa Maria Chronicles, 1963–1969.

32 Zemba, *A Life Like Nun Other*, 3.

33 UNDA/CHJC, 157/12, Historical Data, 1921–1968, 9. In Ancilla Domini, aspirants were allowed to send two letters and two cards to the outside world on the Sundays when there were no visitors.

34 Zemba, *A Life Like Nun Other*, 3.

35 Howe, *A Change of Habit*, 24, 28, 29.

36 UNDA/CHJC, 157/12, Historical Data, 1921–1968, 9.

37 UNDA/CHJC, 157/13, Villa Maria Chronicles, 1963–1969.

38 Conversation with Sister Marianne Mader, St Mary-of-the-Woods, Indiana, 23 May 2013.

39 SPSMWA, Record Group 1630, Juniorate/Aspirancy Group 6, Sister M. Angelica to Mother Superior, 31 March 1954. The survey conducted by the Sisters of St Joseph showed that twenty-one aspirancies out of fifty allowed their students home on Thanksgiving, while twenty-three allowed an Easter vacation.

40 UNDA/CHJC, 157/12, Historical Data, 1921–1968, 5.

41 Senieur, *Vocational Replies*, 95.

42 SPSMWA, Record Group 1630, Juniorate/Aspirancy, Publications III, *The High Road*, June 1946.

43 Howe, *A Change of Habit*, 30.

44 Sister Mary Alene, "The Adolescent Girl and the Aspirancy," 365.

45 Gilligan Wong, *Nun*, 126, 138–9.

46 Senieur, *Vocational Replies*, 95.

47 UNDA/CHJC, 158/10, collection of term papers on the history of the aspirancy, 1951.

48 The congregation was established in Steyl, the Netherlands, in 1889 by Rev. Arnold Janssen. The Sisters arrived in the United States in 1901. McCarthy, *Guide to the Catholic Sisterhoods*, 207.

49 Poage, *Recruiting for Christ*, 175–6.

50 UNDA/CHJC, 157/12, Historical Data, 1921–1968, no page number.

51 Gilligan Wong, *Nun*, 87–8.

52 Howe, *A Change of Habit*, 26.

53 Poage, *Recruiting for Christ*, 120.

54 UNDA/CHJC, 157/12, Historical Data, 1921–1968, 9.

55 Conversation with Sister Marianne Mader, St Mary-of-the-Woods, Indiana, 23 May 2013.

56 SPSMWA, Record Group 1630, Juniorate/Aspirancy, Publications III, *The High Road*, April 1939.

57 Conversation with Sister Marianne Mader, St Mary-of-the-Woods, Indiana, 23 May 2013.

58 SPSMWA, Record Group 1630, File 4, Formation. Academic and extra-curricular materials, 1935–1966.

59 SPSMWA, Record Group 1630, Juniorate/Aspirancy, Publications III, *The High Road*, June 1946.

60 Poage, *Recruiting for Christ*, 175–6.

61 Gilligan Wong, *Nun*, 76. Conversation with Sister Joseph Fillenworth, St Mary-of-the-Woods, Indiana, 22 May 2013.

62 UNDA/CHJC, 157/13, Villa Maria Chronicles, 1963–1969.

63 Senieur, *Vocational Replies*, 87–9.

64 Thering, "The Aspirancy," 40–1.
65 Senieur, *Vocational Replies*, 96–7.
66 Gilligan Wong, *Nun*, 119.
67 Senieur, *Vocational Replies*, 97–8.
68 Gilligan Wong, *Nun*, 110.
69 Ibid., 52.
70 Ibid., 64–7.
71 Howe, *A Change of Habit*, 30.
72 Zemba, *A Life Like Nun Other*, 2.
73 Gilligan Wong, *Nun*, 60.
74 UNDA/CHJC, 157/13, Villa Maria Chronicles, 1963–1969.
75 UNDA/CHJC, 158/10, collection of term papers on the history of the aspirancy, 1951.
76 Carroll, *Catholic Cults and Devotions*, 11–12.
77 SPSMWA, Record Group 1630, Juniorate/Aspirancy, Publications III, *The High Road*, October 1937.
78 Carroll, *Catholic Cults and Devotions*, 106–8.
79 SPSMWA, Record Group 1630, Juniorate/Aspirancy, Publications III, *The High Road*, February 1936.
80 SCPA, Constitutions of the Daughters of Charity, Servants of the Poor. Providence Mother House, Montreal, 1925. Chapter 1, Rule 63, pages 70, 71.
81 SPSMWA, Record Group 1630, Juniorate/Aspirancy, Publications III, *The High Road*, May 1947.
82 Ibid., Spring 1937.
83 Ibid., Easter 1943.
84 Ibid., Easter 1944.
85 Ibid., December 1936.
86 Senieur, *Vocational Replies*, 81–2.
87 Gilligan Wong, *Nun*, 72–3.
88 Senieur, *Vocational Replies*, 94.
89 UNDA/CHJC, 157/13, Villa Maria Chronicles, 1963–1969. See Orsi, *Between Heaven and Earth*, 103–7, on the important role played by angels as ever-present moral vigilantes in Catholic children's lives.
90 UNDA/CHJC, 113/03, Register of Sisters, Entrance Book, graduating 1960; SPSMWA, Record Group 1630, Juniorate/Aspirancy, Yearbooks, with notes on individual students.
91 SPSMWA, Record Group 1630, Juniorate/Aspirancy, Yearbooks, with notes on individual students.
92 Gilligan Wong, *Nun*, 88, 117, 142.
93 SPSMWA, Record Group 1360, Juniorate/Aspirancy, File 6, Materials re. entrance, miscellaneous brochures.
94 SPSMWA, Record Group 1360, Juniorate/Aspirancy, File 6, Lists and statistics, 1953–83.

95 Fichter, *Religion as an Occupation*, 21.
96 Sister Mary Alene, "The Adolescent Girl and the Aspirancy," 366.
97 SPSMWA, Record Group 1360, Juniorate/Aspirancy, File 6, Lists and statistics, 1953–83, "Information about Providence Aspirancy," one-page typescript from 1963.
98 Forbes, "The Aspirancy: Foundation for Renewal?" 491.
99 SPSMWA, Record Group 1360, Juniorate/Aspirancy, File 2, correspondence, 1930–1976, Sister Rose Angela Horan to Sister Wilma Sehr, 4 November 1976; Mother Rose Angela to "My dear Sisters," 29 April 1966.
100 Levack, *The Devil Within*, 174.

CHAPTER 6

1 Griffin, *The Courage to Choose*, 17.
2 UNDA, CHJC, 50/05, Chapters Taken from the Holy Rule, 1928–1932: "On Simplicity."
3 Peters, *The 1917 Pio-Benedictine Code of Canon Law*, 209 (Canon 539), 222 (Canon 573).
4 Farrell, St John, and Elkisch, *The Education of the Novice*, 4–7.
5 Reilly, *What Must I Do?* 20–1.
6 Larsen, *The Tulip and the Pope*, 47.
7 This was the usual arrangement. In some larger convents, the postulants and novices were housed separately.
8 DeFrees, *The Springs of Silence*, 20–1.
9 Whitney, *The Calling*, 166.
10 Gilligan Wong, *Nun*, 155; Howe, *A Change of Habit*, 40.
11 Larsen, *The Tulip and the Pope*, 27.
12 Kuhns, *The Habit*, 26–8.
13 DeFrees, *The Springs of Silence*, 17.
14 Lynch, *Triptych*, 26.
15 Reilly, *What Must I Do?* 22.
16 O'Donnell-Gibson, *The Red Skirt*, 67–8. The separation is vividly portrayed in the 1959 feature film, *The Nun's Story*.
17 DeFrees, *The Springs of Silence*, 27.
18 Gilligan Wong, *Nun*, 169.
19 Morkovsky, *Living in God's Providence*, 346.
20 DeFrees, *The Springs of Silence*, 25, 36.
21 Howe, *A Change of Habit*, 43.
22 Reilly, *What Must I Do?* 26.
23 Stolz, *Convent Life and Beyond*, 18, 22.
24 Masterson, *One Nun's Story*, 85.

25 MSA, Mother Mary Joseph Rogers Papers, Conferences, Box 10, folder 10/3, "Morning talks for the benjamins of the flock, 18 November 1925."

26 For example, the Sisters of Charity of Our Lady of Mercy, the Sisters of the Precious Blood, the Sisters of Divine Providence, the Sisters of St Francis, the School Sisters of the Third Order of St Francis, the Missionary Sisters of Our Lady of Africa, the Society of Mary Reparatrix, and the Sisters, Servants of the Immaculate Heart of Mary. McCarthy, *Guide to the Catholic Sisterhoods*, 41, 65, 94, 101, 149, 174, 202, 231.

27 Ibid., the Bernardine Sisters and the School Sisters de Notre Dame, respectively, 72, 214.

28 Henderson, *Out of the Curtained World*, 52.

29 Whitney, *The Calling*, 46, 53.

30 Ibid., 49. Performing mortifications in honour of Mary on Saturdays was a long-established convent practice and was championed by St Alfonso di Ligouri. See Di Ligouri, *The True Spouse of Jesus Christ*, 636, 637.

31 Howe, *A Change of Habit*, 43–4.

32 Turk, *The Buried Life*, 9.

33 Masterson, *One Nun's Story*, 72–3.

34 Larsen, *The Tulip and the Pope*, 51, 61–2.

35 Ethier Rosenbaum, *The Unmaking of a Nun*, 19.

36 Masterson, *One Nun's Story*, 75, 103.

37 O'Donnell-Gibson, *The Red Skirt*, 74–5.

38 DeFrees, *The Springs of Silence*, 64.

39 Masterson, *One Nun's Story*, 70. Marta Danylewycz, in her study of two congregations in nineteenth-century Quebec, described the isolation of nuns-in-training as a measure to shelter them "from the negative influences of some of the less exemplary professed members of the community." Danylewycz, *Taking the Veil*, 49.

40 DeFrees, *The Springs of Silence*, 60; Masterson, *One Nun's Story*, 66–7.

41 O'Donnell-Gibson, *The Red Skirt*, 73.

42 Larsen, *The Tulip and the Pope*, 32.

43 Stolz, *Convent Life and Beyond*, 33.

44 Masterson, *One Nun's Story*, 91–2.

45 Lynch, *Triptych*, 33; Masterson, *One Nun's Story*, 91–2; McCann, *Out of the Habit*, 39–42.

46 Gilligan Wong, *Nun*, 185.

47 Turk, *The Buried Life*, 29.

48 Masterson, *One Nun's Story*, 92.

49 Bassler, *Removing the Habit of God*, 41; Grueninger Beasley, *The Tears I Couldn't Cry*, 11; O'Donnell-Gibson, *The Red Skirt*, 69–70.

50 DeFrees, *The Springs of Silence*, 38; Lynch, *Triptych*, 30; Turk, *The Buried Life*, 9.

51 When Joanne Howe became a postulant with the Sisters of St Joseph in 1953, she found herself in a bleak and austere dormitory to be shared with eleven others. There were mirrors in the bathrooms for general use, but personal ones were forbidden. At St Mary-in-the-Woods Mary Gilligan discovered that mirrors had only been approved shortly before her arrival in 1958. Postulants were permitted to use them for combing their hair. Gilligan Wong, *Nun*, 156; Howe, *Change of Habit*, 42–4.

52 Masterson, *One Nun's Story*, 76.

53 Ibid., 77–8.

54 Reilly, *What Must I Do?* 23–4.

55 Turk, *The Buried Life*, 26–7.

56 Bassler, *Removing the Habit of God*, 49; O'Donnell-Gibson, *The Red Skirt*, 98–9.

57 Turk, *The Buried Life*, 26–7.

58 For example, Thurston and Attwater, *Butler's Lives of the Saints*, vol. 1, 696–7, tells the story of St Barachisius and his martyrdom; Masterson, *One Nun's Story*, 83–4.

59 Masterson, *One Nun's Story*, 80–1.

60 O'Donnell-Gibson, *The Red Skirt*, 81–2.

61 DeFrees, *The Springs of Silence*, 42–4.

62 Griffin, *The Courage to Choose*, 19.

63 Hollingsworth, *Ex-Nuns*, 11, 15–16.

64 Reilly, *What Must I Do?* 27.

65 DeFrees, *The Springs of Silence*, 46–7.

66 For background on this important figure, see Krieg, *Romano Guardini*.

67 Larsen, *The Tulip and the Pope*, 66–7; O'Donnell-Gibson, *The Red Skirt*, 73–4.

68 Masterson, *One Nun's Story*, 102.

69 SCPA, Formation Series, Box 3, File: Formation History, Sister Martin, notebook.

70 Masterson, *One Nun's Story*, 97.

71 Tanqueray, *The Spiritual Life*, 116–17. Tanqueray (1854–1933) was a native of France and later in his career taught at St Mary's Seminary and University in Baltimore. He was a priest of the Sulpician Order.

72 Stolz, *Convent Life and Beyond*, 34–5.

73 Gilligan Wong, *Nun*, 171; Hollingsworth, *Ex-Nuns*, 11–12.

74 Senieur, *Vocational Replies*, 99–100.

75 The Sister Formation Conference is discussed in Chapter 1.

76 Turk, *The Buried Life*, 9.

77 Mullaly, *Spiritual Reflections for Sisters*, 90.

78 Di Ligouri, *The True Spouse of Jesus Christ*, 219, 220.
79 SCPA, Constitutions and Rules of the Sisters of Providence, Box 2, Constitutions of the Daughters of Charity, Servants of the Poor, Montreal, 1925: 30–1. See also DeFrees, *The Springs of Silence*, 59–60; Di Ligouri, *The True Spouse of Jesus Christ*, 478; Gilligan Wong, *Nun*, 170; Larsen, *The Tulip and the Pope*, 57–8, 68; O'Donnell-Gibson, *The Red Skirt*, 122–3; Whitney, *The Calling*, 49.
80 Grueninger Beasley, *The Tears I Couldn't Cry*, 19; Masterson, *One Nun's Story*, 97–8; Turk, *The Buried Life*, 34–5.
81 DeFrees, *The Springs of Silence*, 59, 60.
82 Lynch, *Triptych*, 31.
83 Grueninger Beasley, *The Tears I Couldn't Cry*, 13.
84 Gilligan Wong, *Nun*, 170, 179; Hollingsworth, *Ex-Nuns*, 13–15.
85 Masterson, *One Nun's Story*, 73.
86 Senieur, *Vocational Replies*, 105–6.
87 Morkovsky, *Living in God's Providence*, 348.
88 Frederic, *And Spare Me Not in the Making*, 34.
89 Reilly, *What Must I Do?* 28.
90 Dr J.T. Nix, in commenting on the health and eating habits of nuns, had this to say: "The absence of other worldly pleasures in the lives of sisters tends to accentuate the palatability of food, with resultant obesity. A final word on the subject is the 'Mother Provincial Syndrome' or recurrent acute gallbladder. During the visitation of the mother provincial, each mission serves her delicacies of a high fat content. She is unable to follow any dietary restrictions in her travels to the various houses and operative removal of the gallbladder frequently results." Nix, "The Physical Health of Religious," 224.
91 Ibid., 23.
92 Bassler, *Removing the Habit of God*, 43.
93 Hollingsworth, *Ex-Nuns*, 12–20.
94 Bissell, *The Scent of God*, 57–62.
95 Grueninger Beasley, *The Tears I Couldn't Cry*, 14; Stolz, *Convent Life and Beyond*, 43; Whitney, *The Calling*, 47–8.
96 Larsen, *The Tulip and the Pope*, 76–7.
97 DeFrees, *The Springs of Silence*, 50.
98 Howe, *A Change of Habit*, 43.
99 Gilligan Wong, *Nun*, 172–3.
100 Grueninger Beasley, *The Tears I Couldn't Cry*, 17, 24; O'Donnell-Gibson, *The Red Skirt*, 74.
101 Bassler, *Removing the Habit of God*, 52; Grueninger Beasley, *The Tears I Couldn't Cry*, 14, 20; DeFrees, *The Springs of Silence*, 65; Masterson, *One Nun's Story*, 105; O'Donnell-Gibson, *The Red Skirt*, 75–6; Turk, *The Buried Life*, 34–5.

102 Gilligan Wong, *Nun*, 189.
103 Larsen, *The Tulip and the Pope*, 86; Masterson, *One Nun's Story*, 106–8; Turk, *The Buried Life*, 42–3.
104 Grueninger Beasley, *The Tears I Couldn't Cry*, 13.
105 Griffin, *The Courage to Choose*, 22; Turk, *The Buried Life*, 31–3, 44–5.
106 O'Donnell-Gibson, *The Red Skirt*, 117–18.
107 Frederic, *And Spare Me Not in the Making*, 18–19.
108 Lynch, *Triptych*, 36.
109 Gilligan Wong, *Nun*, 172.
110 DeFrees, *The Springs of Silence*, 55.
111 Lynch, *Triptych*, 36–7.
112 Turk, *The Buried Life*, 38–41.
113 Grueninger Beasley, *The Tears I Couldn't Cry*, 22.
114 O'Donnell-Gibson, *The Red Skirt*, 77–8, 128–9.
115 Gilligan Wong, *Nun*, 172, 175–6.
116 UNDA/CHJC, 113/03, Entrance Book/Postulants' Book; MSA, Lists, Series 5: Box 15, Folder 15/8, Reports, Internal, Entrance, Statistics 1948–1974.
117 Frederic, *And Spare Me Not in the Making*, 21–3.
118 Masterson, *One Nun's Story*, 97.
119 Howe, *A Change of Habit*, 46; McCann, *Out of the Habit*, 35–6; Reilly, *What Must I Do?* 29.
120 Reilly, *What Must I Do?* 30–1; Quinonez and Turner, *The Transformation of American Catholic Sisters*, 34. Some priests who specialized in conducting retreats for nuns and nuns-in-training turned their lectures into books that usually found their way into convent libraries. See, for example, Hagspiel, *Live in the Holy Spirit*; Hoeger, *The Convent Mirror*; and Moffatt, *Listen Sister*.
121 Frederic, *And Spare Me Not in the Making*, 27.
122 Father Joseph Fichter admitted that large numbers of young women entered novitiates with doubts about their vocations but felt obliged to give it a try nonetheless. Fichter, *Religion as an Occupation*, 189.

CHAPTER 7

1 Association of the Monasteries of Nuns of the Order of Preachers, *Vocation in Black and White*, 82. Sister Mary began her career in religion with the Franciscans, then switched later to the Religious of the Sacred Heart, and finally settled on the Dominicans.
2 SCPA, Box 2, Constitutions of the Daughters of Charity, Servants of the Poor, Chapter 3, 191. These constitutions were in effect with some modifications between 1925 and 1959.

3 The Dominican Sisters of the Sacred Heart in Texas listed a "procuratrix general" in their constitution. In 1914 the title was changed to bursar. Hackett, *Dominican Women in Texas*, 201.

4 Sullivan, *The Inner Lives of Medieval Inquisitors*, 85.

5 Giem, *A River Flows from Eden*, 88; O'Hara, *The Scent of Roses*, 236; Catherine Thomas, *My Beloved*, 88. There was also a congregation known as Instituto Suore Zelatrici del Sacro Cuore, or, in English, the Missionary Zelatrices of the Sacred Heart. Founded in Italy in 1894, they arrived in the United States in 1902 to serve Italian immigrants and established their headquarters in Hamden, Connecticut. In the latter half of the 1950s, they changed their name to the Apostles of the Sacred Heart of Jesus, by which they are still known. McCarthy, *Guide to the Catholic Sisterhoods*, 208. The word "bellatrix," or female warrior, is probably better known. It has been used to name a star, a Canadian energy company, and a character in Harry Potter.

6 Mary Francis, *A Right to Be Merry*, 69.

7 Ibid.

8 Gilligan Wong, *Nun*, 200.

9 Frederic, *And Spare Me Not in the Making*, 48–9.

10 Kelley, *Love Is Not for Cowards*, 68.

11 Among the Presentation Sisters who conducted the first school I attended in Cork, Ireland, there was a certain Sister Stanislaus. Since nobody of my generation had ever heard of Poland's patron saint and martyr, everyone called her Sister Santa Claus. Other Latinized names of nuns I have encountered are: Charitina, Consolata, Eucharista, Illuminata, Perpetua, and Salvatora.

12 MSA, Native Novitiates, Box 5, Motherhouse (1943–1955), File 5.2, "Ceremony of the Reception of the Habit and the first Profession of Vows of the Maryknoll Sisters," March 1948.

13 Reilly, *What Must I Do?* 34.

14 Howe, *A Change of Habit*, 51; Gilligan Wong, *Nun*, 203.

15 Hinsdale, "'The Roughest Kind of Prose,'" 135.

16 Griffin, *The Courage to Choose*, 23, 24.

17 Mary Francis, *A Right to Be Merry*, 71.

18 Giem, *A River Flows from Eden*, 58.

19 Catherine Thomas, *My Beloved*, 101, 102. Mother Catherine Thomas was born in Monticello, New York, in 1907. She entered the Discalced Carmelites in January 1928. Her book, *My Beloved* (1955), sold well and was translated into four languages. McGaw, "Sister Catherine Thomas, OCD," 47, 48.

20 Frederic, *And Spare Me Not in the Making*, 51–2.

21 Masterson, *One Nun's Story*, 124.

22 Gilligan Wong, *Nun*, 206.
23 For example, Midge Turk described her habit as "heavy, confining, and terribly hot." Turk, *The Buried Life*, 54, 55.
24 Grueninger Beasley, *The Tears I Couldn't Cry*, 45, 46.
25 O'Donnell-Gibson, *The Red Skirt*, 176, 183.
26 Howe, *A Change of Habit*, 58; Larsen, *The Tulip and the Pope*, 101.
27 Gilligan Wong, *Nun*, 209.
28 Kuhns, *The Habit*, 17.
29 Glisky, "The Official IHM Stance on Friendship, 1845–1960," 169.
30 Peters, *The 1917 Pio-Benedictine Code of Canon Law*, 217, 218.
31 Philippe, *The Novitiate*, 14, 75, 85.
32 Sisters of Our Lady of Charity of the Good Shepherd, *Rule of St Augustin*, 115.
33 Grueninger Beasley, *The Tears I Couldn't Cry*, 44.
34 Kelley, *Love Is Not for Cowards*, 72, 73.
35 Henderson, *Out of the Curtained World*, 99–102.
36 Griffin, *The Courage to Choose*, 26; Hinsdale, "'The Roughest Kind of Prose,'" 132, 133; Hollingsworth, *Ex-Nuns*, 13, 15, 20; Larsen, *The Tulip and the Pope*, 127.
37 SCPA, Personnel File of Sister Adelaide of Jesus (Ethel Cecilia Burchfield), 1891–1962.
38 Masterson, *One Nun's Story*, 128.
39 Lynch, *Triptych*, 42, 44.
40 Peters, *The 1917 Pio-Benedictine Code of Canon Law*, 216, 218, 219.
41 SCPA, Constitutions of the Daughters of Charity, Servants of the Poor, 1925. Chapter 3, Rule 236: 188.
42 DeFrees, *The Springs of Silence*, 74.
43 Grueninger Beasley, *The Tears I Couldn't Cry*, 64–5.
44 Ethier Rosenbaum, *The Unmaking of a Nun*, 61.
45 Giem, *A River Flows from Eden*, 56.
46 Henderson, *Out of the Curtained World*, 88, 89.
47 Larsen, *The Tulip and the Pope*, 136–7.
48 Wedl and Nalevanko, *Forever Your Sister*, 8.
49 Di Ligouri, *The True Spouse of Jesus Christ*, 277–86.
50 Gilligan Wong, *Nun*, 211.
51 Hollingsworth, *Ex-Nuns*, 14, 15; Larsen, *The Tulip and the Pope*, 106; Stolz, *Convent Life and Beyond*, 57.
52 Hinsdale, "'The Roughest Kind of Prose,'" 142.
53 D'Arienzo, "My Pact with Camillus," 25. Camille D'Arienzo entered the Sisters of Mercy Convent, Syosset, New York, on 8 September 1952, as a postulant, later becoming a novice and professed nun.
54 Grueninger Beasley, *The Tears I Couldn't Cry*, 47, 55–6.

55 Lord, *Letters to a Nun*, 34.
56 Howe, *A Change of Habit*, 57. On the importance of Purgatory and the custom of praying for the souls who found themselves there, see Orsi, *Between Heaven and Earth*, 100, 101.
57 Giem, *A River Flows from Eden*, 55, 56.
58 Henderson, *Out of the Curtained World*, 121.
59 Sister Claver was interviewed by Ray Steward in his documentary, *Why Is a Nun?*
60 Howe, *A Change of Habit*, 55–7; Larsen, *The Tulip and the Pope*, 102.
61 Lynch, *Triptych*, 46.
62 Grueninger Beasley, *The Tears I Couldn't Cry*, 64–5; Howe, *A Change of Habit*, 53; Lynch, *Triptych*, 47.
63 Hinsdale, "'The Roughest Kind of Prose,'" 131. *See also*, Cotel, Jombart, and McCabe, *Catechism of the Vows for the Use of Religious.*
64 MSA, Native Novitiates, Box 5, Motherhouse, 1927–1972, File 5.1, examinations. Unfortunately, there are no surviving examples of answers to these questions.
65 SCPA, Novitiate File, Theology Sylabbi.
66 Kirsch, *The Spiritual Direction of Sisters*, 53.
67 Sisters of Our Lady of Charity of the Good Shepherd, *The Rule of St Augustin*, 115.
68 SCPA, Formation Series, Box 3, Sister Martin Conferences. File: Formation History, "Thoughts on the Rule for Novices," Vancouver Novitiate, 1923.
69 Philippe, *The Novitiate*, 73, 126. Father Philippe was a well-known Dominican friar and later was appointed Secretary for the Sacred Congregation of Religious.
70 Grueninger Beasley, *The Tears I Couldn't Cry*, 63–4; Howe, *A Change of Habit*, 55–6, 59.
71 Larsen, *The Tulip and the Pope*, 150–1.
72 Turk, *The Buried Life*, 61, 62.
73 Lord, *Letters to a Nun*, 205.
74 Larsen, *The Tulip and the Pope*, 147–8.
75 SCPA, Constitutions and Rules of the Sisters of Providence, 1925–1977, Chapter 10, No. 69: 76.
76 SCPA, Formation Series, Box 3, Formation Models, File: Sr Martin, Conferences. The legal form is not actually filed here, but rather some of Sister Martin's notes are scribbled on the back of them.
77 Grueninger Beasley, *The Tears I Couldn't Cry*, 51.
78 Mullahy, "Sanctification Through the Vows," 94.
79 Fisher, *In the Name of God Why?* 199.
80 Gass, *Unconventional Women*, 176–7.

81 Fisher, *In the Name of God Why?* 190, 259.

82 Larsen, *The Tulip and the Pope*, 105. Deborah Larsen was nineteen years old in 1960 when she entered the novitiate of the Sisters of Charity of the Blessed Virgin Mary in Dubuque, Iowa. She left in 1965.

83 Stolz, *Convent Life and Beyond*, 210.

84 Bassler, *Removing the Habit of God*, 77, 78.

85 Larsen, *The Tulip and the Pope*, 132–6.

86 Henderson, *Out of the Curtained World*, 161, 162.

87 Lynch, *Triptych*, 60–1.

88 Relying on celibate nuns, priests, or even bishops for instruction on sexual matters could be problematic. Consider the following description of intercourse from Karol Wojtyla, Bishop of Cracow, who later became Pope John Paul II:

> It is in the very nature of the act that the man plays the active role and takes the initiative, while the woman is a comparatively passive partner, whose function it is to accept and to experience. For the purposes of the sexual act it is enough for her to be passive and unresisting, so much so that it may even take place without her volition while she is in a state in which she has no awareness at all of what is happening – for instance while she is asleep, or unconscious.

Wojtyla, *Love and Responsibility*, 271.

89 McGoey, *The Sins of the Just*, 118.

90 Provera, *Live Your Vocation*, 111.

91 Alberione, *The Superior Follows the Master*, 73.

92 Hoeger, *The Convent Mirror*, 86, 87.

93 Gilligan Wong, *Nun*, 221, 225–6.

94 Glisky, "The Official IHM Stance on Friendship," 153–71.

95 Alberione, *The Superior Follows the Master*, 73. Father James Alberione (1884–1971) was no obscure cleric. The Italian was known as the priest of the media for his energetic use of magazines and periodicals to promote the interests of the Church. He was also the founder of no less than four female religious congregations: the Daughters of St Paul, the Pious Disciples of the Divine Master, the Sisters of Jesus the Good Shepherd (Pastorelle Sisters), and the Queen of Apostles Institute for Vocations (Apostoline Sisters). On 25 June 1996, Pope John Paul II declared Alberione "Blessed." http://www.vatican.va/news_services/liturgy/saints/ns_lit_doc_20030427_alberione_en.html (accessed 19 June 2012).

96 Kirsch, *The Spiritual Direction of Sisters*, 406–7.

97 Philippe, *The Novitiate*, 34–9.

98 Alberione, *The Superior Follows the Master*, 111–12.

99 Hoeger, *The Convent Mirror*, 132.

100 Biot and Galimard, *Medical Guide to Vocations*, 210. The book was translated from the original French and given an imprimatur by Archbishop Francis Keough of Baltimore.

101 Van Zeller, *The Yoke of Divine Love*, 53.

102 Moffatt, *Step This Way, Sister*, 80.

103 Turk, *The Buried Life*, 59.

104 Bassler, *Removing the Habit of God*, 58.

105 Howe, A *Change of Habit*, 53; Masterson, *One Nun's Story*, 128.

106 Bartlett and Bestul, eds., *Cultures of Piety*, 8.

107 Di Ligouri, *The True Spouse of Jesus Christ*, 208.

108 Sisters of the Good Shepherd, *The Rule of St Augustin*, 118.

109 Gilligan, *Nun,* 220; Howe, *A Change of Habit,* 53, 59; McCann, *Out of the Habit,* 51, 52.

110 Grueninger Beasley, *The Tears I Couldn't Cry*, 60.

111 Howe, *A Change of Habit*, 53.

112 Hansberry, *Life Is Not Hard*, 24–5.

113 Bassler, *Removing the Habit of God*, 63.

114 Ethier Rosenbaum, *The Unmaking of a Nun*, 49.

115 Philippe, *The Novitiate*, 111, 112.

116 Howe, *A Change of Habit*, 53.

117 Mary Francis, *A Right to Be Merry*, 134.

118 MSA, Native Novitiates, Box 5, Motherhouse, 1927–1972, file 5.2, Sister Paul Miriam to Mother, 4 July 1949; Mother M. Columba to Sister Paul Miriam, 30 July 1949; Mother M. Columba to Sister Paul Miriam, 22 January 1951.

119 D'Arienzo, "My Pact with Camillus," 25.

120 Hollingsworth, *Ex-Nuns*, 17.

121 Ibid.

122 Grueninger Beasley, *The Tears I Couldn't Cry*, 52.

123 Lynch, *Triptych*, 43; Stolz, *Convent Life and Beyond*, 58–9.

124 Hollingsworth, *Ex-Nuns*, 19.

125 Reilly, *What Must I Do?* 39.

126 Gilligan Wong, *Nun*, 227–8.

127 Grueninger Beasley, *The Tears I Couldn't Cry*, 58–9.

128 Frederic, *And Spare Me Not in the Making*, 58–9.

129 Catherine Thomas, *My Beloved*, 84.

130 Stoltz, *Convent Life and Beyond*, 53.

131 Larsen, *The Tulip and the Pope*, 128–30.

132 Gass, *Unconventional Women*, 266, 267, 270–3, 277, 278.

133 UNDA/CHJC, 114/39, "Register of Sisters who left the PHJC Community, 1926–1983": 80–9.

134 MSA, A6.6, Valley Park, correspondence, 1947–1949, Sister Mary Helen to Mother Mary Columba, 9 October 1948.

135 MSA, Series 5, Reports, Entrance, Valley Park, 1947–56, Box 15, file 14/11, Valley Park candidates, 1951–1956.
136 Gilligan Wong, *Nun*, 225–6.
137 Garibaldi Rogers, *Habits of Change*, 264.
138 Howe, *A Change of Habit*, 63.
139 D'Arienzo, "My Pact with Camillus," 25.
140 MSA, Lists, Series 5: Box 15, Folder 15/18, Reports, Internal, Entrance, Statistics, 1948–1974.
141 MSA, Motherhouse, 1960–1970, File 5-3, Sister Miriam Anthony to Sister Mary Xavier, 2 September 1967.
142 Frederic, *And Spare Me Not in the Making*, 67–71.
143 O'Donnell-Gibson, *The Red Skirt*, 258–60, 283.
144 Sylvester, "PFs: Persistent Friendships," 184–7.
145 Rapley, *A Social History of the Cloister*, 164–82, Reynes, *Couvents de femmes*, 57–76. Carmen Mangion also provides a chapter on the postulancy and novitiate in her study of convents in nineteenth-century England and Wales, and it shows a similar unchanging pattern. Mangion, *Contested Identities*, 89–108.

CHAPTER EIGHT

1 Hagspiel, *Live in the Holy Spirit*, 83. Hagspiel was priest of the Divine Word Missionaries. The initials SVD stand for Societas Verbi Divini. He was an experienced retreat master for religious congregations of women. *Non serviam* is the Latin for "I will not serve."
2 Frederic, *And Spare Me Not in the Making*, 65. The reference is to Exodus 16:3, in which the Israelites grumbled about the lack of food in the Sinai desert while remembering fondly how well they had been fed in Egypt. Today the term "fleshpots of Egypt" is taken to mean a desire for hedonistic pleasure.
3 http://www.cathnewsusa.com/2013/12/vanishing-nuns-100-year-tradition-ends-convents-closing/ (accessed 10 April 2017); "The vanishing nuns: 100-year tradition ends with convent's closing," FoxNews.com, 1 December 2013: http://www.foxnews.com/us/2013/12/01/vanishing-nuns-100-year-tradition-ends-with-convents-closing/ (accessed 30 January 2014).
4 A similar crisis is afflicting the Church in Canada, and even in the province of Quebec, a major supplier of nuns to the United States for over a century. "Convent's Demise Marks the End of an Era," *Globe and Mail*, 30 March 2013, A4.
5 The chart is constructed from figures provided in the Center for Applied Research in the Apostolate, "Frequently Requested Church

Statistics": http://cara.georgetown.edu/CARAServices/requested
churchstats.html (accessed 6 October 2016).

6 "The Vanishing of the Nuns," *New York Times*, 2 December 2012:
http://www.nytimes.com/2012/12/02/booming/the-vanishing-of-the-
nuns.html (accessed 24 February 2014).

7 "Nuns, a 'Dying Breed,' Fade from Leadership Roles at Catholic Hospitals," *New York Times*, 20 August 2011: http://www.nytimes.com/
2011/08/21us/21nuns.html (accessed 24 February 2014).

8 Center for Applied Research in the Apostolate, "Frequently Requested Church Statistics": http://cara.georgetown.edu/CARA
Services/requestedchurchstats.html (accessed 23 January 2015).

9 A number of sociologists, some of them nuns and ex-nuns, in attempting to address these questions, become bogged down in "correlation
coefficients," "the processual nature of role occupancy," and other
jargon, making their "explications" and "delineations" less than helpful. See, for example, Ebaugh, Lorence, and Chafetz, "The Growth
and Decline of the Population of Catholic Nuns Cross-Nationally."

10 Ebaugh, *Women in the Vanishing Cloister*, 49.

11 Briggs, *Double-Crossed*, 132; Fichter, "Vanishing Church Professionals," 100, 101.

12 Kirsch, *The Spiritual Direction of Sisters*, 263, 264, 357–60.

13 Congregations "of diocesan right" were those usually founded by a
bishop, located in one diocese and perhaps a few adjoining ones, and
were responsible to the bishop. Congregations "of pontifical right"
tended to have a wider geographical reach and were often international in scope. They were directly responsible to the Pope through
a Mother General. In 2009, a full 87 per cent of American congregations were of pontifical right. Johnson, Wittberg, and Gautier, *New
Generations of Catholic Sisters*, 36, 37.

14 Peters, *The 1917 Pio-Benedictine Code of Canon Law*, 243–6.

15 Gass, *Unconventional Women*, 276–9.

16 Ebaugh, *Out of the Cloister*, 5.

17 Quinonez and Turner, *The Transformation of American Catholic Sisters*,
66, 67.

18 Morkovsky, *Living in God's Providence*, 350.

19 Wakin and Scheuer, "The American Nun: Poor, Chaste, and Restive,"
37.

20 Sherman, "Fewer Vocations: Crisis or Challenge?" 5, 6.

21 McDannell, *The Spirit of Vatican II*, 55–71.

22 Gillis, *Roman Catholicism in America*, 141, 142.

23 Dwyer-McNulty, *Common Threads*, 170–5; Suenens, *The Nun in the
World*.

24 Briggs, *Double-Crossed*, 70–2.

25 Paul VI, *Perfectae Caritatis*.
26 Paul VI, *Gaudium et Spes*.
27 Wittberg, *The Rise and Fall of Catholic Religious Orders*, 214.
28 Briggs, *Double-Crossed*, 78–81; Sherman, "Fewer Vocations: Crisis or Challenge?" 7.
29 Briggs, *Double-Crossed*, 103–5, 108, 109; McGuinness, *Called to Serve*, 168, 169; Wombacher, "Religious Life, 1965–1985," 64.
30 Briggs, *Double-Crossed*, 84–100; Dwyer-McNulty, *Common Threads*, 13, 187; McGuinness, *Called to Serve*, 166–8.
31 SanGiovanni, *Ex-Nuns*, 42, 43, 52.
32 Schmid, "'These Dear, Faithful Helpers,'" 5.
33 Garibaldi Rogers, *Habits of Change*, 120–2 (interview with Sister Vilma Seelaus).
34 Ebaugh, *Women in the Vanishing Cloister*, 52.
35 Ibid., 70; McGuinness, *Called to Serve*, 170; Wittberg, *The Rise and Fall of Catholic Religious Orders*, 242–4.
36 Ebaugh, Women in the Vanishing Cloister, 70–1; Wittberg, *The Rise and Fall of Catholic Religious Orders*, 247–9, 254.
37 Ebaugh, *Out of the Cloister*, 51.
38 Denham and Wilkinson, *Cloister of the Heart*, 100; Garibaldi Rogers, *Habits of Change*, 120–6 (interview with Sister Vilma Seelaus); Paul VI, *Venite Seorsum*.
39 Briggs, *Double-Crossed*, 147.
40 Ebaugh, *Women in the Vanishing Cloister*, 144, 145. Amy Koehlinger points out that nuns came late to the civil-rights movement and that their impact was largely symbolic. Nonetheless, from their own point of view, agitation for social justice gave new meaning to their vocations – something only possible after the reforms of Vatican II. Koehlinger, *The New Nuns*, 3, 4.
41 Wittberg, *The Rise and Fall of Catholic Religious Orders*, 216. For a detailed and personal account of this dispute, see Caspary, *Witness to Integrity*.
42 Quinonez and Turner, *The Transformation of American Catholic Sisters*, 107.
43 Ibid., 85–7; Wittberg, *The Rise and Fall of Catholic Religious Orders*, 218.
44 These terms are all taken from the names of actual congregations.
45 Wittberg, *The Rise and Fall of Catholic Religious Orders*, 217.
46 The chart is constructed from figures provided in Ebaugh, *Women in the Vanishing Cloister*, 48, 49.
47 McGuinness, *Called to Serve*, 173–5.
48 Ebaugh, *Women in the Vanishing Cloister*, 48, 49.
49 Fichter, "Vanishing Church Professionals," 101.

50 Ebaugh, *Out of the Cloister*, 109.
51 Hollingsworth, *Ex-Nuns*, 44.
52 Briggs, *Double-Crossed*, 121–2; McGuinness, *Called to Serve*, 174.
53 Ebaugh, *Out of the Cloister*, 110.
54 SanGiovanni, *Ex-Nuns*, 30.
55 Ibid.
56 Gass, *Unconventional Women*, 289, 290.
57 Willingham, "Why I Quit the Convent," 64–74.
58 Turk, *The Buried Life*, 190–9.
59 Gass, *Unconventional Women*, 279, 280, 290, 291.
60 Hollingsworth, *Ex-Nuns*, 41.
61 SanGiovanni, *Ex-Nuns*, 69.
62 Kelley, *Love Is Not for Cowards*, 120.
63 Ebaugh, *Women in the Vanishing Cloister*, 78–9; Wittberg, *The Rise and Fall of Catholic Religious Orders*, 239–40.
64 Turk, *The Buried Life*, 62, 63.
65 Halstead and Halstead, "A Sexual Intimacy Survey of Former Nuns and Priests," 83–90. There is a lot of sloppy data in this survey. In some instances, for example, the responses from nuns and priests are not separated. It was only possible to calculate the percentage of nuns who had masturbated by assuming that 100 per cent of the priests had done so.
66 Turk, *The Buried Life*, 64. For multiple descriptions of "particular friendships" in convents, see Curb and Manahan, *Lesbian Nuns: Breaking Silence*. For statistics on sexual harassment and exploitation in convents, see Chibnall, Wolf, and Duckro, "A National Survey of the Sexual Trauma Experiences of Catholic Nuns."
67 Bissell, *The Scent of God*, 168–72.
68 Gilligan Wong, *Nun*, 279, 280.
69 Kelley, *Love Is Not for Cowards*, 98, 116–21, 155–9.
70 SanGiovanni, *Ex-Nuns*, 44–6.
71 "Philip Berrigan, Former Priest and Peace Activist in the Vietnam War Era, Dies at 79." *New York Times*, 8 December 2002.
72 Garibaldi Rogers, *Habits of Change*, 224–30 (interview with Theresa Padovano).
73 Briggs, *Double-Crossed*, 120, 121.
74 Gass, *Unconventional Women*, 279–300. Of the fifty-six former nuns who departed during the 1960s and 1970s, fourteen, or 25 per cent, gave a desire for a human relationship as their reason.
75 Hollingsworth, *Ex-Nuns*, 44. Twenty-six of her informants explained their departure from religious life, and of these, eight, or 30 per cent, attributed it to falling in love or wanting to.

76 Ethier Rosenbaum, *The Unmaking of a Nun*, 188, 236, 245.

77 UNDA/CHJC, 114/39, Register of Sisters who left the PHJC Community, 1926–1983.

78 "The People of N.Y. vs. Sister Maureen," *Los Angeles Times*, 27 February 1977, G1; Breslin, "Nun on Trial for Infanticide"; "Nun Cleared of Charge She Killed Newborn Son," *New York Times*, 5 March 1977. John Pielmeier wrote a play, *Agnes of God*, based on the story. The play was turned into a feature film under the same name in 1985.

79 Bergant, "The Profound Changes in Religious Life Since Vatican II," 77, 78.

80 McGuinness, *Called to Serve*, 175.

81 Fichter, "Vanishing Church Professionals," 112.

82 SanGiovanni, *Ex-Nuns*, 35–7.

83 Ibid., 38.

84 Ebaugh, *Out of the Cloister*, 89–94.

85 McGuinness, *Called to Serve*, 172.

86 Grace Stoltz, who left in 1968, took up teaching in the public-school system of Atlanta, Georgia. Margaret Lynch, who joined the exodus a year later, began to teach high-school English in Trenton, New Jersey. Stoltz, *Convent Life and Beyond*, 186; Lynch, *Triptych*, 172–82.

87 Briggs, *Double-Crossed*, 116, 117; Ebaugh, *Out of the Cloister*, 117.

88 Hollingsworth, *Ex-Nuns*, 80, 81.

89 Garibaldi Rogers, *Habits of Change*, 242, 243.

90 Conversation with Sister Rosemary Dillman, Seattle, 3 December 2013.

91 Conversation with Sister Mariane Mader, St Mary-of-the-Woods, Indiana, 23 May 2013.

92 The chart is constructed from figures provided in Ebaugh, *Women in the Vanishing Cloister*, 48, 49.

93 Ebaugh, *Out of the Cloister*, 71.

94 Maryknoll Archives, Lists, Series 5: Box 15, Folder 15/8, Reports, Internal, Entrance, Statistics 1948–1974.

95 Wittberg, *The Rise and Fall of Catholic Religious Orders*, 259.

96 Donovan, "A More Limited Witness," 91.

97 For example, "Another Nun Defects," *Time* magazine, 20 January 1967, 59. The subject of the story was Sister Jacqueline Grennan, president of Missouri's Webster College. Grennan left the Sisters of Loretto after eighteen years in the congregation. She had a problem with the Church's position on birth control, which she believed hampered attempts to combat poverty. See also, "Religion: Priests and Nuns: Going Their Way," *Time* magazine, 23 February 1970, 59.

98 Padberg, "The Contexts of Comings and Goings," 27.

99 Donovan, "A More Limited Witness," 93; Ebaugh, *Women in the Vanishing Cloister*, 96.

100 Wittberg, *The Rise and Fall of Catholic Religious Orders*, 259.

101 Hennessey, "A Look at the Institution Itself," 37.

102 Stuhlmeuller, "Biblical Observations on the Decline of Vocations to Religious Life," 162.

103 Owram, *Born at the Right Time*. See, in particular, Chapter 10, "Sexual Revolutions and Revolutions of the Sexes, 1965–1973," 248–79.

104 Sullivan, *Visual Habits*, 37, 38.

105 Sherman, "Fewer Vocations: Crisis or Challenge?" 14.

106 Donovan, "A More Limited Witness," 85, 86; Ebaugh, *Women in the Vanishing Cloister*, 95.

107 Sullivan, *Visual Habits*, 56.

108 Wittberg, *The Rise and Fall of Catholic Religious Orders*, 258.

109 Walsh, "Objections to a Sister's Vocation: Point of View of a Teenager," 599, 600.

110 Wittberg, *The Rise and Fall of Catholic Religious Orders*, 221, 230.

111 Ebaugh, *Women in the Vanishing Cloister*, 152, 153.

112 Johnson, Wittberg, and Gautier, *New Generations of Catholic Sisters*, 68.

113 Ibid., 22, 67, 68.

114 http://www.cathnewsusa.com/2013/12/vanishing-nuns-100-year-tradition-ends-convents-closing/ (accessed 10 April 2017).

115 National Catholic Educational Association, *United States Catholic Elementary Schools, 2013–2014: The Annual Statistical Report on Schools, Enrolment, and Staffing*, http://www.ncea.org/data-information/catholic-school-data (accessed 11 January 2015).

116 "Struggling Catholic schools strategize to draw new students," *Reuters*, 2 May 2013: http://www.reuters.com/article/2013/05/02/us-usa-education-idUSBRE9410PN20130502 (accessed 28 January 2014).

117 Ebaugh, *Women in the Vanishing Cloister*, 85, 165; Ellis, *American Catholicism*, 193, 194.

118 The chart is constructed from figures provided in the Center for Applied Research in the Apostolate, "Frequently Requested Church Statistics": http://cara.georgetown.edu/CARAServices/requested churchstats.html (accessed 6 October 2016).

119 "Struggling Catholic schools strategize to draw new students," *Reuters*, 2 May 2013: http://www.reuters.com/article/2013/05/02/us-usa-education-idUSBRE9410PN20130502 (accessed 28 January 2014).

120 Ibid.

121 "Complaints of Sex Abuse by Nuns Begin to Emerge," *Minneapolis Star Tribune*, 25 June 2006.

122 "Anguish has never healed for natives physically, sexually abused at St Ignatius mission," *The Missoulian*, 5 June 2011; "Lawsuit against St. Ignatius Ursuline Academy to proceed, lawyers say," *The Missoulian*, 31 January 2014; "Nuns agree to pay $4.45 million to settle abuse claims,

including from Yakima plaintiff," *Yakima Herald-Republic*, 4 February 2015.

123 Gillis, *Roman Catholicism in America*, 117, 118.

124 "A decade later, struggle for accountability within LCWR on abuse continues," *National Catholic Reporter*, 11 August 2014.

125 "Vouchers Breathe New Life into Shrinking Catholic Schools," *Wall Street Journal*, 14 June 2012.

126 "For Catholic Schools, Crisis and Catharsis," *New York Times*, 18 January 2009, A29; National Catholic Educational Association, *United States Catholic Elementary Schools, 2013–2014: The Annual Statistical Report on Schools, Enrolment, and Staffing*, http://www.ncea.org/data-information/catholic-school-data (accessed 11 January 2015).

127 Gillis, *Roman Catholicism in America*, 207.

128 "The State of Catholic Schools in the U.S.," *The Catholic World Report*, 31 May 2011.

129 While the literature on this topic is extensive, two works in particular are noteworthy: Berger, *The Sacred Canopy* (1967), and Bruce, ed., *Religion and Modernization* (1992).

130 Stark, "Secularization, R.I.P."

131 See, for example, John Fea, *Was America Founded as a Christian Nation: A Historical Introduction* (2011). Fea is a professor of history at Messiah College, Mechanicsburg, Pennsylvania, an institution that was originally founded as a Bible school by the Brethren in Christ Church.

Bibliography

· ·

ARCHIVAL SOURCES

Sisters of Charity of Providence Archives, Seattle, Washington (SCPA).
Sisters of Providence of St Mary-of-the-Woods Archives, Terre Haute, Indiana (SPSMWA).
Catholic University of America, The American Catholic History Research Center and University Archives, Washington, DC. Records of the National Catholic Education Association (ACHRCUA/NCEA).
Maryknoll Sisters Archives, Ossining, New York (MSA).
University of Notre Dame Archives, South Bend, Indiana. Records of the Poor Handmaids of Jesus Christ (UNDA/CHJC).

CATHOLIC UNIVERSITY OF AMERICA, MULLEN LIBRARY,
RARE BOOKS AND SPECIAL COLLECTIONS

Gillard, John T. *More Colored Nuns!* Baltimore: Josephite Press, 1938.
In My Book These Are the Stars: Observations on Vocation by Bing Crosby and Others. Cincinnati, OH: Catholic Students' Mission Crusade, 1947.
Lord, Daniel A. *Shall I Be a Nun?* St Louis: The Queen's Work, 1927.
– *Shall My Daughter Be a Nun?* St Louis: The Queen's Work, 1947.
Poage, Godfrey. *Vocational Club Handbook.* Chicago: St John Bosco Vocational Club, 1943.

PAPAL DOCUMENTS

Paul VI, *Gaudium et Spes*, 1965.
– *Lumen Gentium*, 1964.
– *Perfectae Caritatis*, 1965.
– *Venite Seorsum*, 1969.
Pius XI, *Ad Catholici Sacerdotii*, 1935.
– *Divini Illius Magistri*, 1929.

– *Sacra Virginitas*, 1954.
– *Sponsa Christi*, 1950.

DISSERTATIONS AND THESES

Barrett, Sister Mary Mark. "A Study of the Influences of Catholic High-School Experiences on Vocational Decisions to the Sisterhoods." PhD dissertation, Catholic University of America, 1960.
Bowdern, Thomas S. "A Study of Vocations: An Investigation into the Environmental Factors of Vocation to the Priesthood and the Religious Life in the United States from 1919 to 1929." PhD dissertation, St. Louis University, 1936.
Cahill, Sister Marie William. "Factors in Religious Vocations of a Dominican Community." MA thesis, Catholic University of America, 1955.
Desmond, Sister Ellen Mary. "A Study of the Social Background Factors in Vocations to the Sisters of Charity of Saint Elizabeth, Convent, New Jersey." MA thesis, Catholic University of America, 1955.
Hoedl, Marie Therese (Sister M. Celestine). "A Study of the Relationship of Several Types of Secondary Schools to the Development of Religious Vocations." PhD dissertation, St John's University, 1961.
Thering, Sister Mary Rose Albert. "The Aspirancy: A Guidance School for the Adolescent Girl Aspiring to the Religious Life." MEd thesis, University of St Thomas, 1958.
Willenbring, Sister Rose. "The Origin and Development of Vocations to the Sisterhoods in North Dakota." MA thesis, Catholic University of America, 1954.

NEWSPAPERS AND MAGAZINES

Chicago Tribune
Globe and Mail
Huffington Post
Los Angeles Times
Minneapolis *Star Tribune*
Missoulian
National Catholic Reporter
New York Times
Ottawa Citizen
Pittsburgh Post-Gazette
Time
Wall Street Journal
Yakima Herald-Republic

FILM AND VIDEO

Agnes of God, 1985 (Norman Jewison, director)
God Is the Bigger Elvis, 2013 (Rebecca Cammissa, director)
La religieuse, 2013 (Guillaume Nicloux, director)
The Nun's Story, 1959 (Fred Zinnemann, director)
Why Is a Nun? early 1960s (Ray Stewart, director)

ARTICLES AND BOOKS

Adelbert James, Brother. "Interviews and Vocations." *National Catholic Educational Association Bulletin* 57, no. 1 (August 1960): 491–2.
Ahern, Father Barnabas Mary. "The Role of the Elementary School Teacher in Fostering Vocations." *National Catholic Education Association Bulletin* 48, no. 1 (August 1951): 417–22.
Alberione, James. *The Superior Follows the Master*. Boston: The Daughters of St Paul, 1965.
André, Brother. "The Development of a Religious Vocation." *National Catholic Educational Association Bulletin* 47, no. 1 (August 1950): 342–8.
Association of the Monasteries of Nuns of the Order of Preachers of the United States of America. *Vocation in Black and White: Dominican Contemplative Nuns Tell How God Called Them*. Bloomington: i Universe, 2008.
Bartlett, Anne Clark, and Thomas Howard Bestul, eds., *Cultures of Piety: Medieval English Devotional Literature in Translation*. Ithaca, NY: Cornell University Press, 1999.
Bassler Pickford, Susan. *Removing the Habit of God: Sister Christina's Story*. Charleston, SC: Createspace, 2012.
Beane, Marjorie Noterman. *From Framework to Freedom: A History of the Sister Formation Conference*. Lanham, MD: University Press of America, 1993.
Bergant, Dianne. "The Profound Changes in Religious Life Since Vatican II." In *The Crisis in Religious Vocations*, edited by Felknor, 74–83.
Berger, Peter L. *The Sacred Canopy: Elements of a Sociological Theory of Religion*. New York: Doubleday, 1967.
Bergh, E. "Canonical Impediments." In *Religious Life II*, translated by Mitchell, 85–95.
Bernoville, Gaetan. *Saint Mary Euphrasia Pelletier: Foundress of the Good Shepherd Sisters*. Dublin: Clonmore and Reynolds, 1959.
Bernstein, Marcelle. *Nuns*. London: Collins, 1976.
Best-Colgan, Helen. *Two Girls from the Bay*. St John's, Newfoundland: DRC Publishing, 2012.
Bestor, Arthur E. *Educational Wastelands: The Retreat from Learning in Our Public Schools*. Urbana, IL: University of Illinois Press, 1953.

Biot, René, and Pierre Galimard. *Medical Guide to Vocations.* Translated by Robert P. Odenwald. Westminster, MD: Newman Press, 1956.

Bireley, Robert. *The Refashioning of Catholicism, 1450–1700: A Reassessment of the Counter Reformation.* Washington, DC: Catholic University of America Press, 1999.

Bissell, Beryl Singleton. *The Scent of God.* New York: Counterpoint, 2006.

Bonduelle, A. "The Recognition of a Vocation." In *Religious Life II*, translated by Mitchell, 37–47.

Bradley, Sister Ritamary, ed. *The Juniorate in Sister Formation.* New York: Fordham University Press, 1960.

Breslin, Catherine. "Nun on Trial for Infanticide." *Ms.* magazine, March 1977: 68–71; 99–103.

Brewer, Eileen Mary. *Nuns and the Education of American Catholic Women, 1860–1920.* Chicago: Loyola University Press, 1987.

Briggs, Kenneth. *Double-Crossed: Uncovering the Catholic Church's Betrayal of American Nuns.* New York: Doubleday, 2006.

Brother of the Christian Schools. *Instructions on Vocations.* New York: La Salle Bureau, 1938.

Bruce, Steve, ed. *Religion and Modernization: Sociologists Debate the Secularization Thesis.* Oxford: Oxford University Press, 1992.

Bruno-Jofré, Rosa. *The Missionary Oblate Sisters: Vision and Mission.* Montreal and Kingston: McGill-Queen's University Press, 2005.

Butler, Anne M. *Across God's Frontiers: Catholic Sisters in the American West, 1850–1920.* Chapel Hill: University of North Carolina Press, 2012.

Calhoun, Craig, ed. *Sociology in America: A History.* Chicago: University of Chicago Press, 2007.

Camilleri, Nazareno. *The Problem of Teen-Age Purity: The Teachings of Pope Pius XII.* New Rochelle, NY: Salesiana Publishers, 1961.

Carey, Ann. *Sisters in Crisis: The Tragic Unraveling of Women's Religious Communities.* Huntington, IN: Our Sunday Visitor, 1997.

Carroll, Michael P. *Catholic Cults and Devotions: A Psychological Inquiry.* Montreal and Kingston: McGill-Queen's University Press, 1989.

Caspary, Anita. *Witness to Integrity: The Crisis of the Immaculate Heart Community of California.* Collegeville, MN: Liturgical Press, 2003.

Cassilly, Francis Bernard. *What Shall I Be? A Chat with Young People.* New York: The America Press, 1914.

Catherine Thomas, Mother. *My Beloved: The Story of a Carmelite Nun.* New York, Toronto, London: McGraw-Hill Book Company, 1955.

"Catholic University Research Abstracts." *The Catholic Educational Review* 49, no. 1 (January 1951): 267.

Center for Applied Research in the Apostolate, Georgetown University, "Frequently Requested Church Statistics." http://cara.georgetown.edu.

Chabot, Marie-Emmanuel. "Guyart, Marie, dite Marie de l'Incarnation." *Dictionary of Canadian Biography,* vol. 1, 351–9. Toronto: University of Toronto Press, 1966.

Chibnall, John T., Ann Wolf, and Paul N. Duckro. "A National Survey of the Sexual Trauma Experiences of Catholic Nuns." *Review of Religious Research* 40, no. 2 (December 1998): 142–67.

Cicognani, Most Reverend Amleto Giovanni. "The Religious in the U.S. – Past, Present, Future." In *Religious Community Life in the United States: Proceedings of the Sisters' Section of the First National Congress of Religious of the United States*, 11–18.

Clifford, Geraldine J. *Those Good Gertrudes: A Social History of Women Teachers in America*. Baltimore, MD: Johns Hopkins University Press, 2014.

Coburn, Carol K., and Martha Smith. *Spirited Lives: How Nuns Shaped Catholic Culture and American Life, 1836–1920*. Chapel Hill: University of North Carolina Press, 1999.

Cohen, Sherrill. *The Evolution of Women's Asylums Since 1500: From Refuges for Ex-prostitutes to Shelters for Battered Women*. Oxford: Oxford University Press, 1992.

Collins, A. Leonard, ed. *Proceedings of the 1955 Sisters' Institute of Spirituality*. South Bend, Indiana: University of Notre Dame Press, 1956.

Congregation of the Sisters of St Joseph, Cleveland, Ohio. "Symposium on Religious Life." *National Catholic Educational Association Bulletin* 48, no. 1 (August 1951): 256–68.

Cotel, Pierre, Emile Jombart, and William Hugh McCabe. *Catechism of the Vows for the Use of Religious*. New York: Benzinger Brothers, 1945.

Cullinan, John J. "The Quest for Vocations." *National Catholic Educational Association Bulletin* 29, no. 1 (November 1932): 268–76.

Curb, Rosemary, and Nancy Manahan, eds. *Lesbian Nuns: Breaking Silence*. Tallahassee, FL: The Naiad Press, 1985.

Cushing, Richard J. *That They May Know Thee: Selected Writings on Vocations*. Westminster, MD: Newman Press, 1965.

Danylewycz, Marta. *Taking the Veil: An Alternative to Marriage, Motherhood, and Spinsterhood in Quebec, 1840–1920*. Toronto: McClelland and Stewart, 1987.

D'Arienzo, Camille. "My Pact with Camillus." In *Midwives of the Future*, edited by Ware, 24–30.

Davidson, James D. "The Catholic Church in the United States: 1950 to the Present." In *The Church Confronts Modernity*, edited by Tentler, 177–207.

Deady, Carroll F. "The Role of the Religious Teacher in America." In *Religious Community Life in the United States, Proceedings of the Sisters' Section of the First National Congress of Religious of the United States*, 126–33.

DeFrees, Madeline (Sister Mary Gilbert). *The Springs of Silence*. London: The Catholic Book Club, 1954.

De Hueck, Catherine. "What Sisters Can Do." In *Meeting the Vocation Crisis*, edited by Kane, 139–48.

Di Ligouri, Saint Alphonso. *The True Spouse of Jesus Christ*. New York: Benziger Brothers, 1888.

Del Ray Danforth, Sister Maria, and George Barris. *Bernie Becomes a Nun*. New York: Farrar, Straus and Cudahy, 1956.

Del SS.mo Rosario, Anastasio. "The Theology of Religious Vocations." In *Today's Vocation Crisis*, edited by Poage and Lievin, 147–68.

Denham, Ann, and Gert Wilkinson. *Cloister of the Heart*. Bloomington, IN: Xlibris, 2009.

De Sainte-Marie, François. "The Recognition of a Contemplative Vocation." In *Religious Life II*, translated by Mitchell, 48–67.

Diekmann, Godfrey. "Living with the Church in Prayer and Reading." In *Proceedings of the 1955 Sisters' Institute of Spirituality*, edited by Collins, 159–243.

Dolan, Jay P. *The American Catholic Experience: A History from Colonial Times to the Present*. Garden City, NY: Doubleday, 1985.

– *The Immigrant Church: New York's Irish and German Catholics, 1815–1865*. Baltimore, MD: Johns Hopkins University Press, 1975.

Donovan, Mary Ann. "A More Limited Witness: An Historical Theologian Looks at the Signposts." In *The Crisis in Religious Vocations*, edited by Felknor, 84–98.

Dorcy, Sister Mary Jean. "Some Call It Madness, Some Call It Love." In *Convent Life*, edited by Lexau, 44–50.

Dukehart, Rev. J. Cyril. "Guidance of Prospective Candidates to the Priesthood and Religious Life." *National Catholic Educational Association Bulletin* 55, no. 1 (August 1958): 357–60.

Dwyer-McNulty, Sally. *Common Threads: A Cultural History of Clothing in American Catholicism*. Chapel Hill: The University of North Carolina Press, 2014.

Ebaugh, Helen Rose Fuchs. *Out of the Cloister: A Study of Organizational Dilemmas*. Austin and London: University of Texas Press, 1977.

– *Women in the Vanishing Cloister: Organizational Decline in Catholic Religious Orders in the United States*. New Brunswick, NJ: Rutgers University Press, 1993.

– Jon Lorence, and Janet Saltzman Chafetz. "The Growth and Decline of the Population of Catholic Nuns Cross-Nationally, 1960–1990: A Case of Secularization as Social Structural Change." *Journal of the Scientific Study of Religion* 35, no. 5 (1996): 171–83.

Ehrman, Bart H. *Forgery and Counterforgery: The Use of Literary Deceit in Early Christian Polemics*. Oxford: Oxford University Press, 2013.

Ellis, John Tracy. *American Catholicism*. 2nd edition. Chicago and London: The University of Chicago Press, 1969.

Ethier Rosenbaum, Rachel. *The Unmaking of a Nun.* Privately printed, 2013.

Evangelisti, Sylvia. *Nuns: A History of Convent Life, 1450–1700.* Oxford: Oxford University Press, 2007.

Ewens, Mary. *The Role of the Nun in Nineteenth-Century America: Variations on the International Theme.* Thiensville, WI: Caritas Communications, 2014.

Farrell, Ambrose, Henry St John, and F.B. Elkisch. *The Education of the Novice.* Westminster, MD: Newman Press, 1956.

Fea, John. *Was America Founded as a Christian Nation: A Historical Introduction.* Louisville, KY: Westminster John Knox Press, 2011.

Felknor, Laurie, ed. *The Crisis in Religious Vocations: An Inside View.* New York: Paulist Press, 1989.

Ferrer, William J. "The Church's Need for Vocations." *National Catholic Educational Association Bulletin* 41, no. 1 (August 1944): 289–98.

Fichter, Joseph H. *Parochial School: A Sociological Study.* South Bend, IN: University of Notre Dame Press, 1958.

– *Religion as an Occupation: A Study in the Sociology of Professions.* South Bend, IN: University of Notre Dame Press, 1961.

– "Vanishing Church Professionals." In *The Crisis in Religious Vocations,* edited by Felknor, 99–115.

Fisher, Fran. *In the Name of God, Why? Ex-Catholic Nuns Speak Out About Sexual Repression, Abuse, and Ultimate Liberation.* Granite Bay, CA: Griffin Publishing, 2012.

Florence, Mother Mary, ed. *Religious Life in the Church Today: Prospect and Retrospect.* South Bend, IN: University of Notre Dame Press, 1962.

Forbes, Sister M. Rita Anne. "The Aspirancy: Foundation for Renewal?" *National Catholic Educational Association Bulletin* 63, no. 1 (August 1966): 490–1.

Frederic, Sister M. Catherine. *And Spare Me Not in the Making: Pages from a Novice's Diary.* Milwaukee: The Bruce Publishing Co., 1953.

Freeman, Charles. *The Closing of the Western Mind: The Rise of Faith and the Fall of Reason.* London: Pimlico, 2003.

Frison, Basil. *Selection and Incorporation of Candidates for the Religious Life.* Milwaukee: The Bruce Publishing Co., 1961.

Garesché, Edward J. "The Influence of Schools on Religious Vocations." *The Catholic Educational Review* 40, no. 1 (April 1942): 193–8.

Garibaldi Rogers, Carole. *Habits of Change: An Oral History of American Nuns.* New York: Oxford University Press, 2011.

Gass, Marie Therese. *Unconventional Women: 73 Ex-Nuns Tell Their Stories.* Clackamas, OR: Sieben Hill, 2001.

Giem, Sylvia. *A River Flows from Eden.* Bloomington, IN: Xlibris, 2005.

Gilligan Wong, Mary. *Nun: A Memoir.* New York: Harper Colophon, 1984.

Gillis, Chester. *Roman Catholicism in America.* New York: Columbia University Press, 1999.

Glisky, Joan. "The Official IHM Stance on Friendship, 1845–1960." In *Building Sisterhood*, Sisters, Servants of the Immaculate Heart of Mary, 153–71.

Goyeneche, Servus. "The States of Perfection in the Church Today." In *Today's Vocation Crisis*, edited by Poage and Lievin, 133–46.

Greeley, Andrew M. *The American Catholic: A Social Portrait*. New York: Basic Books, 1977.

Griffin, Mary. *The Courage to Choose: An American Nun's Story*. Boston, Toronto: Little, Brown and Co., 1975.

Grout, Donald Jay, and Claude V. Palisca. *A History of Western Music*, 5th edition. New York: W.W. Norton, 1996.

Grueninger Beasley, Patricia. *The Tears I Couldn't Cry: Behind Convent Doors*. Bloomington, IN: Authorhouse, 2009.

Guardini, Romano. *The Art of Praying: The Principles and Methods of Christian Prayer*. Manchester, NH: Sophia Institute Press, 1994.

Hackett, Sheila. *Dominican Women in Texas: From Ohio to Galveston and Beyond*. Houston: Sacred Heart Convent, 1986.

Hagan, John R. "Some Factors in the Development of Religious Vocations of Women." *Journal of Religious Instruction* 15, no. 8 (April 1945): Part 1, 621–8; Part 2, 712–18; Part 3, 794–800.

Hagspiel, Bruno. *Live in the Holy Spirit*. Milwaukee: The Bruce Publishing Co., 1957.

Haley, Joseph E., ed. *Proceedings of the 1959 Sisters' Institute of Spirituality*. South Bend, IN: University of Notre Dame Press, 1960.

Halstead, Margaret M., and Lauro S. Halstead. "A Sexual Intimacy Survey of Former Nuns and Priests." *Journal of Sex and Marital Therapy* 4, no. 2 (1978): 83–90.

Hansbery, Sister Canisius Mary. *Life Is Not Hard: A Nun's Story*. Montgomery, AL: E-Book Time, LLC, 2007.

Harris, Charles W. "Virginity." *National Catholic Educational Association Bulletin* 55, no. 1 (August 1958): 346–50.

Hart, Mother Dolores, and Richard DeNeut. *The Ear of the Heart: An Actress' Journey from Hollywood to Holy Vows*. San Francisco: Ignatius Press, 2013.

Henderson, Nancy. *Out of the Curtained World*. New York: Pyramid Books, 1972.

Hennesey, James L. *American Catholics: A History of the Roman Catholic Community in the United States*. Oxford: Oxford University Press, 1981.

– "A Look at the Institution Itself." In *The Crisis in Religious Vocations*, edited by Felknor, 32–9.

Herbst, Winfrid. "Doubts About Vocation." *The Ecclesiastical Review* 7, no. 2 (February 1932): 113–27.

– *Girlhood's Highest Ideal: Helpful Chapters to Catholic Girls at the Parting of the Ways*. 10th edition. St Nazianz, WI: Society of the Divine Saviour, 1946.

Hinsdale, Mary Ann. "'The Roughest Kind of Prose': IHM Socialization, 1869–1960." In *Building Sisterhood*, Sisters, Servants of the Immaculate Heart of Mary, 119–50.

Hoeger, Frederick T. *The Convent Mirror: A Series of Conferences for Religious.* New York and Cincinnati: Frederick Pustet Co., 1951.

Hollingsworth, Gerelyn. *Ex-Nuns: Women Who Have Left the Convent.* Jefferson, NC, and London: McFarland, 1985.

Houtart, François. "The Sociology of Vocations." In *Today's Vocation Crisis*, edited by Poage and Lievin, 21–48.

Howe, Joanne. *A Change of Habit: The Autobiography of a Former Catholic Nun.* Nashville, TN: Christian Communications, 1986.

Hoy, Suellen. *Good Hearts: Catholic Sisters in Chicago's Past.* Urbana and Chicago: University of Illinois Press, 2006.

– "The Journey Out: The Recruitment and Emigration of Irish Religious Women to the United States, 1812–1914." *Journal of Women's History* 6, nos 4/7 (Winter/Spring 1995): 64–98.

Hulme, Katherine. *The Nun's Story.* New York: Little, Brown, 1956.

Hunter, David G. *Marriage, Celibacy, and Heresy in Ancient Christianity: The Jovinianist Controversy.* Oxford: Oxford University Press, 2007.

Jansen, Katherine Ludwig. *Making the Magdalen: Preaching and Popular Devotion in the Later Middle Ages.* Princeton, NJ: Princeton University Press, 2000.

Jean Clare, Sister. "A Primary Objective of Christian Education – Developing a Sense of Vocation." *National Catholic Education Association Bulletin* 58, no. 1 (August 1961): 444–9.

Johnson, Mary, Patricia Wittberg, and Mary L. Gautier. *New Generations of Catholic Sisters: The Challenge of Diversity.* Oxford: Oxford University Press, 2014.

Josephine, Sister. "One Reason for the Dearth of Religious Vocations." *Sponsa Regis* 5, no. 3 (November 1933): 70–2.

Kane, George L., ed. *Meeting the Vocation Crisis.* Westminster, MD.: Newman Press, 1956.

– ed. *Why I Became a Priest.* Dublin: Browne and Nolan, 1954.

– ed. *Why I Entered the Convent.* Westminster, MD: Newman Press, 1953.

Kelley, Shirley Dyckes. *Love Is Not for Cowards.* Englewood Cliffs, NJ: Prentice-Hall, 1978.

Kirsch, Felix M. *The Spiritual Direction of Sisters: A Manual for Priests and Superiors.* New York: Benziger Brothers, 1931.

Koehlinger, Amy L. *The New Nuns: Racial Justice and Religious Reform in the 1960s.* Cambridge, MA: Harvard University Press, 2007.

Krieg, Robert Anthony. *Romano Guardini: A Precursor of Vatican II.* South Bend, IN: University of Notre Dame Press, 1997.

Kuhns, Elizabeth. *The Habit: A History of the Clothing of Catholic Nuns.* New York: Image/Doubleday, 2003.

Larsen, Deborah. *The Tulip and the Pope: A Nun's Story.* New York: Vintage, 2006.

Laven, Mary. *Virgins of Venice: Broken Vows and Cloistered Lives in the Renaissance Convent.* New York: Viking-Penguin, 2003.

Lazerson, Marvin. "Understanding American Catholic Educational History." *History of Education Quarterly* 17 (1977): 297–317.

Leahy, Karen. *The Summer of Yes: An Ex-Nun's Story.* North Charleston, SC: CreateSpace, 2013.

LeMay, Michael C. *From Open Door to Dutch Door: An Analysis of U.S. Immigration Policy Since 1820.* Westport, CT: Praeger, 1987.

Levack, Brian P. *The Devil Within: Possession and Exorcism in the Christian West.* New Haven and London: Yale University Press, 2013.

Lexau, Joan M., ed. *Convent Life: Roman Catholic Religious Orders for Women in North America.* New York: Dial Press, 1964.

Lord, Daniel A. *Letters to a Nun.* St. Louis: The Queen's Work, 1947.

Lynch, Margaret. *Triptych: A Memoir.* Bloomingham, IN: Authorhouse, 2005.

MacCulloch, Diarmaid. *Christianity: The First Three Thousand Years.* New York: Viking Penguin, 2010.

MacDonald, Heidi. "Entering the Convent as Coming of Age in the 1930s." In *Changing Habits*, edited by Smyth, 86–102.

Mangion, Carmen M. *Contested Identities: Catholic Women Religious in Nineteenth-century England and Wales.* Manchester: Manchester University Press, 2008.

M. Annette, Sister. "An Environment Conducive to Mental and Physical Health." In *Proceedings of the 1959 Sisters' Institute of Spirituality*, edited by Haley, 75–162.

M. Christina, Sister. "Study of the Catholic Family Through Three Generations." *American Catholic Sociological Review* 3, no. 3 (October 1942): 144–53.

M. Claudette, Sister. "I Remember My Last Date." In *In My Book These Are the Stars: Observations on Vocation by Bing Crosby and Others*, 48–52.

M. Madeleva, Sister. "The Education of Our Young Religious Teachers." *National Catholic Educational Association Bulletin* 46, no. 1 (August 1949): 253–6.

Marian Elizabeth, Sister. "Methods of Recruiting Vocations Among High School Students." *National Catholic Educational Association Bulletin* 46, no. 1 (August 1949): 308–10.

Marie Helene, Mother. "The Spiritual Possibilities of Teaching as a Vocation." In *Religious Community Life in the United States: Proceedings of the*

Sisters' Section of the First National Congress of Religious of the United States,
117–25.

Martinez, Demetria. "Drydyk's Life a Paradigm for Justice." *National Catholic Reporter,* 6 October 1995.

Mary Alene, Sister. "The Adolescent Girl and the Aspirancy." *National Catholic Educational Association Bulletin* 54, no. 1 (August 1957): 364–9.

Mary Blaise, Sister. "Fostering Vocations in Grades Six, Seven, and Eight." *National Catholic Educational Association Bulletin* 52, no. 1 (August 1955): 103–6.

Mary Corona, Sister. "Recruiting for Vocations to the Sisterhood." *National Catholic Educational Association Bulletin* 43, no. 1 (August 1946): 323–32.

Mary Daniel, Sister. "Successful Vocation Programs." *National Catholic Educational Association Bulletin* 64, no. 1 (August 1967): 215–17.

Mary Emil, Sister. "The Survey Report on Teacher Preparation." *National Catholic Educational Association Bulletin* 50, no. 1 (August 1953): 224–9.

Mary Francis, Mother. *A Right to Be Merry.* Chicago: Franciscan Herald Press, 1956.

Mary George, Sister. "Proper Relationship Between Teacher and Prospective Vocation." *National Catholic Educational Association Bulletin* 56, no. 1 (August 1959): 385–6.

Mary Isabel, Sister. "A Plan for Fostering Vocations in the Elementary School." *National Catholic Educational Association Bulletin* 49, no. 1 (August 1952): 254–61.

Mary James, Sister. *Providence: A Sketch of the Sisters of Charity of Providence in the Northwest, 1856–1931.* Seattle: Sisters of Charity of Providence, 1931.

Mary Jean, Sister. "In Search of God." In *Why I Entered the Convent,* edited by Kane, 55–61.

Mary Joanne, Sister. "Our Lady of Good Counsel Clubs." *National Catholic Educational Association Bulletin* 51, no. 1 (August 1954): 172–7.

Mary Patrick, Sister. "Share the Sisters." In *Religious Community Life in the United States: Proceedings of the Sisters' Section of the First National Congress of Religious of the United States,* 134–47.

Mary of St Teresita, Sister. *The Social Work of the Sisters of the Good Shepherd.* Cleveland, OH: Cadillac Press, 1938.

Masterson, Sister Mary Jane. *One Nun's Story: Then and Now.* Salt Lake City: Millennial Mind Publishing, 2009.

McAllister, Joseph. "The Recognition and Preservation of Vocations to the Priesthood and the Religious Life Among High School Students." *National Catholic Educational Association Bulletin* 33, no. 1 (November 1936): 346–53.

McCann, Shirley. *Out of the Habit: A Young Woman's Experiences Joining, Loving, and Ultimately Leaving a Convent in the 1940s.* Self-published, 2011.

McCarthy, Rebecca Lea. *Origins of the Magdalene Laundries: An Analytical History*. Jefferson, NC: McFarland, 2010.

McCarthy, Thomas P. *Guide to the Catholic Sisterhoods in the United States*. Washington: Catholic University of America Press, 1958.

McCorry, Vincent P. "Basic Concepts of Vocation." *National Catholic Educational Association Bulletin* 54, no. 1 (August 1957): 355–9.

– *Most Worthy of All Praise*. New York: Declan X. McMullen Co., 1946.

McDannell, Colleen. *The Spirit of Vatican II*. New York: Basic Books, 2011.

McGaw, Sister Martha Mary. "Sister Catherine Thomas, OCD." *Carmelite Digest* 4, no. 3 (Summer 1989): 47, 48.

McGoey, John H. *The Sins of the Just*. Milwaukee: The Bruce Publishing Co., 1963.

McGoldrick, Desmond F. *The Martyrdom of Change: Simple Talks to Postulant Sisters on the Religious Mentality and Ideal*. Pittsburgh: Duquesne University Press, 1961.

McGuinness, Margaret M. *Called to Serve: A History of Nuns in America*. New York: New York University Press, 2013.

McLoughlin, Emmett. *American Culture and Catholic Schools*. New York: Lyle Stuart, 1960.

McNally, Robert E. "Religious Vocations: A Crisis of Religion." *National Catholic Educational Association Bulletin* 64, no. 1 (August 1967): 206–11.

McNamara, Jo Ann Kay. *Sisters in Arms: Catholic Nuns Through Two Millennia*. Cambridge, MA: Harvard University Press, 1996.

Meyer, Fulgence. "Training in Purity." *National Catholic Educational Association Bulletin*, 29, no. 1, (November 1932): 684–709.

Meyers, Sister Bertrande. *The Education of Sisters: A Plan for Integrating the Religious, Social, Cultural and Professional Training of Sisters*. New York: Sheed and Ward, 1941.

Mitchell, Penny Blaker. *Mother Theodore Guerin – Saint of God*. St Mary-of-the-Woods, IN: Sisters of Providence, 2006.

Mitchell, Walter, trans. *Religious Life II: Vocation*. Westminster, MD.: Newman Press, 1952.

Moffatt, John E. *Listen Sister*. New York: McMullen Books, 1952.

– *Step This Way, Sister: Reflections for Nuns, Young and Less Young*. New York: Farrar, Strauss and Cudahy, 1960.

Morkovsky, Sister Mary Christine. *Living in God's Providence: History of the Congregation of Divine Providence of San Antonio, Texas, 1943–2000*. San Antonio: Congregation of the Divine Providence, 2009.

Motte, A. "The Obligation to Follow a Vocation." In *Religious Life II*, translated by Mitchell, 18–36.

Mullahy, Bernard I. "Sanctification Through the Vows." In *Proceedings of the 1955 Sisters' Institute of Spirituality*, edited by Collins, 91–158.

Mullaly, Charles J. *Spiritual Reflections for Sisters*. New York: Apostleship of Prayer, 1937.

Neal, Marie Augusta. *Catholic Sisters in Transition: From the 1960s to the 1980s*. Wilmington, DE: Michael Glazier, 1984.

Nelson, Sioban. "'The Harvest That Lies Before Us': Quebec Women Religious Building Health Care in the U.S. Pacific Northwest, 1858–1900." In *Changing Habits*, edited by Smyth, 151–71.

Nix, J.T. "The Physical Health of Religious." In *Religious Life in the Church Today: Prospect and Retrospect*, edited by Florence, 221–33.

Oates, Mary J. "Catholic Female Academies on the Frontier." *U.S. Catholic Historian* 12, no. 4 (Fall 1994): 121–36.

O'Donnell, M. "The Lay Teacher in Catholic Education." *National Catholic Educational Association Bulletin* 58, no. 1 (August 1961): 93–6.

O'Donnell-Gibson, Patricia. *The Red Skirt: Memoirs of an Ex Nun*. Watervleit, MI: StuartRose Publishing, 2011.

O'Donoghue, Thomas. *Catholic Teaching Brothers: Their Life in the English-Speaking World, 1891–1965*. New York: Palgrave Macmillan, 2012.

– *Come Follow Me and Forsake Temptation: Catholic Schooling and the Recruitment and Retention of Teachers for Religious Orders, 1922–1965*. Bern: Peter Lang, 2004.

O'Hara, Mary. *The Scent of Roses*. London: Fontana Collins, 1981.

Omez, Reginald, "Negative Criteria of Vocation." In *Religious Life II*, translated by Mitchell, 96–100.

Orsi, Robert A. *Between Heaven and Earth: The Religious Worlds People Make and the Scholars Who Study Them*. Princeton, NJ: Princeton University Press, 2005.

– *Thank You, St. Jude: Women's Devotion to the Patron Saint of Hopeless Causes*. New Haven and London: Yale University Press, 1996.

Owram, Doug. *Born at the Right Time: A History of the Baby-Boom Generation*. Toronto: University of Toronto Press, 1996.

Packard, Vance. *The Hidden Persuaders*. New York: Pocket Books, 1957.

Padberg, John W. "The Contexts of Comings and Goings." In *The Crisis in Religious Vocations*, edited by Felknor, 19–31.

Palmer, Ben. "The Natural Law and International Relations," *Proceedings of the American Catholic Philosophical Association* 24 (1950): 33–40.

– *Parents and Vocations*. St Louis: The Queen's Work, 1958.

Peckham Magray, Mary. *The Transforming Power of Nuns: Women, Religion, and Cultural Change in Ireland, 1750–1900*. Oxford: Oxford University Press, 1998.

Peters, Edward N. *The 1917 Pio-Benedictine Code of Canon Law*. San Francisco: Ignatius Press, 2001.

Philippe, Paul. *The Novitiate: Religious Life in the Modern World*, vol. 2. South Bend, IN: University of Notre Dame Press, 1961.

Pius XII. *Selected Encyclicals and Addresses*. Harrison, NY: Roman Catholic Books, nd.

– "Women's Duties in Social and Political Life." In *Selected Encyclicals and Addresses*.

Poage, Godfrey. *For More Vocations*. Milwaukee: The Bruce Publishing Co., 1955.

– *Recruiting for Christ*. Milwaukee: The Bruce Publishing Co., 1950.

– *Secrets of Successful Recruiting: The Principles of Religious Vocational Guidance and Tested Techniques of America's Most Successful Religious Recruiters*. Westminster, MD.: Newman Press, 1961.

– "The Better Part." In *Why I Became a Priest*, edited by Kane, 103–16.

– and Germain Lievin, eds. *Today's Vocation Crisis: A Summary of the Studies and Discussions at the First International Congress on Vocation to the States of Perfection, December 1961*. Westminster, MD: Newman Press, 1962.

– and John P. Treacy. *Parents' Role in Vocations*. Milwaukee: The Bruce Publishing Co., 1959.

Poluse, Martin. "Archbishop Joseph Schrembs's Battle to Obtain Public Assistance for the Parochial Schools of Cleveland during the Great Depression." *Catholic Historical Review* 83, no. 3 (July 1997): 428–51.

Praszalowicz, Dorota. "Polish American Sisterhoods: The Americanization Process." *U.S. Catholic Historian* 27, no. 3 (Summer 2009): 45–57.

Provera, Paulo. *Live Your Vocation*. Translated by Thomas F. Murray. St Louis: B. Herder, 1959.

Quinonez, Lora Ann, and Mary Daniel Turner. *The Transformation of American Catholic Sisters*. Philadelphia: Temple University Press, 1992.

Ralenkotter, Howard. "Winning Parents." *National Catholic Education Association Bulletin* 51, no. 1 (August 1954): 190–5.

Rapley, Elizabeth. *The Dévotes: Women and the Church in Seventeenth Century France*. Montreal and Kingston: McGill-Queen's University Press, 1990.

– *The Lord as Their Portion: The Story of the Religious Orders and How They Shaped Our World*. Toronto: Novalis, 2001.

– *A Social History of the Cloister: Daily Life in the Teaching Monasteries of the Old Regime*. Montreal and Kingston: McGill-Queen's University Press, 2001.

Redemptorist Father, A. *A Treatise on Religious Vocation, According to the Teachings of the Holy Doctors, St Thomas and St Alphonsus, to Which Is Added a Series of Prayers for Those of Us Who Are Called to the Religious State*. Market Weighton: St William's Press, nd.

Reilly, Sister Mary Paul. *What Must I Do? Complete Information on Convent Life and What It Means to Be a Sister*. Milwaukee: The Bruce Publishing Co., 1950.

Religious Community Life in the United States: Proceedings of the Sisters' Section of the First National Congress of Religious of the United States. New York: Paulist Press, 1952.

Reynes, Geneviève. *Couvents de femmes: La vie des religieuses cloitrées dans la France des XVIIe et XVIIIe siècles.* Paris: Fayard, 1987.

Roby, Yves. "Les Canadiens français des États-Unis (1860–1900): Dévoyés ou missionnaires." *Revue d'histoire de l'Amérique française* 41, no. 1 (1987): 3–22.

SanGiovanni, Lucinda. *Ex-Nuns: A Study of Emergent Role Passage.* Norwood, NJ: Ablex Publishing, 1978.

Schmid, Peter F. "'These Dear, Faithful Helpers': The Coadjutrix Sisters of Providence." *Past Forward* (Providence Archives Newsletter, Seattle) 15, no. 3 (Summer 2008): 2–5.

Schneider, Mary L. "American Sisters and the Roots of Change: The 1950s." *U.S. Catholic Historian* 7, no. 1 (Winter 1988): 55–72.

Schultz, Nancy Lusignan, intro. *Veil of Fear: Nineteenth-Century Convent Tales.* West Lafayette, IN: Notabell Books, 1999.

Senieur, Jude. "Why Do Parents Object?" In *Meeting the Vocation Crisis*, edited by Kane, 80–8.

– *Vocational Replies.* Paterson, NJ: St Anthony Guild Press, 1954.

Shahar, Shulamith. *The Fourth Estate: A History of Women in the Middle Ages.* London and New York: Methuen, 1983.

Sherman, Sarah Marie. "Fewer Vocations: Crisis or Challenge?" In *The Crisis in Religious Vocations*, edited by Felknor, 5–18.

Sisters of Our Lady of Charity of the Good Shepherd. *Rule of St Augustin and the Constitutions for the Religious of the Congregation of Our Lady of Charity of the Good Shepherd of Angers (1890).* Whitefish, MT: Kessinger Publishing (reprint), 2007.

Sisters, Servants of the Immaculate Heart of Mary. *Building Sisterhood: A Feminist History of the Sisters, Servants of the Immaculate Heart of Mary.* Syracuse, NY: Syracuse University Press, 1997.

Smyth, Elizabeth M., ed. *Changing Habits: Women's Religious Orders in Canada.* Ottawa: Novalis, 2007.

Spring, Joel. *The American School, 1642–1996.* New York: McGraw-Hill, 1997.

Sprows Cummings, Kathleen. *New Women of the Old Faith: Gender and American Catholicism in the Progressive Era.* Chapel Hill: University of North Carolina Press, 2009.

– "'The Wageless Work of Paradise': Integrating Women into American Religious History." *Journal of Religion and Society*, Supplementary Series 5 (2009): 114–28.

Stark, Rodney. "Secularization, R.I.P." *Sociology of Religion* 60, no. 3 (1999): 249–73.

Steinmetz, George. "American Sociology Before and After World War II: The (Temporary) Settling of a Disciplined Field." In *Sociology in America: A History*, edited by Calhoun, 314–66.

Stevens, Martin. "Picketing the Vineyard." In *Meeting the Vocation Crisis*, edited by Kane, 73–9.

Stewart, George C. *Marvels of Charity: History of American Sisters and Nuns*. Huntington, IN: Our Sunday Visitor, 1994.

Stolz, Grace E. *Convent Life and Beyond*. Denver: Outskirts Press, 2007.

Stuhlmueller, Carroll, "Biblical Observations on the Decline of Vocations to Religious Life." In *The Crisis in Religious Vocations*, edited by Felknor, 152–64.

Suenens, Léon-Joseph. *The Nun in the World: Religious and the Apostolate*. Westminster, MD: Newman Press, 1963.

Sullivan, Karen. *The Inner Lives of Medieval Inquisitors*. Chicago: University of Chicago Press, 2011.

Sullivan, Rebecca. "Blasphemes of Modernity: Scandals of the Nineteenth-Century Quebec Convent." In *Changing Habits*, edited by Smyth, 103–28.

– *Visual Habits: Nuns, Feminism, and American Postwar Popular Culture*. Toronto: University of Toronto Press, 2005.

Sylvester, Nancy. "PFs: Persistent Friendships." In *Building Sisterhood*, Sisters, Servants of the Immaculate Heart of Mary.

Swatos, William H., ed. *The Encyclopedia of Religion and Society*. Walnut Creek, CA: AltaMira Press, 1998.

Tanqueray, Adolphe. *The Spiritual Life: A Treatise of Ascetical and Mystical Theology*. Trans. Herman Branderis. Tournai: Desclée, 1930.

Tentler, Leslie Woodcock, ed. *The Church Confronts Modernity: Catholicism Since 1950 in the United States, Ireland, and Quebec*. Washington: Catholic University of America Press, 2007.

Thérèse of Lisieux. *The Story of a Soul*. Trans. John Beevers. New York: Doubleday, 1957.

Thurston, Herbert J., and Donald Attwater, eds. *Butler's Lives of the Saints*. Westminster, MD: Christian Classics, 1956.

Titley, Brian. "Heil Mary: Magdalen Asylums and Moral Regulation in Ireland." *History of Education Review* 35, no. 2 (2006): 1–15.

Turk, Midge. *The Buried Life: A Nun's Journey*. London: New English Library, 1972.

Valeri, Cardinal Valerio. "Introduction." In *Today's Vocation Crisis*, edited by Poage and Lievin.

Van Zeller, Hubert. *The Yoke of Divine Love: A Study of Conventual Perfection*. Springfield, IL: Templegate, 1957.

Vaughan, Richard P. "The Psychological Screening of Candidates." In *Religious Life in the Church Today*, edited by Mother Mary Florence, 209–19.

Villet, Barbara, and Grey Villet. *Those Whom God Chooses*. New York: Viking, 1966.

Vincentian Father, A. *Vocations Explained: Matrimony, Virginity, the Religious State, and the Priesthood*. New York: Benziger Brothers, 1897.

Wakin, Edward, and Joseph F. Sheuer. "The American Nun: Poor, Chaste, and Restive." *Harper's* magazine, August 1965: 35–40.

Walch, Timothy. *Parish School: American Catholic Parochial Education from Colonial Times to the Present*. New York: Crossroad Publishing, 1996.

Walsh, Eileen Judith. "Objections to a Sister's Vocation: Point of View of a Teen-ager." *National Catholic Educational Association Bulletin* 62, no. 1 (August 1965): 599–600.

Ward, W. Reginald. *Christianity Under the Ancien Régime, 1648–1789*. Cambridge: Cambridge University Press, 1999.

Ware, Ann Patrick, ed. *Midwives of the Future: American Sisters Tell Their Story*. Kansas City, MO: Leaven Press, 1985.

Weakley, Mary Ann. *Monastery to Matrimony: A Woman's Journey*. Bloomington, IN: Balboa Press, 2014.

Wedl, Janice, and Eileen Maas Nalevanko, eds. *Forever Your Sister: Reflections on Leaving Convent Life*. St Cloud, MN: North Star Press of St Cloud, 1998.

Whitney, Catherine. *The Calling: A Year in the Life of an Order of Nuns*. New York: Crown Publishers, 1999.

Willingham, Saundra. "Why I Quit the Convent." *Ebony*, December 1968: 64–74.

Wittberg, Patricia. *The Rise and Fall of Catholic Religious Orders: A Social Movement Perspective*. Albany: State University of New York Press, 1994.

Wojtyla, Karol. *Love and Responsibility*. Trans. H.T. Willetts. San Francisco: Ignatius Press, 1981.

Wolf, Hubert. *The Nuns of Sant'Ambrogio: The True Story of a Convent in Scandal*. New York: Knopf Doubleday, 2015.

Wombacher, Kristin. "Religious Life, 1965–1985." In *The Crisis in Religious Vocations*, edited by Felknor, 63–73.

Woods, Thomas E. *The Church Confronts Modernity: Catholic Intellectuals and the Progressive Era*. New York: Columbia University Press, 2004.

Wulston, Mother Mary. "Overcoming the Prejudice to Vocation Clubs." *National Catholic Education Association Bulletin* 51, no. 1 (August 1954): 166–71.

Zemba, Joyce. *A Life Like Nun Other*. Bloomington: Authorhouse, 2010.

Index

· · · · · · · · · · · · · · · · · · · ·

Serra Club, 75

Servants of the Pierced Hearts of Jesus and Mary, 10

Seton, Elizabeth, 19

Seven Cities of Gold, 110

sex abuse scandal, 199, 203

sex education, 95, 96, 161–3

Sex and the Single Girl (Gurley Brown), 196

Shall My Daughter Be a Nun? (Lord), 99

Sheen, Fulton J., bishop, 69, 109

Sherman, Sister Sarah Marie, 196

singularity, 151

Sister Formation Conference, 32, 33, 34, 137, 178, 180, 183, 192

Sisters Adorers of the Most Precious Blood, 10

Sisters of the Assumption of the Blessed Virgin Mary, 27

Sisters of the Blessed Sacrament for Indians and Colored People, 40

Sisters of Charity of the Blessed Virgin Mary, 10, 30, 77, 124, 125, 130, 131, 134, 135, 154

Sisters of Charity of the Incarnate Word, 10

Sisters of Charity of Montreal, 10, 27

Sisters of Charity of Nazareth, 21, 72

Sisters of Charity of Providence, 20, 28, 42, 49, 68, 89, 90, 135, 146, 152, 153, 157, 158, 159, 182, 193

Sisters of Charity of St Elizabeth, 65, 127, 143, 152, 156, 162

Sisters of Charity of St Joseph, 19

Sisters of Charity of St Vincent de Paul, 10, 17, 60, 76, 189

Sisters of Divine Providence, 108, 127, 139, 179, 197

Sisters of the Good Shepherd, 20, 39, 152, 158, 166

Sisters of the Holy Cross, 86, 148, 152, 189

Sisters of the Holy Family, 21

Sisters of the Holy Names of Jesus and Mary, 20, 90, 126, 142, 153

Sisters of the Humility of Mary, 77

Sisters of the Immaculate Conception, 132

Sisters of the Immaculate Heart of Mary, 24, 130, 141, 143, 159, 184, 188

Sisters' Institute of Spirituality, 34, 158

Sisters of Mercy, 20, 40, 48, 61, 72, 104, 155, 171

Sisters of the Most Precious Blood, 10

Sisters of Notre Dame, 187

Sisters of Notre Dame de Namur, 70

Sisters of Our Lady of Charity of the Refuge, 10, 17, 20

Sisters of the Precious Blood, 10

Sisters of Providence, 20, 25, 32, 67, 69, 105, 112, 122, 131, 142, 147, 151, 163, 171, 193

Sisters of the Sacred Heart, 189

Sisters of St Casimir, 27

Sisters of Saints Cyril and Methodius, 27

Sisters of St Francis, 107, 199

Sisters of St Joseph, 17, 20, 24, 56, 58, 65, 74, 77, 105, 128, 130, 141, 152, 155, 165, 167, 171, 191

Sisters of St Joseph of the Third Order of St Francis, 27

Sisters of St Mary of the Presentation, 128, 131, 136

Sister Servants of the Holy Ghost and Mary Immaculate, 24